DAILY LIFE IN

Elizabethan England

Recent Titles in
The Greenwood Press Daily Life through History Series

DAILY LIFE IN

Elizabethan England

Second Edition

Jeffrey L. Forgeng

The Greenwood Press Daily Life Through History Series

GREENWOOD PRESS
An Imprint of ABC-CLIO, LLC

A B C CLIO

Santa Barbara, California • Denver, Colorado • Oxford, England

Library of Congress Cataloging-in-Publication Data
Forgeng, Jeffrey L.
    Daily life in Elizabethan England / Jeffrey L. Forgeng. — 2nd ed.
        p. cm. — (The Greenwood Press Daily Life through History Series)
    Includes bibliographical references and index.
    ISBN 978-0-313-36560-7 (hard copy : acid-free paper) —
ISBN 978-0-313-36561-4 (ebook) 1. England—Social life and customs—
16th century. 2. Great Britain—History—Elizabeth, 1558–1603. I. Title.
    DA320.S56   2010
    942.05'5—dc22   2009027600

14   13   12   11   10   1   2   3   4   5

This book is also available on the World Wide Web as an eBook.
Visit www.abc-clio.com for details.

ABC-CLIO, LLC
130 Cremona Drive, P.O. Box 1911
Santa Barbara, California 93116-1911

This book is printed on acid-free paper ∞

Manufactured in the United States of America

Copyright Acknowledgments

The publisher has done its best to make sure the instructions and/or recipes in this book are
correct. However, users should apply judgment and experience when preparing recipes,
especially parents and teachers working with young people. The publisher accepts no
responsibility for the outcome of any recipe included in this volume.

Contents

Preface to the Revised Edition

When *Daily Life in Elizabethan England* first came out, I was 32 years old and publishing my first book. A dozen years and half as many books later, one would certainly hope that I bring something more to the table for this revised edition. The intervening time has given me a good deal of new experience to work with: during the late 1990s, I continued my involvement in living history, culminating in a stint at Plimoth Plantation, and since that time I have been teaching about this period both to undergraduates at Worcester Polytechnic Institute and to the general public as Paul S. Morgan Curator at the Higgins Armory Museum.

The outcome has been a book substantially revised from the first edition. Based on my work on other volumes in the Greenwood Daily Life series, I have reconceived the chapters in ways that should make them flow better while also allowing expansion in crucial areas—for example, the chapter on the Living Environment has been broadened as Material Culture. I have also deepened both descriptions and discussions, particularly in areas like the chapter on Society, which has grown substantially relative to its previous iteration.

In particular, I am very glad that Greenwood asked me to include side-bars outside of the main narrative. There is a massive amount of primary-source material to offer the reader compelling glimpses of Elizabethan daily life, but it does not always fit well into the main text of a book such as this, precisely because it offers integrated views of the historic environment and loses much of its value when it is shoehorned into a specific slot in the narrative. I am sure readers will agree that the passages from

Claude Hollyband's dialogues, Lady Margaret Hoby's diary, and Phillip Stubbes's *Anatomy of Abuses* add hugely to this second edition.

One of the biggest changes between the worlds of 1995 and today has been the exponential growth of the Internet, which figured only marginally in the appendices of the first edition. The Net offers an outstandingly powerful tool to those who want to go deeper into the topics covered in this book, but finding a way to accommodate the ever-shifting geography of virtual space within the rigid format of the printed page is a formidable challenge—it would be all too easy to produce what would soon amount to no more than a list of dead links. Instead of trying to compile a comprehensive guide to Internet sites, I have tried to lay out a strategy of digital research that should remain useful even when some of the URLs are no longer valid.

While much has changed, I hope that the features that made the first edition so popular continue to remain in place. In particular, I feel that the first-person perspective of the living-history practitioner continues to make this work uniquely valuable in offering the reader a compelling sense of what life in the Elizabethan world was like for the people who lived it.

I also feel that this perspective has proved especially pertinent to a 21st-century readership. One of the issues I most tried to address in the first edition was the material basics that are often glossed over in accounts of daily life but that are crucial to the actual functioning of individuals and societies: food, water, light and heat, sanitation, and the production and life cycles of materials. These topics are much more in the public eye than they were a decade ago, and I feel that this book offers perspectives in this area that can still be relevant today. In fact, I made personal changes in my own lifestyle as a result of writing the first edition, such as altering my daily schedule to the Elizabethan practice of rising with the sun—helpful to anyone who has an ambitious publication agenda, but also one of the many things all of us could be doing to reduce our ecological footprint.

It is perhaps also worth emphasizing here that any broad-reaching portrait of the past will inevitably oversimplify its subject. The on-the-ground realities in any society are vastly more complex than can possibly be captured in writing, and the broader one's topic, the more violence one has to do to these realities to squeeze them into the space available. Yet the exercise is eminently worthwhile. Even if this book can never do justice to the complexity—and the fascination—of the Elizabethan world, a general introduction of this sort fulfills an essential function as a guidebook for the first-time traveler to this unfamiliar country and will hopefully inspire some readers to get to know the environment a bit more deeply. I have also found my works in this series to be personally helpful when I need to look up technical details—monetary values, agricultural practices, populations, and life expectancies—that are rarely brought conveniently together between two covers.

I would like to thank the people without whom this second edition would never have been possible—Sarah Kolba, as fine a research assistant as one could ever hope for; Laura Hanlan, a magus among ILL librarians; and Christine Drew, whose sage counsel and unfailing patience have been essential in bringing this project to completion.

Acknowledgments

The author wishes to thank the Centre for Renaissance and Reformation Studies at the University of Toronto for permission to reproduce various illustrations in this volume and for their help in obtaining them.

I would also like to thank Sandra Marques of the Museum of London for her unflagging assistance with the illustration by the late Peter Jackson.

Special credit is due to David Hoornstra for several of the illustrations in this book. Special credit is also due to Victoria Hadfield for her work on the illustrations in this volume, some of which are her own.

Thanks also to David Kuijt for providing the rules for Primero.

Daily Life in Elizabethan England is in part a revision of *The Elizabethan Handbook*, a manual for Elizabethan living history produced by the University Medieval and Renaissance Association (now the Tabard Inn Society) at the University of Toronto for its "Fencing, Dancing, and Bearbaiting" event in June 1991, and subsequently revised and expanded for private publication by the present author. Although relatively little of the original text survives, some credit is due to the people who originally produced it, or who had a hand in later revisions, including Susan Carroll-Clark, Maren Drees, Victoria Hadfield, Lesley Howard, Shona Humphrey, A.J.S. Nusbacher, Tricia Postle, and Tara Jenkins.

A Chronology of Tudor England

1561   Return of Mary Stuart (Mary Queen of Scots) from France to
          Scotland

1562   First religious war between Catholics and Protestants in
          France

1563   Plague

1564   Birth of William Shakespeare

1567   Second religious war in France

          Rebellion against Spain in Flanders is ruthlessly suppressed
          by the Duke of Alva

1568   Mary Stuart flees to England

1569   Northern rebellion

          Third religious war in France

1570   Pope Pius V excommunicates Elizabeth

1571   Ridolfi plot against Elizabeth

1572   St. Bartholomew's Day massacre of Protestants in France

1574   Beginning of covert Roman Catholic mission in England

1576   First permanent theater built in London

1577   Sir Francis Drake sets out on a voyage around the globe

1578–79   Plague

1580   Beginning of Jesuit mission in England

          Return of Sir Francis Drake

1581   Parliament enacts harsh anti-Catholic legislation

1582   Plague

1583   Sir Humphrey Gilbert attempts to found an English colony in
          Newfoundland

          Throckmorton conspiracy to overthrow Elizabeth

1585   Sir Walter Raleigh attempts to found an English colony in
          Virginia (Roanoke Colony, modern North Carolina)

          Sack of Antwerp by Spanish troops

          English troops are sent to fight Spain in the Netherlands

1586   Babington conspiracy to overthrow Elizabeth

          Poor harvests

1587	Execution of Mary Stuart
	Birth of Virginia Dare at Roanoke, the first English child born in America
	Poor harvests and famine
1588	Spain's Invincible Armada is defeated by the English fleet
	Poor harvests
1590	Edmund Spenser begins publishing *The Faerie Queene*
1592	Plague
ca. 1592	Shakespeare's early plays
1593	Death of Christopher Marlowe in a tavern brawl
	Plague
1594–95	Poor harvests
1596	Poor harvests
	English expedition under the Earl of Essex against Spanish port of Cadiz
	Irish rebellion under Hugh O'Neill
1597–98	Poor harvests and famine
1598	First performance of Ben Jonson's *Every Man in His Humour*
1599	Globe Theater opens
	Earl of Essex's expedition to Ireland
1601	Rebellion and execution of the Earl of Essex
1603	Plague
	Death of Elizabeth

Introduction

The reign of Elizabeth is for many people one of the most fascinating periods in the history of the English-speaking world. Our images of the Elizabethan age, whether derived from the stage, screen, or books, have an enduring romantic appeal: the daring impudence of the sea-dogs, the chivalric valor of Sir Philip Sidney at Zutphen or the Earl of Essex at the gates of Cadiz, the elegant clash of steel as masters of the rapier display their skill. In addition to its imaginative appeal, the period is one of considerable historical importance. In political terms, Elizabeth's reign saw the definitive emergence of England as a significant naval power, as well as the growth of England's commercial and colonial activities: the British Empire, which so shaped the world in which we live, had its roots in the reign of Elizabeth. In the cultural sphere, England's achievements were no less significant, most notably in the person of William Shakespeare.

Elizabethan daily life has received a good deal of attention during the past 200 years. Yet although many books have been written on the subject, this volume is very different in one fundamental respect, which has influenced its shape in many ways.

This is the first book on Elizabethan England to arise out of the practice of living history. In its broadest sense, living history might be described as the material re-creation of elements of the past. In this sense, it includes a wide variety of activities. People who play historical music (especially on reproduction instruments) or who engage in historical crafts are practicing a form of living history.

An English army on the march. [*Shakespeare's England*]

In its fullest sense, living history involves the attempt to re-create an entire historical setting. Perhaps the most outstanding example is the historical site of Plimoth Plantation in Massachusetts, where the visitor will find not only reconstructed houses of the pilgrim settlers of 1627, but also a staff of highly trained interpreters who represent the individual men and women who were at the settlement in that year, even down to the dialect of English likely to have been spoken by the persons they are portraying.

This book began life as *The Elizabethan Handbook*, a brief guide written by the University Medieval and Renaissance Association of Toronto (an amateur living-history group based at the University of Toronto), to accompany its "Fencing, Dancing, and Bearbaiting" Elizabethan living history event in 1991. It was privately published in expanded and revised form in 1993, as part of a series of manuals geared for living-history use. Very little of the original text still remains, but the underlying connection with living history is very much present.

The living-history background of this book gives it two particular advantages over previous works. The first is its hands-on approach. In addition to telling the reader what sort of foods people ate, what sort of clothes they wore, and what sort of games they played, this book includes actual recipes, patterns, and rules, based on sources from the period. We ourselves have had great fun reproducing such aspects of the past and hope that readers will enjoy them too.

The second important advantage is the perspective that living history affords. This book is not only based on the author's reading about the Elizabethan period. It is also informed by time spent living in thatched cottages, cooking over open hearths, and sleeping on straw mattresses. The simple act of doing these things cannot actually tell you how they were done, but there is no better way to focus your attention on the essential parts of historical daily life than by actually trying to live it. As a result, this book offers a uniquely clear, focused, and detailed account of the Elizabethan world. Many fundamental topics that other books mention only briefly (if at all) are given full attention here: water supply, sanitation, sources of heat and light.

This book is also distinguished by its attention to the daily life of ordinary people. Books about Elizabethan England often focus on the world of the aristocracy, leaving the impression that every man in Elizabethan England wore an enormous starched ruff, every woman wore a rich brocade gown, and they all lived in huge brick mansions. Yet the lives of ordinary people can be just as interesting and informative. This book tries to give the other 98 percent of the population a degree of attention more in keeping with their numbers.

Another important feature of this book is that it attempts to incorporate a high quality of scholarly research in a form that is accessible to a broad readership. There tends to be a great divide between scholarly and popular accounts of the past. Scholarly accounts generally offer high-quality information based on primary sources—primary sources being sources of information contemporary with the period in question, as opposed to secondary sources, which are modern works that make use of primary sources, or tertiary sources, which are modern works that rely on secondary sources. The information in scholarly works is generally superior, since the authors are in closer contact with the original sources of information, but their language and content tend to be geared toward the specialist, and they often assume a great deal of background knowledge on the part of the reader. On the other hand, popular works are written for a broader audience but often rely on inferior secondary and even tertiary sources of information.

As far as has been possible with so vast a subject, this book relies directly on primary sources; in particular, it has made use of some original books and manuscripts that are especially rich sources of information but are not well known even in scholarly circles (the rules for games, for example, derive from a forgotten 17th-century treatise on the subject). This is particularly true in the hands-on sections of the book: the patterns, recipes, rules, and so on are all based as far as possible on primary sources. Where primary sources are impractical, the book strives to make use of the best and most recent secondary work on the period.

At the same time, I have attempted to present this information in a format that will be accessible and enjoyable for a wide audience. After all, the greatest value of the past lies in its interaction with the present. If history only touches the historians, it is truly a lifeless form of knowledge. Readers of this book may be surprised to find just how much of Elizabethan life is relevant to the present. The Elizabethans were dealing with many of the same issues that face us today: unemployment resulting from an economy in transition, conflicting views over the relationship between religion and the state, a technological revolution in the media of communication, bitter cultural strife, and a general sense that the established social order was at risk of disintegration. In the modern age, where we are increasingly worried about our ability to sustain our standard of living and about the impact of our activities on the environment, we can benefit by learning how people lived in a period when their material expectations were much lower and the degree of industrialization was still quite limited. This is not to suggest that we should idealize the Elizabethan age—it was also a period of hardship, brutality, and intolerance—but we can acquire a much more meaningful perspective on the present by becoming familiar with the past.

1

A Brief History of Tudor England

The Middle Ages are customarily taken to have ended when Richard III was defeated by Henry Tudor at the Battle of Bosworth in 1485. Henry's accession as Henry VII marked the end of the Wars of the Roses, which had dominated English politics for much of the 15th century. The coronation of the first Tudor monarch was to herald the beginning of an unprecedented period of peace that lasted until the outbreak of civil war in 1642.

Henry VII devoted his reign to establishing the security of his throne, which he passed on to his son Henry VIII in 1509. Henry VIII is best known for having married six wives, but his marital affairs were of great political importance as well. His first wife, Catherine of Aragon, produced only a daughter, named Mary. Desperate for a male heir, Henry applied to the pope to have his marriage annulled. The request was refused, so Henry arranged for Parliament to pass a body of legislation that withdrew England from the Catholic Church, placing the king at the head of the new Church of England.

As head of his own church, Henry had his marriage annulled and married Anne Boleyn. This marriage proved no more successful in Henry's eyes, as it produced only a daughter—little did he know that this daughter, as Elizabeth I, was to become one of England's most successful and best-loved monarchs. Henry had Anne Boleyn executed on charges of adultery. His third wife, Jane Seymour, died of natural causes, but not before bearing him his only son, Edward. Of Henry's three subsequent wives, none bore any heirs.

Henry had no desire to make any significant changes in church teachings, but there was growing pressure in the country to follow the lead of the Continental Protestants such as Martin Luther; English Protestants were later heavily influenced by Jean Calvin, a French Protestant who established a rigidly Protestant state in Geneva.

The English church moved only slightly toward Protestantism in Henry's lifetime. Upon Henry's death in 1547, his son came to the throne as Edward VI. Edward was still underage, and his reign was dominated by his guardians, who promoted Protestant reformation in the English church. Edward died in 1553 before reaching the age of majority. The throne passed to his eldest half-sister, Mary. Mary had been raised a devout Catholic by her mother, and it came as no surprise that Mary brought England back into the Catholic Church. Her reign would prove brief and undistinguished. She committed England to a Spanish alliance by marrying Philip II, who became king of Spain in 1556. The marriage led to English participation in Philip's war against France. The war went poorly and England lost Calais, the last remnant of its once extensive French empire. Mary died shortly after, in 1558. Today she is popularly remembered as Bloody Mary due to her persecution of Protestants—some 300 were executed during her reign, while others escaped into exile in Protestant communities on the Continent.

With Mary's death, the throne passed to Henry's only surviving child, Elizabeth. She was not an ardent Protestant, although she was of Protestant leanings. Even more important, her claim to the throne depended on the independence of the English church. The pope had never recognized Henry's divorce, so in Catholic eyes, Elizabeth was the illegitimate child of an adulterous union and could not be queen. Elizabeth had Parliament withdraw England from the Catholic Church once more and was established as head of the Church of England, as her father had been.

The new queen faced serious international challenges. Her country was still officially at war with France and Scotland. Elizabeth swiftly concluded a peace treaty, but Scotland, now under the governance of a French regent, Mary of Guise, remained a potential threat. Mary reigned in the name of her daughter, Mary Stuart (known today as Mary Queen of Scots), who remained in France, where she was queen consort of the French king Francis II. Elizabeth strengthened her position in Scotland by cultivating relations with the growing number of Scottish Protestants who preferred Protestant England to Catholic France. In 1559 John Knox, the spiritual leader of the militant Scottish Protestants, returned to Scotland from exile in Geneva, and the country rose against the regent. After some hesitation, Elizabeth sent military support. The French were expelled from Scotland, and the Protestant party took effective control.

France too had a growing Protestant movement, and the death of Francis II in 1560 led to a civil war between Protestants and Catholics. Elizabeth sent troops to Normandy in 1562 to support the Protestant cause, hoping to reestablish the foothold on the Continent that her sister had lost, but the army was ravaged by illness and had to be withdrawn the following year. Religious conflict between French Catholics and Protestants erupted intermittently throughout Elizabeth's reign, substantially undermining France's influence in international affairs.

The death of Francis II impacted Scotland as well, as the widowed Mary Stuart returned to her native country. Her reign was tumultuous, and relations with her subjects were not helped by her firm Catholicism. After a series of misadventures, Mary's subjects rose against her, and she was ultimately forced to seek refuge in England in 1568.

The situation was extremely awkward for Elizabeth, who believed in the divine right of a monarch to occupy her throne, but who was also dependent on the Protestant party in Scotland to keep England's northern border secure. To make matters worse, Mary had some claim to the English throne by right of her grandmother, a sister of Henry VIII. According to the Catholic Church, Elizabeth was illegitimate and Mary was the rightful queen. Mary remained in comfortable confinement in England during a series of fruitless negotiations to restore her to the Scottish throne.

Unfortunately for Mary, she was unable to resist meddling in English politics. Many Catholics wanted to see her replace Elizabeth as Queen of England, and Mary was only too willing to entertain the idea. Northern England was still home to large numbers of Catholics, and in 1569 several of the northern earls led a rebellion against Elizabeth, thinking to place Mary on the throne. The rebels were swiftly suppressed, but the incident was a reminder of the threat posed by Elizabeth's Catholic rival. The following year, the pope issued a Bull, or papal decree, excommunicating Elizabeth and declaring her deposed, a move that further strained relations between the two queens.

Mary's interactions with Catholic conspirators only intensified after the Northern Rebellion. During 1570–71 a plot was organized by Roberto Ridolfi, a Florentine banker, to have Mary wed the Duke of Norfolk, the highest-ranking nobleman in England, with an eye to creating a powerful Catholic alliance to topple the Queen. The plot was discovered, and Norfolk, already under suspicion for his involvement with the rebellion of 1569, was executed for treason. Many people urged Elizabeth to have Mary executed as well, but she was extremely reluctant to kill a queen, knowing the implications to herself.

In the meantime, relations with Spain were deteriorating. At first Elizabeth had worked to preserve something of the alliance between England and Spain created by her sister's marriage to Philip II, but the atmosphere of religious conflict on the Continent made this increasingly difficult. In the Low Countries, a population that had come to embrace Protestantism was still under the rule of the Catholic Philip II. Rebellion erupted in ˋ1566–67. At first Protestantism was widely spread throughout the area, but over time a successful Spanish counteroffensive succeeded in regaining the southern provinces (equivalent to modern-day Belgium), leaving only the northern provinces (the modern Netherlands) in a state of rebellion. Popular sentiment in England was strongly in support of the Protestant rebels, and many Englishmen volunteered to fight in the Netherlands against Spain, even though Spain and England were still officially friends. Even Elizabeth, who still wanted to eke out what remained of the Spanish alliance, was not happy about the presence of a large Catholic force suppressing Protestantism practically on England's doorstep.

Spain's very size and power made it a threat, and the situation was made worse by Spain's vast and profitable empire in the New World. Elizabeth was reluctant to undertake the risks and expense of war, but she turned to more subtle means of undermining Spanish power. In particular, she gave her support to the sea-dogs, privateers who preyed on Spanish shipping. Perhaps the greatest was Francis Drake, who circled the globe in 1577–80, wreaking havoc on Spanish shipping and colonies and returning home with a phenomenal 4,700 percent profit for those who had invested in the voyage. The Queen herself was the largest shareholder.

By 1584 the international situation was becoming extremely ominous. A Catholic fanatic had assassinated William of Orange, the leader of the Dutch Protestants, reminding Elizabeth that Europe's mounting religious conflict could threaten her very life. The Catholic faction that dominated France was negotiating an alliance with Spain, and Antwerp was on the verge of falling to a Spanish siege. Elizabeth concluded a treaty with the Dutch Protestants and sent an English army to aid them in their cause.

Under the circumstances, Mary Stuart was a grave liability. She continued to be at the center of plots against Elizabeth. In 1583 a Catholic Englishman named Francis Throckmorton was arrested and found to be carrying a list of leading Catholics and potential landing places for an invading army. Under torture, he revealed plans for a major Spanish invasion of England.

The Queen's advisors urged the death of Mary, but still Elizabeth resisted. In 1586 a further plot was uncovered in which a young Catholic gentleman named Anthony Babington had engaged with several accomplices to assassinate the Queen. Mary had given her explicit assent to the scheme. After a trial and prolonged vacillation by Elizabeth, an order was sent in 1587 for Mary's execution; but after Mary was beheaded, Elizabeth denied that she had ordered the execution and made a show of punishing those involved.

All this while, Spain had been making preparations to remove Elizabeth by force, gathering a massive fleet in various Spanish ports. The fleet was to sail to the Spanish Netherlands, rendezvous with the Spanish army stationed there, and make the short crossing to England. In the summer of 1588, the Invincible Armada set sail.

The expedition was a disastrous failure. The English ships, smaller, more agile, better crewed, and more heavily armed with cannons, harassed the Spanish fleet as it sailed up the English Channel. In the face of bad weather,

A fight at sea. [Holinshed]

the Spanish anchored at Calais; during the night the English set several of their own ships on fire and sent them in among the Spanish ships, forcing the Armada to disperse. The next day there was heavy fighting off the Flemish coast, as winds from the west forced the Spanish ships eastward, and several of them were lost to the coastal shoals. It proved impossible to rendezvous with the army, and the adverse winds made it impossible for the Armada to sail back into the Channel. The fleet was forced to make its way around the British Isles, battered by storms and decimated by malnutrition and disease, until about half the original fleet finally made it back to Spain in mid-September.

The war with Spain dragged on inconclusively for the rest of Elizabeth's reign. The Spanish sent several subsequent armadas, but none met with any success; the English sent raids to Spanish ports, with minimal effect. In the mean time, England's military entanglements spread. The Dutch provinces continued their war for independence with English assistance. The Protestant Henri of Navarre inherited the French crown as Henri IV in 1589, and Elizabeth sent multiple expeditions to help him secure his throne.

Elizabeth's greatest problem was in Ireland, where centuries of resistance to English domination were coming to a head. Already in 1579–83 there had been a protracted rebellion by one of the leading Irish lords in the southern part of the country. In 1580 the Spanish had sent a small and unsuccessful expedition to Kerry. In 1596 Hugh O'Neill, the Earl of Tyrone and perhaps the most powerful man in northern Ireland, began a major revolt against England, assisted by Spanish supplies. In 1599 Elizabeth sent Robert Devereux, the Earl of Essex, to suppress the revolt, but he proved thoroughly incompetent as a military commander. He was recalled and promptly became embroiled in a plot to take over the government. The scheme failed miserably: Essex was imprisoned and, ultimately, executed.

The money and supplies required for supporting these military efforts strained the English economy in the 1590s. The situation was exacerbated by a series of bad harvests in 1594–97. A likely contributing factor in these repeated crop failures was a climatic downturn that began around the time of Elizabeth's accession and would last through the 1600s. Known to historians as the Little Ice Age, the trend brought colder and wetter weather, even freezing the Thames River in 1565 and 1595. Grain shortages in the mid-1590s led to runaway inflation, famine, and civil unrest. Repeated visitations of the plague only worsened the sense of crisis.

Yet these years of domestic troubles were also in many ways the cultural pinnacle of Elizabeth's reign. England's first permanent theater was built in London in 1576; in 1598–99 it was moved to the south bank of the Thames and renamed the Globe. The Globe and the other burgeoning theaters of late Elizabethan London would host the works of some of the most renowned playwrights in the English language: Christopher Marlowe was at the apex in the late 1580s and early 90s, Ben Jonson was on the rise by 1600, and William Shakespeare penned many of his most famous plays during the final decade of Elizabeth's reign. Poetry too was enjoying a golden age: Edmund Spenser's *The Faerie Queen* appeared in 1590, and Shakespeare's earliest published poetry in 1593. At the geopolitical level, some of the initial groundwork was laid that would lead to the emergence of the British Empire: the first attempt to found an overseas colony was in 1585 in Roanoke—although the colony did not survive, the English claim to Virginia (named for Elizabeth as the Virgin Queen) would be revived with colonies at Jamestown and Plymouth under Elizabeth's successor. In 1600 Elizabeth chartered the East India Company, which would ultimately become the agent for Britain's imperial expansion in Asia.

By the time Elizabeth died in 1603, having lived 69 years and ruled for almost half a century, many of her subjects were ready to see someone new on the throne. Willful to the end, the Queen refused to take to her bed: she passed away upright in her chair. She had never married, and there were no immediate heirs. The crown passed peacefully to James VI, son of Mary Stuart. Already king of Scotland, James now ruled England as James I, the first of the country's Stuart kings. His subjects were delighted to have a man on the throne again, but he and his heirs proved less adept at managing England than Elizabeth. James's son Charles would lose the throne and his life through civil war in the 1640s, and his grandson James II would be overthrown in a bloodless coup in 1688. Under the Stuarts, Elizabeth's reign came to be idealized as a lost golden age, and the mythology of Elizabeth's "merrie England" persists even into the 21st century.

2

Society

The underlying reality that shaped English society during Elizabeth's reign is the shape of the land itself. England is topographically complex, but at the broadest level, the country can be roughly divided into Lowland and Highland zones. Most of England falls in the Lowland zone, which consists of the central, southern, and eastern parts of the country. The land here is relatively gentle and fertile, supporting intensive agriculture and higher concentrations of population. The Highland zone lies in the north and west: the land here is rougher, more mountainous, and less fertile, supporting lower population densities. This distinction played out in various ways in the story of Elizabethan England: the Lowland zone was more densely populated, provided the bulk of the country's staple grains, and was wealthier and more subject to social and cultural change. The Highland zone had fewer people, relied more heavily on pastoralism, and was poorer and culturally more conservative.

Local divisions within this broad framework were shaped by geographical factors. Rough and mountainous country divided populations from each other, as did marshes. But rivers acted less as boundaries and more as unifying thoroughfares. Communication was easier up and down a river than across the highlands that separated one river valley from another, so rivers and their tributaries created integrated economic and cultural zones: such was the region unified by the Thames River, which incorporated the central area of southern England from London to the Cotswolds, and the Severn River watershed, which included the adjoining areas to the west, stretching into Wales.

THE POPULATION

England's overall population was probably over 3 million when Elizabeth came to the throne in 1558, growing to over 4 million by the time of her death in 1603. These figures represent roughly 1/10 of the population of England today. The overwhelming majority lived in rural areas, although London was growing rapidly.

Not all of this population were ethnically or culturally English. Wales and western Cornwall were subject to the English crown: Cornwall was normally reckoned as a part of England, and Wales was integrated into the English system in many respects. Yet these regions still spoke Welsh and Cornish—languages distantly related to Gaelic and unintelligible to the English—and their linguistic distinctiveness mirrored a very distinct society and culture. Ireland was also officially under English rule, although effective English control was limited to the eastern part of the country. The population of Ireland included Englishmen and English-speaking Irishmen in the east, with the remainder of the country inhabited by Gaelic-speaking Irishmen. Scotland was still an independent kingdom, although England and Scotland came to be under a single ruler when the Scottish king, James VI, inherited the English throne in 1603. Southern Scotland spoke its own dialect of English, whereas the northern and western parts of the country still spoke Scottish Gaelic, a close relative of Irish.

Within England itself there was a significant population of foreign immigrants, typically Protestants who had fled the Continent because of wars or religious persecution. These immigrants came primarily from the Low Countries (especially Flanders), Germany, and France, with a few from Spain and Italy. The proportion of foreigners was highest in London—perhaps around 3 percent of the population. It was much lower in other areas, and there were few in the countryside, except in areas with growing mining or cloth-making industries. Finally, by this period the Romany, or gypsies, had come across the Channel to England. The Romany were a culture largely to themselves; they had a language of their own and led wandering lives on the fringes of society. They did not generally assimilate to mainstream English society, although they had a significant impact on the culture of vagrancy and the underworld.[1]

THE MEDIEVAL HERITAGE

A modern person looking to understand Elizabethan society needs to begin by digging even further back in history, into the Middle Ages. Although many of the definitive features of medieval feudalism and manorialism had died out by the late 1500s, Elizabethan England was deeply shaped by its feudal heritage, and many of the key structures of Elizabethan society cannot be understood without understanding their medieval roots.

During the Middle Ages, society and the economy had been organized around people's relationship to farmland. The relationship was understood as *holding* rather than owning: landholders at every level were called *tenants*, literally "holders." (Technically this still holds true, as land ultimately belongs to the state that holds sovereignty over it, a fact occasionally exercised through the legal principle of eminent domain.)

A medieval landholder inherited the right to occupy and use a certain landholding under terms established by custom. Theoretically, all land actually belonged to the sovereign monarch, and was passed downward in a hierarchical chain, each landholder providing payment to his overlord in exchange for the landholding. Landholdings were inherited like other forms of property, but they were not owned outright: they could not be freely bought or sold, and it was very difficult in the Middle Ages to acquire land by any means other than inheritance. Since feudalism emerged at a time when there was limited cash in circulation, payment was in the form of service rather than money.

At the upper ranks of society, landholding was by *feudal* tenure, meaning that it was theoretically paid for with military service. When their lord called upon them, feudal tenants were expected to serve as mounted and armored knights with a following of soldiers. This was the aristocratic form of service, and landholders who held their land by feudal tenure were considered to be of gentlemanly birth, along with everyone in their families. Feudal landholdings carried with them a measure of legal authority over the landholding and its inhabitants, and gentle status in general went hand-in-hand with political influence, social privilege, and cultural prestige.

The smallest unit of aristocratic landholding was the manor, typically consisting of hundreds of acres of farmland. The manor often coincided physically with a village settlement and its farmlands, and it might also correspond to a parish in the hierarchy of the church. The medieval manor lord parceled out landholdings to his peasant tenants, keeping a portion in his own hands as *demesne*. The villagers held their land by *manorial* tenure, paying for it in annual rents of cash and goods, but above all through labor services that provided the manor lord with manpower to cultivate the demesne.

Everyone below the level of the manor lord was considered a commoner, although there were subdivisions of status among them. Some were freeholding peasants, whose rents and services were minimal and who were free to leave the manor if they chose. The majority were villeins or serfs, who owed several days of labor service a week and had limited personal rights and freedoms—they were not quite slaves, but they were in a position of servitude to their lord.

The functionality of this system rested on the culture's respect for custom and inheritance. For aristocrat and commoner alike, the terms of a landholding were not negotiated personally, but were established by the

THE CLASS SOCIETY

In London, the rich disdain the poor; the courtier the citizen; the citizen the country man. One occupation disdaineth another: the merchant the retailer; the retailer the craftsman; the better sort of craftsmen the baser; the shoemaker the cobbler; the cobbler the carman [carter]. One nice dame disdains her next neighbour should have that furniture to her house or dainty dish or device which she wants. She will not go to church, because she disdains to mix herself with base company, and cannot have her close pew by herself. She disdains to wear that everyone wears, or hear that preacher which everyone hears.

Thomas Nashe, *Christ's Tears over Jerusalem* (London: James Roberts, 1593), fols. 70v-71r.

traditional customs associated with that holding, passed down from parent to child across the generations.

The on-the-ground realities of medieval feudalism and manorialism were complex, varying heavily with local circumstances, traditions, and history: it was never an organized system, but a characteristic pattern of organization that arose out of a shared set of circumstances. By the late Middle Ages, feudalism was being substantially transformed. By 1290, intermediate levels of feudal tenure had been eliminated, and all feudal land was held directly from the crown. At about the same period, military service was being replaced by cash payments: the king preferred to collect money to hire his own troops, rather than relying on the traditional service of feudal knights.

At the manorial level, customary service-rents proved similarly unsatisfactory to both lords and tenants in a rapidly changing economy, and labor services were being replaced by cash rents. As labor services declined, so too did serfdom, which was largely gone by the 1500s. When Henry VIII abolished the monasteries during the 1530s, a great deal of monastic land came onto the market; unlike traditional medieval holdings, this land could be freely bought and sold, further loosening the older strictures of feudal landholding. By Elizabeth's day, feudal tenants and village freeholders were the effective owners of their land, while serfs had been transformed into renters.

THE ELIZABETHAN ARISTOCRACY

Although England was no longer a feudal society by the time Elizabeth came to the throne, feudal and manorial structures still played a major part in the social fabric. At the upper levels, feudalism provided the vocabulary of personal status that shaped the aristocratic hierarchy. This elaborate hierarchy embraced only a tiny minority of the population: noblemen, knights, and squires together accounted for well under 1 percent of the population, and ordinary gentlemen for about 1 percent.

At the top of this hierarchy was the monarch, the titular sovereign owner of all land in the kingdom, and still one of the biggest actual landowners in the country. Below her was the peerage, heirs to the great nobles of the Middle Ages who had been able to ride to war with large followings of knights at their command. Titles of nobility were inherited: the eldest son inherited the title when his father died, while his siblings ranked slightly below. In descending order of rank, the titles were duke, marquis, earl, viscount, and baron or lord; their wives were called duchess, marchioness, countess, viscountess, and baroness or lady. The actual title was not the only criterion of aristocratic status. Many titles were relatively recent creations—nearly half the peerage were first or second generation when Elizabeth came to the throne—so the longer a title had been in the family, the more respect it enjoyed.

The total number of peers was never much above 60. This was a highly exclusive sector of society, but in contrast to the medieval peerage, heavily dependent on the favor of the monarch. Attempts to raise medieval-style aristocratic rebellions failed miserably in 1569 and 1601. Medieval peers had expected to occupy the highest positions in government, but Elizabeth preferred to rely on lower-ranking gentlemen to help shape and implement her policies. Nonetheless, families at this level of society enjoyed tremendous landed wealth—their annual incomes were typically thousands of pounds a year—as well as prestige and influence at a national level, and the peers were entitled to sit in the House of Lords when Parliament was in session.

A substantial gap separated the peers from the knights, the next level down in the feudal hierarchy. The title of knight was never inherited: it had to be received from the monarch or a designated military leader. Knighthood in the Middle Ages had been a military title, but by the Elizabethan period, it had become a general mark of honor. As a knight, Sir William Cecil was addressed as Sir William, and his wife as Lady Mildred or Lady Cecil. There were probably about 300 to 500 knights at any given time: they were invariably wealthy landowners with substantial regional influence.

At the bottom of the feudal hierarchy were esquires (also called squires) and simple gentlemen. The distinction between the two was not always clear-cut. In theory, an esquire was a gentleman who had knights in his ancestry, but he might also be a gentleman of especially prominent standing.

Knights, squires, and gentlemen and their families were sometimes referred to collectively as the *gentry*—the total number of people in this category at the end of Elizabeth's reign may have been around 16,000. The gentry enjoyed considerable power and prestige in their local regions, and

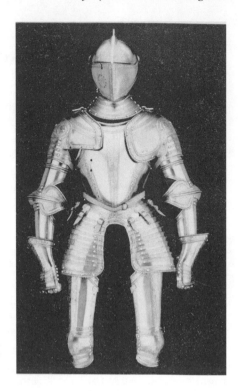

A cavalry armor of Henry Herbert, Earl of Pembroke, c. 1565. [Higgins Armory Museum]

the central government relied very heavily on them as a class to implement national policies at the local level, particularly through those who were chosen to serve as justices of the peace.

Although the gentry ranked far below the peerage in the Elizabethan hierarchy, contemporary culture saw the two as sharing the fundamental characteristic of gentle status that set them apart from commoners. The concept of the gentleman had been inherited from the Middle Ages, when gentle birth had meant belonging to the military class—those who fought on horseback in full armor. Such people had required sufficient income to allow them to purchase their expensive equipment and sufficient leisure to be able to practice the complex physical skills of mounted and armored combat. By the late 1500s, the military importance of the armored horseman was marginal, but the medieval tradition still shaped the concept of what made a gentleman. A classic Elizabethan definition of the gentleman is offered by Sir Thomas Smith in his treatise on English society, *De Republica Anglorum:*

Who can live idly and without manual labor and will bear the port, charge, and countenance of a gentleman, he shall be called "master," for that is the title which men give to esquires and other gentlemen, and shall be taken for a gentleman.[2]

As Smith suggests, the principal characteristic of the gentleman was a leisured and comfortable lifestyle supported without labor. Traditionally, this meant having enough land to live off the rents. Gentry landholdings were large—50 to 1,000 acres represented the lower end of the scale, supporting an income of hundreds of pounds a year.

The manor remained the basic unit of landholding among the privileged classes. Manor lords still retained some legal jurisdiction over their manors—courts held in their name still ratified land transfers in the manor, promulgated bylaws, and resolved minor disputes in the community. But the manor lord rarely exercised legal powers in person, and for most, the manor was above all a source of income. Manorial land was now part of any ambitious investor's portfolio. It offered a relatively stable annual income, as well as the social status that came with being a landowner. It could potentially be resold at profit when the market was favorable: old feudal manors were effectively sold through legal fictions and stratagems that circumvented feudal restrictions on property transfer, and former monastic landholdings were bought and sold freely.

A rich man and a beggar. [Traill and Mann]

Absentee manor lords had become common, leaving manorial administration in the hands of hired stewards. Some manors were actually owned by consortiums of investors. Other manor lords took a more proactive approach to estate management, looking for ways to maximize the yield on their land through new farming techniques or by restructuring their tenants' landholdings.

Although gentle status was associated with land ownership, not all gentlemen were landowners. In Smith's formulation, gentlemen were expected to live comfortably without manual labor, but this did not necessarily require landed income. Government service was considered an acceptable occupation for a gentleman. Many gentlemen supplemented their income through commercial activity, while successful merchants moved into the gentry class by acquiring rural land. Military service, although no longer required, was still a gentlemanly occupation: the officers of Elizabeth's army and navy were drawn from the gentry. In addition, anyone with a university education or working in a profession was considered a gentleman: such people included clergymen, physicians, lawyers, teachers, administrators, and secretaries (who were invariably men).

THE RURAL COMMUNITY

Below the gentry in the manorial hierarchy were the landholding commoners. Land could be held in various ways, deriving from the customs of the medieval manor. The most secure form of tenancy was the freehold. Freeholders held their lands in perpetuity: their holdings were passed from generation to generation with no change in terms. The rent charged for freehold lands had been fixed in the Middle Ages, and inflation had rendered the real cost of these holdings minimal. Few manor lords even bothered to collect freehold rents, and they consequently fell out of use: a freeholder was the effective owner of his landholding.

Less secure than a freeholding was leasehold land. Leasehold tenancies were for fixed periods, sometimes a lifetime or more—for example, for the life of the leaseholder, his wife, and his son—sometimes as little as a year. Leasehold land might be manorial demesne land, rented out by the manor lord as a source of cash, but villagers often leased to each other, sometimes subletting their own leaseholds. When a lease ended, it was subject to renegotiation. Manor lords often simply renewed the existing lease for the lessor, or for the heir in the case of a lifetime lease. But the end of a lease offered an opportunity for an ambitious landlord: he might take the land back into his own hands as part of his estate management strategy, or insist on a higher rent.

The heirs of medieval serfs were the copyholders, also called customary tenants. A copyhold was a landholding that had once been held under villeinage tenure. At the beginning of Elizabeth's reign, there were actually a few hundred villeins in the country, but villeinage was rapidly dying out, and had all but vanished by 1600. Although the copyholder was no longer in a state of personal servitude, copyhold tenure could be precarious. The terms of a copyhold were dictated by custom—the holder was supposed to have a copy of the manorial records that confirmed the right to the holding, but many essential features of the holding were never committed to writing. The rent, fees, and ancillary rights associated with the holding might be based purely on unwritten tradition, and it could be hard to prove which customs carried legal force and which did not.

In principle, a copyhold was a perpetual right that was passed on in the family like other heritable property, although the heir had to pay an entry fee at the beginning of the tenancy. However, when the copyhold changed hands, the landlord might try to raise the entry fee or the rent—sometimes with the deliberate intent of driving the heir out of the landholding. When conflicts arose, the tenant had no recourse to the Common Law courts, which had no jurisdiction over copyhold tenure. The matter might be brought before an Equity court, but the tenant still needed the resolve and the money to prosecute a case. In general, landlords were finding ways to replace copyhold tenancies with leaseholds, allowing them more flexibility in managing their estates.

For all forms of tenure, the land itself might be only a part of the rights associated with the holding. Villages typically had uncultivated areas of *commons* such as pasture and woodlands, shared collectively by the residents. A landholding often came with rights of commons: these might a quota of firewood from the woods; pasturage for a certain number of livestock; grazing animals on the village fields at certain times of year; or gathering leftovers from the fields after harvest—a custom called *gleaning* that was a significant source of food for the poorest villagers.

Tenants found themselves under increasing pressure in an age of inflation when many manor lords were looking to increase the yields from their lands. The simplest way was to raise fees and rents. Contemporaries called this *rack-renting*, and traditionalists saw it as exploitative, at least if the increase was excessive—naturally, landlords and tenants often disagreed on what was excessive.

Rack-renting could also be used to drive tenants out of their holdings. For many manor lords, the way to increase income was higher productivity. This often meant consolidating large blocks of agricultural land for greater efficiency or to implement improved farming techniques. By fair means or foul, many landowners were finding ways to build up consolidated farmlands, enclosing them with hedges to set them apart from the lands held by others. This process of *enclosure* might also incorporate common pastures and woodlands, converting them to farmland to increase their value. Not only did enclosures provoke hostility when tenants were driven out of their holdings by unscrupulous tactics, but the enclosed land was no longer accessible for traditional rights of commons. Many saw enclosure as a violation of sanctioned custom, and for some it constituted a real threat to a livelihood that might be precariously balanced on the rights of commons. In 1601, tenants of Sir Miles Sandys of Willingham (Cambridgeshire) raised a joint fund to challenge at law his efforts to enclose common and fen lands; the following year a number of them broke into a meadow he had enclosed, pasturing cattle there in an act of symbolic protest—the conflict was ultimately settled by arbitration.[3]

This does not mean that all tenants were in constant danger of homelessness or impoverishment. Not all landlords were inclined to raise rents or evict tenants. They too had a vested interest in tradition and social stability, and many were reluctant to engage in behavior that could disrupt the social system. On the other side of the equation, many of the wealthier villagers were themselves buying up or trading landholdings to enclose them for purposes similar to those of the manor lords.

How a villager felt about enclosure might depend less on the terms of his holding and more on its size. These two were independent of each other, although the larger holdings were more likely to be freeholds, and the smaller ones leaseholds or copyholds.

The wealthiest villagers were known as yeomen. Traditionally, the title was supposed to apply to freeholders whose lands yielded revenues of at least 40 shillings a year, a qualification that entitled the holder to vote in Parliamentary elections. In reality, the 40s. qualification was outdated— one contemporary estimated that £6 would be a more realistic minimum— and in practice a leaseholder might also be considered a yeoman if he held enough land. Roughly speaking, the yeomen were landholders who held something on the order of 50 acres or more. At this level they could reliably ride out the tumultuous waves of the Tudor economy and sustain or increase their wealth. Overall, this class probably accounted for around 10 percent of the population. A yeoman's income might amount to dozens of pounds a year, and the wealthier among them had incomes equivalent to the gentry. The yeoman was a dominant figure in village society, and was often called on to serve in such positions as village constable or parish churchwarden.

Tenants whose holdings were smaller but still sufficient to sustain a family were known as husbandmen—a term also used more generally of anyone who worked his own landholding, more or less equivalent to the modern "farmer." A typical husbandman's landholding might be around 30 acres, yielding a normal annual income around £15, enough to maintain his family comfortably under normal circumstances, but potentially at risk in the inflationary and uneven economic environment of the period. Husbandmen may have accounted for about 30 percent of England's population.

The smallest landholders were called cottagers. A cottager might hold no more than the cottage his family lived in and the acre or two on which it sat. A few had some land in the village fields as well, occasionally as much as 10 or 15 acres. A cottager's holding was too small to support a household, so cottagers had to supplement their income by hiring themselves out as laborers. Most did agricultural work, but depending on local opportunities, there might be other options: metalworking (especially making small wares like nails or knives), weaving, pottery, charcoal burning, and mining, were all common sources of income for a rural cottager and would eventually lead to urbanization of some of these rural communities during the Industrial Revolution.

At the very base of the rural hierarchy were the servants and laborers who had no homes of their own and were entirely dependent on others for both lodging and livelihood. Such people may have represented a quarter to a third of the rural population. Servants were common in landholding households at all levels, particularly if the family lacked children of an age to help out with farmwork. Gentry households might have specialized domestic servants, but most rural servants were general workers hired on an annual basis, living in the home and helping out with the daily male or female work of the farm—looking after livestock, tending to the dairying, and helping to cultivate the fields.

Laborers did similar kinds of work, but on a more short-term basis. They might be local cottagers, or they might be itinerant workers traveling from village to village in search of work. The life of such traveling workers was precarious. It was technically illegal for them to leave their home parish without permission from an employer or a local authority, and those who had trouble finding employment could easily find themselves falling into poverty, vagrancy, or crime. Many ended up migrating to a town in search of work.

THE URBAN COMMUNITY

The constant influx of labor from the countryside was essential to the life of the Elizabethan town. Urban living conditions were crowded and unsanitary, and deaths outpaced births. Immigration from the countryside allowed towns not only to maintain their numbers, but to grow substantially over the course of Elizabeth's reign. The fastest expansion was in London, which grew from an estimated 120,000 inhabitants in 1558 to over 200,000 by 1603, overtaking Venice as the third largest city in Europe, after Paris and Naples. Such a rate of growth required an influx of some 3,750 immigrants a year by the end of Elizabeth's reign. London dominated English society to a degree not generally true of other European capitals: about 1 Englishman in 20 lived in London, and few people in the country would be without a friend or relative who lived in London.

Other towns were growing, but none was on the same scale. The second tier of English cities consisted of Norwich, Bristol, and York, with about 10,000–12,000 in 1558 and 15,000 in 1603. Only a handful of other towns, including Newcastle-upon-Tyne, Salisbury, Exeter, and Coventry, had as many as 10,000 inhabitants by 1600. Historians sometimes refer to these

Interior of a shop. [Hindley]

cities as provincial capitals: they acted as hubs in the political and economic life of their respective sections of the country.

Below these were about 100 towns that constituted a significant presence
in their counties: these county centers typically had populations of 1,500 to
7,000, with complex street layouts and city walls, multiple markets in the
course of a week, and annual fairs. The smallest urban centers were the 700
or so local market towns, having populations of no more than 1,000–2,000,
and often fewer, with limited urban features beyond their weekly market.
Most of the boroughs that sent representatives to parliament fell into this
last category. Overall, only about 10 percent of the population lived in
towns of 1,000 or more by the end of Elizabeth's reign.

Although towns varied hugely in size, they shared a number of features
in common. Most held charters that gave them a measure of self-govern-
ment, including the right to choose their governing officers, establish local
by-laws, hold courts to settle civil and petty criminal cases, and to hold
and regulate markets. Land in the towns was normally held by burgage
tenure, a less restrictive form of land ownership that allowed the property
to be freely bought and sold.

Towns often played a role as focal points in the network of royal and
church administration: sheriffs and royal courts worked from the major

town in a shire, and the larger towns might be home to a bishop's cathedral or the seat of an archdeacon. However, the town's own government and social structure operated independently of these authorities.

At the heart of urban government was the concept of town citizenship, usually termed *freedom* of the town. A town's citizens, also called freemen or burgesses, were those who enjoyed the full privileges of belonging to the town. These typically included the right to trade freely and some degree of participation in the town's government. Many towns had some sort of deliberative or legislative body in which freemen were involved. A freeman might also hold civic office, for example serving on a court or as a constable. As a self-governing polity, a town relied on its citizenry to staff the largely unpaid posts in town government, and perhaps one freeman in four or five held some office at any given time. However, real political power typically lay in the hands of an oligarchy drawn from the most wealthy and influential citizens.

Freemen may have accounted for a quarter to a half of the adult male population in some towns; in London the figure appears to have been as much as three-quarters. They were usually male householders who had acquired their status in one of three ways. Patrimony was the right of any citizen's son to become a citizen himself once he came of age. Redemption allowed a person to purchase citizenship. The third route was through apprenticeship: a person who successfully completed apprenticeship in a trade was allowed to become a citizen.

The process of gaining the freedom of the town was commonly administered through the town's guilds, reflecting the close relationship between town government and the guild system. The guilds, often called *companies*, were trade associations that governed the practice of a particular trade in the town, including product quality, working conditions, and who was allowed to ply the trade. The correlation between guild and trade was not always precise. In small towns, many trades might be administered by a single guild: the Mercer's Company in Kingston-on-Thames included haberdashers, grocers, chandlers, painters, cutlers, vintners, glaziers, and barbers. Some towns had only a single guild to which all tradesmen belonged. Even in a large city like London, with its 60-odd different guilds, a person might belong to one guild even though he practiced the trade of another.

Most urban freemen attained their status through a period of apprenticeship. Upon successfully completing the period of training required by the guild, the apprentice became a freeman of the guild and so acquired freedom of the town as well. A freeman initially ranked as a journeyman, meaning that he was free to work in the trade under someone else's employ. Those who had the means and were approved by the guild could set themselves up as independent practitioners, called *masters* or *householders*. All freemen had some participation in the governance of the guild, but as with the town government, real authority typically lay in the hands

Table 2.1.
The Social Hierarchy

Aristocracy and Their Servants	Clergy	Rural Commons	Urban Commons	Others
Queen				
Duke (1, executed 1572)				
Marquis (1–2)				
Earl (ca. 20)	Archbishop (2)		Mayor of London	
Viscount (2)				
Baron (ca. 40)	Bishop (24)			
Knight (ca. 300–500)	Archdeacon		Alderman of London; Mayor of great town	Major legal officer
Esquire, Gentleman (ca. 16,000)	Parish priest (ca. 8,000)		Lesser mayor or civic officer; Merchant	Professional (Physician, Lawyer, etc.)
Yeoman	Deacon, Vicar	Yeoman (ca. 500,000)	Free tradesman	Master of Arts
Groom		Husbandman	Journeyman	
Page		Cottager	Apprentice	
		Laborer, Servant	Laborer, Servant	
		Vagrant	Vagrant	

A schematized table of the social hierarchy. Approximate numbers have been included where available to give a sense of proportions. Ranks at the same horizontal level could be considered roughly equivalent.

of a self-coopting oligarchy of leading masters, often called liverymen. The wealth and status of guild members varied enormously: at the lower end, ordinary freemen might live at a level comparable to a yeoman or husbandman in the country, while the richer merchants in London had incomes that approached that of the peerage.

Outside the guilds were those whose work was not part of the guild system, with limited prospects of advancement: servants, porters, water carriers, day laborers, and other unskilled workers. Nor did all skilled workers belong to a guild. Few guilds were authorized to exercise authority outside the town where they were based, so a tradesman might set up shop beyond the city's jurisdiction in order to avoid guild restriction. The suburbs of London were a magnet for skilled craftsmen, often foreign, who could not break into the guild system, and many crafts were practiced in the countryside beyond the reach of guild supervision.

THE UNDERCLASS

Unskilled laborers were always at risk of falling into the substantial and growing number of unemployed poor. Perhaps 10 percent of the population at any given time were in need of assistance to support themselves, with the rate of poverty higher in the towns than in the country, due to the constant influx of people in need of work. Many of the poor were orphans, widows, abandoned wives, the elderly, and the infirm; but their ranks were increased by growing numbers of unemployed but able-bodied adults displaced by economic change, as well as by men returning from service in the army or navy.

Villagers who were unable to support themselves might turn to the charity of neighbors and relatives. In the towns, there were endowed private institutions, called hospitals, that took in residents for the medium or long term. In London, Christ's Hospital received orphans and foundlings, St. Bartholomew's Hospital provided care for those with curable illnesses, St. Thomas Hospital took in the disabled, and Bethlehem Hospital housed those with mental illnesses. Other foundations provided permanent residences for the elderly poor. Conditions in these institutions were generally spartan at best; all were chronically underfunded, and none had the capacity to accommodate everyone who was in need of a place.

In response to growing concerns over the problems of poverty and vagrancy, Elizabeth's government began to implement laws to punish

---

THE PUNISHMENT OF VAGRANTS, 1573

At High Holborn, county Middlesex and elsewhere in the same county on the same day, Nicholas Welshe, Anthony Musgrove, Hugh Morice, John Thomas, Philip Thomas, Alice Morice and Katherine Hevans, being over fourteen years of age, and strong and fit for labour, were masterless vagrants without any lawful means of subsistence. Whereupon it was decreed that each of the said vagrants should be whipped severely and burnt on the right ear.

Middlesex County Records, cited Arthur F. Kinney, *Rogues, Vagabonds, and Sturdy Beggars: A New Gallery of Tudor and Early Stuart Rogue Literature* (Amherst: University of Massachusetts, 1973), 17.

vagrants while helping those who were genuinely unable to work. Already in 1552 a law had been passed encouraging those of means to contribute to a voluntary parish fund for the support of the poor. In 1563 this contribution was made mandatory, and the first comprehensive Poor Law was issued in 1572, establishing the framework for dealing with poverty that remained in place until the 1800s.

The Poor Laws acknowledged for the first time the existence of involuntary unemployment. Each parish was to take care of its own residents, based on a mandatory tax, called the Poor Rate, levied on those able to pay. Those physically unable to work were to be given regular stipends. The unemployed were to be apprenticed, placed in service, or sent to workhouses where they were given tasks that included pulling apart old ropes to make oakum (used in sealing ships) or operating treadmills to grind flour. Those who shirked labor might be whipped or imprisoned, and vagrants from outside the parish were to be whipped and sent back to their parish of origin. This last provision could be a real problem for the unemployed poor, since anyone leaving their parish in search of work could theoretically be punished as a vagrant (although it was possible to get a license to travel from a local justice of the peace).

The Elizabethan Poor Laws lie behind the dismal and abusive world that Dickens would depict two and a half centuries later in *Oliver Twist*. In their own day, the Poor Laws were a serious and innovative attempt to address a growing problem, but they had little real impact on either poverty or vagrancy. The underlying problem of national-level economic change could not ultimately be resolved by parish-level solutions. Rural communities were unable to support their growing populations, and the rural poor who had no prospects in their villages had no choice but to migrate in search of employment. These migrants would eventually gravitate toward emerging centers of manufacture, providing the labor that supported Britain's industrialization after 1700.

In the mean time, long-term unemployment could lead to a life among the growing number of permanent beggars and vagabonds, who may have numbered as many as 20,000. In combination with the gypsies, they were beginning to create an underworld culture of their own; in fact, the Elizabethans were both fascinated and horrified by the counterculture of the lawless, much as people today are intrigued by the culture of the Mafia or street gangs. A whole genre of literature emerged that purported to offer a glimpse into the alternative society in which these rogues circulated: social organization, tricks of the trade, and the distinctive *cant* in which they spoke to each other. John Awdeley's *Fraternity of Vagabonds* (1561) describes a few types:

An *Abraham Man* is he that walketh bare-armed and bare-legged, and feigneth himself mad, and carrieth a pack of wool, or a stick with bacon on it, or suchlike toy, and nameth himself Poor Tom . . .

A *Prigman* goeth with a stick in his hand like an idle person. His property is to steal clothes off the hedge, which they call "storing of the rogueman," or else to filch poultry, carrying them to the alehouse, which they call the "bousing inn," and there sit playing at cards and dice, till that is spent which they have so filched. . .

A *Kintchin Co* is called an idle runagate boy.[4]

Thomas Harman's *A Caveat for Common Cursitors* (1566) offers a canting conversation between two of these vagabonds:

Bene Lightmans to thy quarroms! In what libken hast thou libbed in this darkmans, whether in a libbege or in the strummel?

Good morrow to thy body! In what house hast thou lain in all night, whether in a bed or in the straw?

I couched a hogshead in a skipper this darkmans.

I lay me down to sleep in a barn this night.

I tour the strummel trine upon thy nab-cheat and togeman. . . . Bring we to Rome-vill, to nip a bung; so shall we have lour for the bousing-ken. And when we bring back to the dewse-a-vill, we will filch some duds off the ruffmans or mill the ken for a lag of duds.

I see the straw hang upon thy cap and coat. . . . Go we to London to cut a purse; then shall we have money for the alehouse. And when we come back again into the country, we will steal some linen clothes off some hedges, or rob some house for a buck [laundry-tub] of clothes.[5]

The cutpurse alluded to here typically wore a horn sheath on his thumb and carried a small knife, so that he could cut people's purses off their

---

WILLIAM FLEETWOOD, CITY RECORDER OF LONDON, DESCRIBES A SCHOOL FOR CUTPURSES IN 1585

One Wotton, a gentleman born, and sometime a merchant man of good credit, who falling by time into decay, kept an alehouse at Smart's Quay, near Billingsgate, and after for some misdemeanor being put down, he reared up a new trade of life, and in this same house he procured all the cutpurses about this city to repair to his same house. There was a school house set up to learn young boys to cut purses. There was hung up two devices: the one was a pocket, the other was a purse. The pocket had in it certain counters and was hung about with hawks' bells, and over the top did hang a little sacring bell; and he that could take a counter without any noise was allowed to be a "Public Foister"; and he that could take a piece of silver out of the purse without the noise of any bells, he was adjudged a "Judicial Nipper." Note that a foister is a pickpocket, and a nipper is termed a pickpurse, or a cutpurse.

R. H. Tawney and Eileen Power, eds., *Tudor Economic Documents* (London: Longmans, 1924), 2.337–8.

belts by slicing against his thumb. Pickpockets would actually filch valuables out of his victims' pockets (the word *filch*, as the dialogue suggests,
comes from the dialect of the Elizabethan rogue). Such thieves especially
frequented crowded places like markets, fairs, and public spectacles.

SOCIAL STABILITY AND AMBITION

In principle, Elizabethan society was a rigid and orderly hierarchy that
discouraged the pursuit of personal advancement. People were expected
to live within the social class of their parents, a man following his father's
vocation or one comparable to it, a woman marrying into a family similar
in status to the one in which she was born. Each person was supposed to
fit into a stable social network, remaining in place to preserve the steady
state of society as a whole.

The realities were much more complex. It was not always easy to be
certain of a person's social status. Formal titles could be verified, as in
the case of a nobleman, a knight, or a freeman in a guild. The less formal
distinctions, such as between an esquire and a gentleman, or between a
gentleman and a yeoman, were not always so clear. A prosperous yeoman
might hold more land than a minor gentleman; by subletting it to tenants
of his own, he could live off the rents and slip into the gentlemanly class.
Successful merchants often used their profits to purchase land and make
themselves gentlemen. For women, the opportunities for advancement
were more limited, since they were generally not in a position to accumulate wealth or power independent of a husband, although a woman
might advance in society if she managed to marry a man of significantly
higher social station. Meanwhile, a gentleman who acquired excessive
debts might slide down the social scale, and enclosure in the countryside
could leave a rural landholder without a livelihood.

The growth of education as a route to gentlemanly status also opened
up opportunities for social advancement and obscured the distinction
between gentleman and commoner. London in particular was a venue
where someone with education, polish, and enough money to afford a
good set of clothing might pass himself off as a gentleman, and perhaps
even win a lasting place in the gentlemanly class. The life story of William Shakespeare is emblematic: born in 1564 as the son of a glover in
the provincial market-town of Stratford-on-Avon, his success in London's
burgeoning entertainment industry allowed him to return in later years to
his home town as a major local landowner and gentleman with his own
coat of arms.

While the official social vocabulary was couched in traditional terms
of hierarchy and status, much of a person's standing actually depended
on a more fluid social asset known as *credit*. Credit reflected the respect
in which a person (particularly a man) was held and the confidence people placed in his ability to deliver on his commitments. A person could

be born into credit by virtue of their family's status or wealth, but credit was less rigid than status and could be more easily gained or lost by the choices a person made. Being able to make good on promises, repay debts, or avenge insults increased a man's credit; failing to do any of these diminished it. In a mobile society where people met strangers on a regular basis, it was possible to garner credit, at least in the short term, through outward appearances: dressing the part, displaying skills or knowledge that suggested a creditable person, carrying oneself with a certain poise and self-confidence. London in particular was a place where Elizabethans were daily negotiating credit among themselves, jockeying for position in an environment where there were opportunities that might make a man's fortune.

THE CHURCH

The Elizabethans inherited from the Middle Ages a social system in which church and state were regarded as inseparable. During the Middle Ages, every country in western Europe had adopted Catholicism as its state religion, and secular authorities worked closely with the church hierarchy to ensure religious conformity. It was widely assumed that without a shared structure of religious belief and practice, no society could survive. As Elizabeth's chief minister, Lord Burghley, put it, "That state could never be in safety, where there was toleration of two religions."[6]

Religious change in the age of Reformation had only deepened the connection between religious and secular authority. When Henry VIII with-

A sermon outside St. Paul's Cathedral in London. [*Shakespeare's England*]

drew England from the Catholic Church, he replaced the pope with the king, making himself head of both church and state. Religious nonconformity was now tantamount to treason.

Henry had no desire to pursue Protestant reform, but there was a growing trend toward Protestant thought in England. The doctrinal differences between Catholicism and Protestantism were complex, but many of them hinged on the contrast between concrete and intellectual approaches to religion. Catholicism affirmed the importance of concrete observances, such as religious ritual, veneration of saints, and charitable deeds; the Catholic Church taught that such things had the power to bring people closer to God. Protestants generally rejected this idea and stressed a more abstract form of religion: a person would not go to heaven by doing good deeds but by having faith in God, and the word of the Bible was to be taken as more important than traditional religious practices. Protestant reformism gained the ascendancy under Edward VI, and during Mary's reign, many English reformers deepened their Protestantism while in exile in Calvin's Geneva.

For a Renaissance monarch, Elizabeth was unusually tolerant in matters of belief—she famously remarked that she had no desire to "make windows into men's souls." Yet like her predecessors she insisted on outward religious conformity, and she was fully prepared to inflict savage physical punishment on those who threatened to undermine her church.

The church that took shape during her reign was Protestant in its doctrine but still retained many of the outward trappings of Catholicism. The number of saints' days was reduced, but they were not entirely eliminated; the garments worn by Elizabethan ministers were simpler than those of Catholic priests, but still more elaborate than the severe gowns worn in Geneva. Religious statuary was removed from the churches and wall paintings were covered over, but stained glass windows were allowed to remain, until normal wear and tear afforded an opportunity to replace them with clear panes. Monks and nuns had been abolished, but bishops and archdeacons continued to fulfill their medieval roles.

Administration of the Elizabethan church remained largely unchanged from the hierarchical structure inherited from Catholicism. At the base of the hierarchy was the parish church, typically serving a village or an urban neighborhood. Everyone was required to attend service at their parish church, and parishioners owed annual tithes amounting to a tenth of their income in money or goods. There were upwards of 9,000 parishes in the country, ranging in size from over 3,000 communicants to fewer than 10; a few dozen households or a couple of hundred people was a fairly typical parish population.

The right to nominate the parish priest and allocate the parish tithes was called an advowson. Many advowsons during the Middle Ages had belonged to monasteries: with the dissolution of the monasteries, these were sold off with other monastic property, so that many Elizabethan advowsons had ended up in secular hands. Others belonged to schools or university colleges, serving as endowments to support the operations of the institution.

The right to collect the principal tithes from the parish church was called the rectory, and whoever held that right was called the rector. In a bit more than half the parishes in the country, the rector was actually the appointed minister. In the rest, the owner of the advowson held onto the rectory and appointed a vicar to minister to the parish. The rector paid the vicar a salary, which in a rural parish might be supplemented by *small tithes*—the less valuable tithed produce of his parishioners—along with income from agricultural land that went with the vicar's position, called the *glebe.*

Inadequate funding could make it difficult for the church to attract skilled parish clergy. In 1576, an investigation in the bishopric of Lincoln found that one parish in six had no clergyman, and that in the archdeaconries of Lincoln and Stow only a third of the clergy had adequate knowledge of scripture for their duties. Such figures were worrisome to a government that feared efforts by Catholic priests and Protestant separatists to win converts from the English church, and concerted efforts by Elizabeth's bishops generally succeeded in raising the quality of the parish clergy over the course of her reign.

The minister was assisted in his work by a clerk who kept the parish records and by a pair of churchwardens who managed the practical affairs of the church building, property, and finances. The churchwardens were also required to report to the church hierarchy on the state of their parish and to present cases of misconduct for prosecution by the church courts. One or both churchwardens might be appointed by the vestry, a self-coopting board of leading parishioners. Upkeep of the parish church was offset by various sources of income such as the rental of pews, and some urban parishes owned substantial property on the side: in such cases the churchwardens had substantial administrative responsibilities that could include collecting rents from tenants, lending money, and buying and selling parish property.

The clergy were fewer in number than they had been during the Middle Ages, especially since there were no longer any monasteries. However, they still enjoyed a measure of prestige. A parish minister enjoyed the status of a low-ranking gentleman, while bishops sat in the House of Lords and had incomes not far below that of the peerage. The church was one of the best avenues by which a commoner might advance in society, and since the Catholic ban on clerical marriage had been lifted as part of the Protestant reformation, a clergyman could pass his status on to his family: Elizabeth's bishops were mostly commoners by birth, but a third of their sons managed to establish themselves as landed gentry.

Activities of the parish priest were overseen by his superiors in the church hierarchy. Parishes were grouped into archdeaconries administered by an archdeacon and his staff. Archdeacons were subject to the authority of a bishop—there were 24 bishoprics and 2 archbishoprics. Each bishop was overseen by one of the two archbishops, Canterbury and York, with the see of Canterbury enjoying some authority over York. At the apex of the hierarchy was the Queen, established by Parliament as supreme governor of the English church.

The medieval heritage of the Elizabethan church was manifested not only in the hierarchy, but in its jurisdiction over many aspects of life that today would be seen as secular matters. The church was charged with ensuring attendance at religious services, enforcing tithes, and punishing heresy, but it also had authority over matters such as marriage, wills, education, sexual behavior, and what could generally be termed personal morality. Marital disputes, disputed wills, paternity suits, and even charges of defamation were handled by the church's consistory courts.

The court of first recourse sat under the authority of the archdeacon; decisions of the archdeacon's court could be reviewed by the consistory court of the bishop or archbishop, with the archbishop of Canterbury's Court of High Commission as the highest authority. Church courts could impose penances, including rituals of public humiliation, but they did not have the authority to inflict punishments of life or limb. Technically they were not even allowed to impose fines, although penances could be commuted into monetary payments, and court costs could be assigned to the defeated party, making for de facto fines.

At every level, the staff of the court were not actually clergymen: laymen trained in civil law sat as judges, administered court business, and served as *proctors* (lawyers) on behalf of the plaintiffs and defendants.

Elizabeth's policies stressed outward conformity of religion, or at least absence of obvious nonconformity. People were required to attend church each Sunday. The fine for nonattendance was initially set at 12 pence, and enforcement was lax in the early years of the reign. Those who failed to attend were known as *recusants* and consisted mostly of Catholics—most Protestants were able to attend in good conscience, even if they felt the church was less reformed than they might wish. People were also required to take communion three times a year. Public officials, teachers, and other persons of authority were required to take the Oath of Supremacy, swearing to uphold the English church and the Queen as its supreme governor. Beyond this, there was little persecution of people for their religious beliefs in the early part of Elizabeth's reign, especially in comparison to the religious wars that were rocking the Continent at this time.

In fact, there were still quite a number of Catholics in England. They may have constituted some 5 percent of the population, and were especially numerous in the north. Elizabeth was inclined to let English Catholics believe as they pleased, but the level of tolerance extended to Catholics diminished from the late 1560s onward, as international tensions between Protestants and Catholics increased, and English Catholics were increasingly seen as a potentially dangerous fifth column. The situation was aggravated with the arrival of Mary Stuart in England as a possible Catholic claimant to the throne, and by Catholic participation in the Northern Rebellion of 1569. In 1570 the pope issued a decree officially deposing Elizabeth from the crown, making it very difficult to maintain loyalty both to the Catholic Church and to the Queen, and it was in this year that the Queen first began to execute Catholics for acts in support of the pope and his policies. Tensions rose even further in the 1580s when the pope sent Jesuit missionaries into England, with the intent of ministering to English Catholics and winning converts. The Jesuits were regarded as the worst of spies, and if caught, they were subject to torture and a protracted and agonizing execution.

Changing attitudes toward English Catholics can be traced in governmental policies: enforcement of recusancy laws began to intensify in the early 1570s; in 1581 the 12d. fine for recusancy was increased to a ruinous £20; in 1593 recusants were forbidden to travel more than five miles from their home without a license from the local bishop or justice of the peace. Yet even amidst these rising tensions a Catholic like the composer William Byrd was able to secure a place as a court musician under the patronage of the queen.

At the other end of the religious spectrum were those who felt that the English church was not Protestant enough. Many English Protestants believed that the Church of England needed to go further along the path of reform; they objected to even the limited degree of ritual retained in the church and wanted a more fully Protestant church like those in Scotland, the Netherlands, and Geneva. Some even felt that bishops should be abolished, since their office was not based on scriptural authority. Such people favored a presbyterian church government, run by assemblies of clergy and godly laymen, an idea that Elizabeth considered a threat to her royal authority.

Opponents of the advocates of further reform called them Precisians or Puritans. The Puritans had no label for themselves, except perhaps generally referring to the *godly* or *reformed*—indeed they were not a cohesive movement but represented a spectrum of reformist thinking within the established church.

There were others who saw the national church as hopelessly flawed and founded clandestine religious groups of their own outside the church's authority, pursuing what they felt was a purer form of Christian worship. Notable among these were the Anabaptists, who had been an underground presence since the days of Henry VIII, and the *Brownists*, as critics labeled the followers of Robert Browne, who founded a clandestine group in Norfolk around 1580, and eventually established a foothold in London and elsewhere in the country. Such sects formed small independent congregations for worship, but their meetings were secretive, since the government regarded separatism as treasonous. Government suppression drove some of these Separatists to the Netherlands, where they would later merge with the emigrants who went on to establish the Plymouth Colony in America in 1620.

A certain measure of religious liberty was allowed for foreigners. French and Dutch (mostly Flemish) Protestants had their own churches in London, although the English were not allowed to attend them. Even the diplomatic representatives of Catholic countries were allowed to celebrate Mass in their residences—again, strictly off-limits to subjects of the English crown. There were even communities of Jews. The Jews had officially been evicted from England in 1290, and would not be officially readmitted until the late 1600s, but there were Spanish and Portuguese Jews in London and other major ports, officially purporting to be Catholics. Such men included Hector Nuñez, an associate of several leading figures in Elizabeth's Privy Council. The most famous was Rodrigo Lopez, who served for a time as personal physician to the earl of Leicester and ultimately to the Queen herself. Changing political tides led to Lopez's trial for treason on fabricated charges of attempting to assassinate the monarch, resulting in his execution in 1594—not long before Shakespeare's *Merchant of Venice* appeared on the stage.

THE STATE

Since the Middle Ages, English government had been organized around the principle of laws. Elizabethan England had a highly developed—in some ways overdeveloped—legal system that guided the roles and operations of the country's various governmental authorities. Law and government were indistinguishable: any given government authority might fulfill political, legislative, and judiciary roles, and the typical Elizabethan court was an administrative and legislative body as well as a court in the modern sense. Yet Elizabethan law was never embodied within a single written code. It consisted of a variety of traditions, practices, and jurisdictions informed but never defined by written documents.

The entire system rested on the principle of custom: things were done in a certain way because they had been done so since time out of mind. This system ensured stability, but also accommodated change, since customs could fall out of use if no one was inclined to enforce them, and new practices could become customary over time. It could also lead to conflict when different elements in society adhered to different ideas of which customary practices had the force of law—this dynamic would be a major factor in the story of Elizabeth's Stuart successors, when conflict between royalist and parliamentarian views of authority came to Civil War in 1642.

Government

The most unambiguously powerful organ of government was the monarch acting in concert with Parliament. Parliament had emerged as a consultative body during the Middle Ages. By the 1500s, one of its most important roles was to approve taxation. Ordinary royal income, based on such sources as crown lands, customs, and legal fines, was never adequate to support extraordinary expenses such as the costs of war. When additional revenue was needed, Parliament might vote a *subsidy*, a tax on property to supplement the crown's ordinary income. Equally important, Parliament had become a forum where the monarch could build support and consensus for royal policies among the privileged classes. Henry VIII had made unprecedented use of Parliament in this way in order to legitimize his transformation of the English church.

Elizabeth inherited from her father a powerful alliance with Parliament, and she managed her relations with Parliament successfully to ensure support from those who had the ability to facilitate or obstruct her will. But this relationship was far from a guaranteed success. The House of Commons in particular had become accustomed to playing a more active part in government under the earlier Tudors, and was becoming increasingly assertive and self-confident. Elizabeth's Stuart successors, lacking her instinct for public relations and political management, would find themselves increasingly at odds with their Parliaments.

Parliament was divided into two houses. The House of Lords was attended by approximately 50 lay peers, 24 bishops, and 2 archbishops. The House of Commons consisted of 2 representatives from each English shire (with the exception of Durham—a holdover from the Middle Ages when this was an independent feudal jurisdiction), 2 from each of about 180 English cities and towns (with some exceptions, including London, which sent 4), plus a single representative from each of 12 Welsh shires and 1 each from 12 Welsh towns; the total was around 450 representatives. The exact means by which the representatives were chosen depended on local practice, but in the shires any holder of lands worth 40 shillings a year was entitled to vote.

A bill passed by both Houses and assented to by the monarch was the highest legal authority in the land. Elizabeth made use of Parliament when she had need of money or of new national initiatives to deal with changing circumstances, but Parliament was not a regular part of the apparatus of her government: only 10 parliaments were summoned during her half-century reign, meeting for less than three years in all.

The actual operation of government revolved around the figure of the monarch, who was the embodiment and guarantor of law, as well as the executive figure at the head of the state. To provide advice and to oversee the day-to-day business of governing, the Queen relied on her Privy Council. The Council numbered a bit over a dozen men, hand-selected by the monarch, and drawing heavily from men of gentry background, in contrast with medieval councils that had been dominated by aristocrats. The Privy Council supervised national defense, regulated commerce, heard sensitive judicial cases, managed government finances, and supervised the operations of government. They also deliberated matters of policy, although the Queen always had the final say. The monarch, and the Council acting in the monarch's name, had some power to issue decrees enforceable at law, but the exact extent of these powers was ill-defined.

Dependent on the crown was a complex network of bureaucracies and jurisdictions. The Privy Councilors generally held office in addition to their role on the Council, heading up bureaucracies of their own in the Queen's name: during the latter half of her reign, Sir William Cecil, Lord Burghley, served as Lord Treasurer; Sir Christopher Hatton was Lord Chancellor; Sir Francis Walsingham was Secretary of State. The treasury and chancery were the largest departments: the former was responsible for administering royal finances; the latter was the chief organ of the administrative and legal bureaucracy. The various government departments were staffed by a modest civil service, numbering about 600 salaried officials, with another 600 serving the monarch in administering crown lands.

Perhaps as important as the formal royal bureaucracies was the informal institution of the court, orbiting around the person of the Queen herself. As modern lobbyists know, face time with people who have power is itself a route to power. Those who were able to speak with the Queen in person could gain access to favors and privileges for themselves and their friends. These people included government officers such as the Privy Councilors, but also many who were not actually a part of government, such as the ladies-in-waiting who kept Elizabeth company and looked after her needs. These leading courtiers were sought after by a subsidiary tier of secondary courtiers, and so on downward in a complex hierarchy of patronage.

Royal government operated at the local level through the country's 39 shires or counties. In the Middle Ages, the crown's main representative in the shire had been the sheriff, but by Elizabeth's day, the sheriffs had been reduced to a managerial role. Each shire also had a Lord Lieutenant, responsible for military matters, and a coroner (literally "crowner"), whose investigated suspicious deaths in case the government needed to pursue a criminal indictment.

The most important organ of government in the shires was the Commission of the Peace. Each year the crown appointed a number of local gentry as justices of the peace for their shire. The justices met four times a year in the chief town of the shire to handle important judicial cases in the Quarter Sessions; there were also more frequent Petty Sessions held locally by smaller groups of justices. Individual justices of the peace were also empowered to deliver summary judgment in minor local cases. At every level the justices of the peace had administrative and quasi-legislative powers in addition to their judiciary functions.

In addition to the local justice of the peace, there were other sometimes overlapping local jurisdictions. Since the Middle Ages, the shires had been subdivided into hundreds (or wapentakes, as they were called in areas once conquered by the Vikings). These had their own courts and officers, although their role had been marginalized by the late 1500s.

At the local level, royal government more often operated through the parish. Each parish had at least one constable, a part-time officer drawn from the yeomanly class. The parish constable was responsible for local law enforcement and worked closely with local justices of the peace in administering law and policy at the community level. Parishes were also responsible for the execution of national laws: there were Surveyors of the Highway to oversee the implementation of the Highway Act of 1555, while from 1598 Overseers of the Poor were charged with administering the Poor Laws. Boroughs and manors also had their own officers and courts with authority over local matters.

At every level, exceptions were common. London was an exception among the boroughs, sending four representatives to Parliament—reflecting its importance, but in no way proportional to the city's wealth, power, or population. The Borough of Southwark on the south bank of the Thames was an exception within London, being administered not by the usual urban forms of government but as a feudal manor owned by the City of London. Within Southwark there were several areas exempted from the legal power of borough authorities: *liberties* such as the environs of the Marshalsea prison, exempted because it was royal land, and *sanctuaries* like Montague Close near London Bridge, which retained privileges from the days when it had been owned by the church.

At all levels government relied heavily on unpaid or underpaid office-holders—by definition drawn from the classes who could afford to spare time from work. Great lords might serve in major offices of the state; local gentlemen served as justices of the peace; and even ordinary tradesmen and yeomen might be called upon to serve in minor local offices of the village, town, or parish. This kind of unpaid work was a cause of governmental corruption; men who had to spend considerable time and money on an unsalaried government office would frequently find other ways to make the post profitable.

Law

One of the most important functions of the royal government was in overseeing a national system of courts to implement the laws. England's Common Law had emerged in the Middle Ages as the result of royal efforts to centralize and standardize the patchwork of jurisdictions and practices that had emerged in the feudal environment. The guiding principles of the Common Law were tradition and precedent: Common Law was seen as the embodiment of centuries-old customs, guided and informed by legal precedent as embodied in the practice of the courts and documented in the records of prior legal cases. Common Law was supplemented by Parliamentary statute, which was seen as a vehicle for dealing with emerging needs that were not already addressed by existing Common Law.

At the national level, both Common Law and Statute Law were implemented by the Court of Common Pleas, which handled civil matters (i.e., between subjects of the crown); the Court of the Exchequer, which handled cases in which the crown was alleged to have a financial interest; and the Court of Queen's Bench, which dealt with criminal cases (i.e., those to which the crown was a party) and could also serve as a de facto court of appeal. All of these courts met at Westminster, within walking distance of the city of London. Judges from these central courts were also sent out twice a year to travel circuits of the country, sitting as courts of Assize in the chief towns of each shire, where they would hear both civil and criminal cases.

Because the Common Law courts could be unwieldy, expensive, and sometimes unduly influenced by the power and wealth of the parties involved, the Crown also had Equity courts. Equity courts functioned under the principles of Civil Law developed by the Romans and were not bound by the often tortuous traditions of Common Law. These courts included the Court of Chancery, the Court of Requests, and the Court of Star Chamber. Sometimes known as prerogative courts, since they were based on royal prerogative as opposed to Common Law, these courts were used by the Tudors to deal with overmighty subjects and were often favored by commoners as a means to seek redress more swiftly and cheaply than might be possible in the Common Law courts—and the Equity courts had the additional advantage of conducting their proceedings fully in English, without the heavy admixture of French and Latin legal jargon that prevailed in Common Law.

Civil Law also governed the operations of the Court of Admiralty, which had jurisdiction over cases relating to the high seas and the ecclesiastical courts of the episcopal hierarchy. In addition to Common, Equity,

---

THE WORK OF A CONSTABLE

If two men be fighting together in a house (the doors being shut), yet may such an officer break open the doors, to cause the peace to be kept, though none of the parties have taken hurt. And . . . such an officer may carry them before a Justice of the Peace, to find surety for the peace, because they have broken the peace already. . . But if any of the parties to an affray have received any dangerous hurt, then ought such officer to arrest him that did the hurt, and to carry him to the gaol, there to remain till he find surety to appear at the next gaol delivery . . . The fact may fall out to be a felony, if so be that he which was hurt do happen to die within one year and a day next following such hurt done.

William Lambard, *The Duties of Constables, Borsholders, Tithingmen, and Other Such Low Officers of the Peace* (London: R. Newberry and H. Bynneman, 1583), 15–16.

and Civil Law, the legal system also embraced *customary* law, consisting of traditional laws and practices that were specific to particular communities or shires, applied in the local courts of boroughs, hundreds, and manors.

Multiple legal jurisdictions and systems of practice made for a complex system that could be exploited to advantage by those who knew its workings. With various courts available as potential avenues for pursuing a case, plaintiffs often steered toward those which they felt would be more advantageous, while defendants might lodge countersuits in alternative courts. Voluminous legal records show that Elizabethan England was a highly litigious society, where even ordinary people were remarkably familiar with the law and willing to use it when they had a grievance, often using legal pressure as a tactic in securing a satisfactory out-of-court settlement. In 1580, the courts of Queen's Bench and Common Pleas handled over 13,000 cases at an advanced stage of litigation—suggesting that 1 household in 10 might have been involved in a case involving one of the central national courts. In 1602, the manor court of Keevil cum Bulkington dealt with over 130 prosecutions, encompassing matters from playing of unlawful games to failure to clean out watercourses.

Professional law enforcement did not exist, and the functions of the modern police force were largely fulfilled by unpaid part-time officials. At the local level, two important institutions were the town watch, responsible for patrolling the streets of a town at night, and the parish constable,

Administering the law. [Furnivall (1879)]

the closest thing to a local policeman. When a crime was alleged, it was the constable's job to apprehend the accused and bring them before the appropriate authority. If the accused evaded capture, the constable was supposed to raise the hue and cry in the parish, calling on all inhabitants to find the suspect, and sending word on to the neighboring parishes as necessary. The actual administration of justice depended on the case. A trivial matter might be handled summarily by a justice of the peace. If the offense was more serious, the accused would need to be brought before a higher court, either being jailed in the meantime, or bound over to appear before the court if there was little reason to fear an attempt to evade justice.

Punishment

The most serious crimes were treason, murder, and a range of crimes classed as felonies, including manslaughter, rape, sodomy, arson, witchcraft, burglary, robbery, and grand larceny (theft of goods worth at least 12 pence). All these offenses carried a mandatory death sentence, making juries sometimes reluctant to convict in felony cases: one Justice complained that "most commonly the simple countryman or woman, looking no further into the loss of their own goods, are of opinion that they would not procure a man's death for all the goods in the world," so that "upon promise to have their goods again [they] will give faint evidence, if they be not strictly looked into by the Justice."[7]

Someone convicted of a capital crime could escape death through a pardon from the crown. In the case of most felonies, it was also possible for men to plead *benefit of clergy* (this option was not open to women). In the Middle Ages the clergy had been exempt from secular punishment for felony, an exemption that extended to any man who could prove he was able to read. A version of the custom was still in use in the late 1500s. Benefit of clergy could only be exercised once: the convict would be branded on the thumb to mark that he had exercised this privilege (technically, he had been defrocked as a clergyman). Benefit of clergy was not available to those convicted of the most serious felonies, such as burglary and robbery.

Most execution was by hanging, although some crimes such as poisoning and heresy were punishable by burning, and treason was punishable by the triple punishment of hanging, drawing (disemboweling), and quartering (cutting the body into quarters). Nonfelonious crimes might be subject to lesser forms of corporal punishment, such as whipping, branding, or loss of a body part such as a hand or ear. Lesser punishments included fines and rituals of public humiliation, including confinement in the stocks or the pillory. The pillory confined both the head and hands: the convict was held immobile in a standing position, and vulnerable to the abuse of passers-by. The stocks confined only the legs, and most of the time only one leg was secured; the stocks were often used simply as a means of restraint rather than punishment.

THE SOCIAL SPECTRUM IN ST. PAUL'S CATHEDRAL, LONDON

What whispering is there . . . how by some slight to cheat the poor country client of his full purse that is stuck under his girdle? What plots are laid to furnish young gallants with ready money (which is shared afterwards at a tavern, thereby to disfurnish him of his patrimony? . . . What swearing is there, yea what swaggering, what facing and out-facing? What shuffling, what shouldering, what jostling, what jeering, what biting of thumbs to beget quarrels, what holding up of fingers to remember drunken meetings, what braving with feathers, what bearding with mustachios, what casting open of cloaks to publish new clothes?. . . For at one time, in one and the same rank, yea foot by foot, and elbow by elbow, shall you see walking the Knight, the Gull [dupe], the Gallant, the Upstart, the Gentleman, the Clown [bumpkin], the Captain, the Apple-Squire, the Lawyer, the Usurer, the Citizen, the Bankrupt, the Scholar, the Beggar, the Doctor, the Idiot, the Ruffian, the Cheater, the Puritan, the Cutthroat, the High-men, the Low men, the True-man, and the Thief.

Thomas Dekker, *The Dead-Terme* (1608), in *The Non-Dramatic Works of Thomas Dekker*, ed. Alexander B. Grosart (New York: Russell and Russell, 1963), 4.50–51.

Imprisonment was not the typical means of punishment, but its use was on the rise. Debtors might be imprisoned until they repaid their debts. Serious misdemeanors might result in time at a House of Correction, a new form of institution of which the most famous was Bridewell in London: here vagrants, prostitutes, and other convicts worked on treadmills to grind grain, picked apart ropes to make oakum, and beat hemp plants to prepare the fibers for spinning. Imprisonment was usually for a matter of months, but sentences of life imprisonment were not unknown.

Ecclesiastical courts might impose public penance, which would involve some form of public ritual in which the wrongdoer would publicly acknowledge his or her offense. It was difficult for the church courts to enforce their punishments against the truly recalcitrant. The ultimate sanction was excommunication, or exclusion from church services. This punishment theoretically excluded the wrongdoer from society, but in practice many people defied such sanctions. Obstinate excommunicates were supposed to be imprisoned by secular authorities until they relented, but the government did not always have the will and means to pursue them, and as many as 5 percent of the population may have lived excommunicate.

A snapshot view of the workings of the law can be found in the story of Jeremy Heckford, a villager from Marks Tey in Essex. In 1584 he was unemployed and in trouble with the local authorities; he fled Marks Tey, to be picked up later the same year as a vagrant in Chelmsford, where he was imprisoned on suspicion of felony. No charges were pressed, and he was eventually released. By 1587 he was back in Marks Tey, where he was tried and acquitted for stealing some grain. In 1589 he was brought before the Essex Quarter Sessions court, where he was indicted for a theft valued at 2s.—enough to qualify as a felony and send him to the gallows. The jury reduced the valuation to the level of a petty larceny, and Heckford was punished by whipping. The following year he was convicted of stealing some hose and petticoats in Marks Tey. This time the valuation of 2s. was not reduced. Heckford tried to plead benefit of clergy, but failed to prove his ability to read, and so ended his life on the gallows.[8]

In a society without a professional police force to enforce its laws, social control relied heavily on the use of spectacles of punishment. Hangings were public events, attended by large crowds of men, women, and children, and the sight of such punishments was considered instructive and essential in teaching the young to behave themselves. Even after execution, the remains of an executed criminal were displayed as a warning. The corpses of murderers were left in cages called gibbets to be picked clean by carrion birds, and the heads of executed traitors were impaled above the gatehouse on London Bridge. Continental visitors were inevitably struck by the grisly spectacle: one Swiss visitor noted the "more than thirty skulls of noble men who had been executed and beheaded for treason and for other reasons—and their descendants are accustomed to boast of this, themselves even pointing out out one their ancestors' heads on this same bridge, believing that they will be esteemed the more because their antecedents were of such high descent that they could even covet the crown."[9]

NOTES

1. On the population of England, see D. M. Palliser, *The Age of Elizabeth* (London: Longman, 1992), chap. 2. For a contemporary atlas of England, see John Speed, *The Counties of Britain* [1616] (London: Pavillion, 1988).

2. Sir Thomas Smith, *De Republica Anglorum* (London: Gregory Seton, 1584), 27.

3. Keith Wrightson, *English Society, 1580–1680* (New Brunswick, NJ: Rutgers University Press, 1982), 176.

4. Arthur F. Kinney, *Rogues, Vagabonds, and Sturdy Beggars: A New Gallery of Tudor and Early Stuart Rogue Literature* (Amherst: University of Massachusetts, 1973), 91–94.

5. Kinney, *Rogues*, 150–52.

6. Palliser, *Age of Elizabeth*, 381.

7. R. H. Tawney and Eileen Power, *Tudor Economic Documents* (London: Longmans, 1924), 2.341.

8. Wrightson, *English Society*, 163.

9. P. Razzell, ed., *The Journals of Two Travellers in Elizabethan and Early Stuart England* (London: Caliban Books, 1995), 13.

3

Households and the Course of Life

THE ELIZABETHAN HOUSEHOLD

Elizabethan England was truly a family oriented society. Society was considered to consist not of individuals but of households, with everyone either a head of household or subject to one. In counting population it was customary only to reckon householders: wife, children, servants, and apprentices were subsumed under the man at the head of the household, who was expected to be the official point of interface between household members and the external world. The household constituted the basic unit not only of the society but of the economy as well—the family business was the rule rather than the exception.

At the core of the household was the nuclear family of father, mother, and children, but it also included resident employees in the form of servants and apprentices. The mean household size was about 4 to 5, with higher figures further up the social scale. According to one 17th-century estimate, a lord might typically have some 40 people in his household; a knight, 13; a squire or gentleman, 10; a merchant, 6 to 8; a freeholder, 5 to 7; and a tradesman, craftsman, or cottager, 3 to 4. In addition to the actual household, many houses, particularly in the towns, accommodated a paying lodger or two.

It was unusual for relatives beyond the nuclear family to live within the household—one region that has been studied in detail shows this happen-

A family, 1563. [*Hymns Ancient and Modern*]

ing in only 6 percent of households, with only 2 percent including more than one married couple in the same household. This was less true in upper-class households, which were more likely to house additional relatives. Due to the high rate of mortality, single-parent families and stepparents were common: in one village in 1599, a quarter of the children living at home had lost one parent.

Women and Men

Gender roles within the household were notionally divided along lines that had been determined millennia before with the emergence of agriculture: the man did the labor of farming at a distance from the home, while the woman was responsible for the work inside and around the house. Even in urban families where the man might actually work at home as a craftsman while the woman left the home daily as a laundress or vendor, the notional distinction between inside and outside the home as the boundary between female and male domains remained powerful. The idea underlies the description of a woman's role as articulated by the Elizabethan political theorist Sir Thomas Smith:

Women . . . nature hath made to keep home and to nourish their family and children, and not to meddle with matters abroad, nor to bear office in a city or commonwealth no more than children or infants.[1]

A DUTCHMAN'S IMPRESSION OF ENGLISH WOMEN, 1575

Wives in England are entirely in the power of their husbands, their lives only excepted . . . yet they are not kept so strictly as they are in Spain or elsewhere. Nor are they shut up, but they have the free management of the house or housekeeping, after the fashion of those of the Netherlands, and others their neighbours. They go to market to buy what they like best to eat. They are well dressed, fond of taking it easy, and commonly leave the care of household matters and drudgery to their servants. They sit before their doors, decked out in fine clothes, in order to see and be seen by the passers-by. In all banquets and feasts they are shown the greatest honour; they are placed at the upper end of the table, where they are the first served; at the lower end, they help the men. All the rest of their time they employ in walking or riding, in playing at cards or otherwise, in visiting their friends and keeping company, conversing with their equals (whom they term gossips) and their neighbours, and making merry with them at childbirths, christenings, churchings, and funerals; and all this with the permission and knowledge of their husbands, as such is the custom.

William Brenchley Rye, ed., *England as seen by Foreigners in the Days of Elizabeth and James the First* (New York: Benjamin Blom, 1967), 72–73.

It was assumed that a well-run home would be managed by the woman, leaving the man free to serve as the chief breadwinner for the household. Women's domestic responsibilities included childrearing, marketing, cooking, cleaning, and basic health care. Yet an Elizabethan housewife also played a significant if secondary role in the economy of the household. She looked after the household garden, which provided vegetables for cooking as well as medicinal herbs. She might also have responsibility for domestic livestock, which were a feature of urban as well as rural households: these might include poultry, pigs, and dairy animals. She was expected to know how to brew ale or beer. All of these activities provided not only food for the table but potentially a surplus for sale.

Women might also take part in men's work. In rural families, female members of the household assisted in the fields at harvest and haymaking time, since the pressures of the season required as many hands as possible. They could also be involved in winnowing the grain after it was harvested. In the towns, a woman might help her husband in his trade, and if he died, she might carry on the business herself. There were even a few instances of women plying trades in their own right.

Women could also engage in part-time work to supplement the family income. Some worked as petty-school teachers or tutors, others engaged in home industries such as spinning and knitting. In towns, women engaged in a wide variety of work: they were especially likely to be employed as seamstresses, laundresses, servants, and street vendors.

The secondary yet significant economic role of the woman in the household mirrored her general status in the family. Officially, she was under the governance of a man for most or all of her life. A girl grew up under the rule of her father or guardian; as a young adult she might go into service under the authority of her employer; and when she married, she was subject to her husband. Only in widowhood was a woman legally recognized as an independent individual. A widow took over as head of her husband's household; if he left her sufficient means to live on, she might do quite well, perhaps taking over his trade, and she would be free to remarry or not as she chose.

Yet the domestic power equation was not a one-way street. The man was supposed to have the final say, but a husband who governed arbitrarily would sooner or later find his home in crisis. A successful family needed the wife's cooperation, and women had routes of recourse if they found their husbands overbearing or abusive. Informally, women had networks of support among themselves, socializing at church, at the alehouse, while laundering, and on other occasions that brought women together. Perhaps even more important were the social networks of family and community that could bring pressure onto a tyrannical husband: neighbors and ministers were known to intervene if a family was clearly dysfunctional. If informal systems failed, women could turn to the law: Common Law courts were not open to married women, but Equity courts were, as were the church courts, which were the primary legal vehicles for addressing issues relating to marriage and family.

Gender relations were heavily constrained by custom, but this was not necessarily an impediment to domestic harmony. Affectionate relations between husbands and wives are attested in correspondence and diaries of the time, and in the day-to-day expressions used by married couples—married couples commonly addressed each other by such pet names as *sweetheart, duck,* and *chuck.* Nicholas Breton offered advice on how a husband should treat a wife:

Cherish all good humors in her: let her lack no silk, crewel, thread, nor flax, to work on at her pleasure, force her to nothing, rather prettily chide her from her labor, but in any wise commend what she doeth: if she be learned and studious, persuade her to translation—it will keep her from idleness, and it is a cunning kind task: if she be unlearned, commend her to housewifery, and make much of her carefulness, and bid her servants take example at their mistress. . . . At table be merry to her, abroad be kind to her, always be loving to her, and never be bitter to her, for patient Griselda is dead long ago, and women are flesh and blood.[2]

In short, women were subordinate but not powerless, and they appear to have enjoyed an unusual measure of freedom compared to other parts of Europe. According to a proverb that was current in Elizabeth's day, England was "the Hell of Horses, the Purgatory of Servants, and the Paradise of Women." The phrase is highly revealing. On the one hand, it supports the observations of contemporary visitors from the Continent who remarked that English women had more power in the home and more freedom abroad compared to women in most other European countries. At the same time, it reminds us that women, like horses and servants, were expected to be in a position of subordination.

Children and Servants

More fully subordinate to the householder were the children and servants. England's rapid population growth meant that a large part of the population at any time were young people: it has been estimated that roughly a third were under the age of 15, a half under age 25. These figures were balanced by a high rate of child mortality: a woman might give birth to a half-dozen children over the course of her childbearing years, but only half of these were likely to see adulthood.

The final component in the household was the servants, who were a ubiquitous feature of Elizabethan society. Both rural and urban families hired servants: a quarter of the population may have been servants at any given time, and a third or more of households may have had servants. The relationship of servants to their employers in many ways resembled that of children to their parents. They were not just paid employees, but subordinate members of their employer's household who actually lived with the family and were subject to the householder's authority much like his own children.

Servants were hired on annual contracts, living within the home of the employer and receiving food, clothing (especially shoes and hose, which wore out quickly), and quarterly wages. In large households they might have specialized functions, such as cooks, chambermaids, or footmen, but in most cases they were generalized hired hands, helping the man and woman of the house in their daily tasks.

THE LIFE CYCLE

Birth and Baptism

Childbirth in the 16th century normally happened at home. There were hospitals in Elizabethan England, but these served primarily to provide long-term care for those in need, rather than short-term treatment of acute medical problems. Nor was a physician likely to be involved in the birthing process. The delivery of babies was primarily the domain of the midwife. Indeed, a number of women might be present—childbirth was often a major social occasion for women.

Childbirth carried a significant level of risk to the mother, although less so than is commonly supposed today. The rate of maternal mortality in childbirth may have been in the region of 1 percent. This would still be quite high by modern standards, very close to the estimated figure for sub-Saharan Africa in 2005. With a 1 percent chance of dying every time she gave birth, a woman who gave birth to five children over the course of her childbearing years would have roughly a 1 in 20 chance of dying in childbed. Given these odds, virtually every woman in Elizabethan England would have known someone who had died in childbirth.

Soon after birth, the baby would be taken to the parish church for baptism, also called christening: this was supposed to happen on a Sunday or holy day within a week or two of the birth. Christenings at home or by anyone but a clergyman were against church law. The only exception was if the child was in imminent danger of death, in which case it was considered more important to ensure that the child did not die unchristened.

The ritual of baptism involved dipping the baby in a font of holy water in the parish church. At the ceremony the child was sponsored by three godparents, two of the same sex and one of the opposite. These godparents became relatives of the child in a very real sense; children would ask their godparents' blessing whenever meeting them, much as they did of their parents every morning and evening.

A christening was a major social occasion and might be followed by a feast. It was customary for people to give presents for the newborn—

THE TROUBLES OF AN EXPECTING FATHER, 1603

There is another humor incident to a woman, when her husband sees her belly to grow big (though peradventure by the help of some other friend), yet he persuades himself it is a work of his own framing; and this breeds him new cares and troubles, for then must he trot up and down day and night, far and near, to get with great cost that his wife longs for; if she let fall but a pin, he is diligent to take it up, lest she by stooping should hurt herself. She on the other side is so hard to please, that it is a great hap when he fits her humor in bringing home that which likes her, though he spare no pains nor cost to get it. And oft times through ease and plenty she grows so queasy stomached, that she can brook no common meats, but longs for strange and rare things, which whether they be to be had or no, yet she must have them. . . . When the time draws near of her lying down, then must he trudge to get gossips, such as she will appoint, or else all the fat is in the fire. Consider then what cost and trouble it will be to him, to have things fine against the Christening day: what store of sugar, biscuits, comfets and carroways, marmalade and marzipan, with all kinds of sweet suckets and superflous banqueting stuff. . . . Every day after her lying down will sundry dames visit her, which are her neighbors, her kinswomen, and other her special acquaintance, whom the goodman must welcome with all cheerfulness, and be sure there be some dainties in store to set before them; where they about some three or four hours (or possibly half a day) will sit chatting with the child-wife.

Thomas Dekker, *The Batchelar's Banquet* (London: T. C., 1603), sig. B3r.

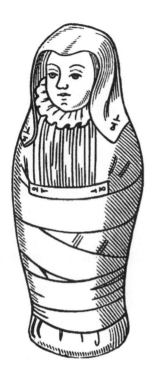

An infant in swaddling clothes. [Clinch]

apostle spoons, having the image of one of the 12 apostles at the end of the handle, were a common choice, as were other gifts of pewter and silver.

Baptism was not only a religious ritual. In the 16th century, to belong to society and to belong to the church were considered one and the same, so that the ceremony of baptism also marked the child's entry into the social community. In fact, the modern birth certificate has its counterpart in the baptismal record entered into the parish register: the law required the child's name and date of baptism to be recorded in the register as a part of the ceremony; this record served as a legal verification of that person's age and origin for the rest of their life.

At the core of the baptismal ceremony was the assigning of a name. The surname was inherited from the child's father. Given names were mostly drawn from traditional stock, but there was more scope for variation than had been the case in the Middle Ages. Perhaps the most common were French names imported during the Middle Ages. For boys, these included (in roughly descending order of popularity) William, Robert, Richard, Humphrey, Henry, Roger, Ralph, Fulk, Hugh, and Walter. Girls' names in this category included Alice, Joan, Jane, Isabel, Maud, Juliana, Eleanor, and Rose. Some French names had been imported more recently, such as Francis for boys and Joyce, Florence, and Frances for girls.

Also popular were the names of saints. Among boys, some of the most common saints' names were (roughly in descending order of popularity) John, Thomas, James, and George. Behind these came Peter, Anthony, Lawrence, Valentine, Nicholas, Christopher, Andrew, Giles, Maurice, Gervase, Bernard, Leonard, and Ambrose. Female saints' names included Catherine, Elizabeth, Anne, Agnes, Margaret (with its variant, Margery), Lucy, Barbara, and Cecily. The name Mary was also used, although it was much less common than on the Continent. Because Protestantism discouraged the veneration of saints, these names had lost much of their religious significance and were more likely to be chosen simply on the basis of family traditions.

Another religious source of names was the Old Testament, from which came such boys' names as Adam, Daniel, David, Toby, Nathaniel, and Zachary. Obscure Old Testament names were especially popular among the more extreme Protestant reformers. For girls, Old Testament names were rarer, although one occasionally finds a Judith. The names Simon and Martha derived from the New Testament.

A few names derived from Greek or Latin, such as Julius, Alexander, Miles, and Adrian for boys, Dorothy and Mabel for girls. Some names were ultimately inherited from the Anglo-Saxons, such as Edward and Edmund for boys, Edith, Winifred, and Audrey for girls. A few names were taken from legend. For boys these included Arthur, Tristram, Lancelot, Perceval, and Oliver. For girls the principal example is Helen or Ellen. Among Puritans there was a growing fashion for creative names with religious themes, such as Flee-Sin and Safe-on-High. By and large, the upper classes and townspeople were most likely to be innovative in naming their children; country folk were likely to use more traditional names.

Then as now, people were often known by shortened forms of their names, many of which are still in use today. Edward might be known as Ned, John as Jack, David as Davy, Robert as Robin, Dorothy as Doll, Mary as Moll, Catherine as Kate or Kit.

A few weeks after the christening, the mother would go to the church for the ceremony called churching. This had originated in the Middle Ages as a purifying ritual, but in Protestant England it was reinterpreted as an occasion for thanksgiving, both for the safe delivery of the child and for the mother's survival of the dangers of childbirth. Churchings were popular social occasions among women.

Childhood

Childhood was a dangerous time in Elizabethan England. The infant mortality rate may have been about 135 in 1,000, and in some places as high as 200 in 1,000. By comparison, a mortality rate of 125 in 1,000 is exceptionally high in the modern developing world; the rate in the United States is around 10 in 1,000. Between the ages of 1 and 4, the mortality rate

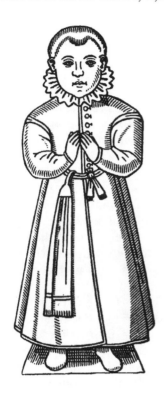

A boy wearing a gown. [Clinch]

was around 60 in 1,000, and about 30 in 1,000 between the ages of 5 and 9. This means that out of every 10 live births, only 7 or 8 children lived to 10 years of age. The high mortality rate was primarily due to disease. Young children have weak immune systems, and the illnesses that send countless modern children to the emergency room in the middle of the night often ended fatally for their Elizabethan counterparts.[3]

It is sometimes supposed that because of the high mortality rate, parents were reluctant to invest emotion in their children, but evidence suggests that love was considered an essential component in the parent-child relationship. The sentiments expressed by Sir Henry Sidney in a letter to his son were not at all uncommon:

I love thee, boy, well. I have no more, but God bless you, my sweet child, in this world forever, as I in this world find myself happy in my children. From Ludlow Castle this 28th of October, 1578. [Addressed:] To my very loving son, Robert Sidney, give these. Your very loving father.[4]

Parents were expected to be strict, but this was seen as a sign of love. Children who were not disciplined properly would not learn how to interact with the rest of society: as one Elizabethan proverb has it, "Better unfed than untaught." Undoubtedly there were cruel parents who abused their power, but there is no evidence to indicate that abusiveness was any more common then than now, and child abuse could be prosecuted in the courts.

For the first six years or so, the Elizabethan child would be at home and principally under female care. Most children were cared for by their own mothers, although privileged children might be in the keeping of a nurse. Young babies were kept in cradles fitted with rockers to help soothe the child to sleep; sometimes they slept in bed with their parents—this could be risky to the child, but it simplified midnight nursing and was probably especially beneficial on cold winter nights.

Old cloths were used as diapers. The baby's head was kept warm with a cap called a *biggin,* and its body was wrapped in bands of linen called *swaddling.* Theorists believed that swaddling kept the limbs straight so that they would grow properly, but more importantly, it kept the baby warm and controlled its mobility: as the infant grew, unsupervised free-dom could be extremely dangerous in a home with open fireplaces and countless other domestic dangers.

Babies were breast-fed and might be nursed in this way for about one or two years—Elizabeth herself had been weaned at 25 months. Aristocratic children often received their milk from a wet nurse, sparing the mother the trouble of nursing, and also raising the aristocratic birth-rate, since she would cease lactating and become fertile once more. The wet nurse was always a woman of lower social standing, and by definition one who had recently given birth herself, so that she was giving milk. With the high rate of infant mortality, there were many poor women able to earn a bit of extra money for a time by nursing someone else's child.

As the child grew, it would be swaddled less restrictively to allow the arms to move, and eventually the swaddling would be dispensed with in favor of a long gown (allowing easy access to the diaper cloths). The child's gown was typically fitted with long straps that dangled from the shoulders. The straps probably derived from the false sleeves sometimes found on adults' gowns, but with children they allowed the garment to double as a harness. Boys and girls alike were dressed in gowns and pet-ticoats akin to the garments of adult women; only after age 6 or so were boys *breeched*—put into the breeches worn by adult men.

For Elizabethan children, like children today, the early years were pri-marily a time for play and learning. During this time children would explore their world and begin to acquire some of the basic tools of social interaction.

Elizabethan English

The first of these tools was the child's mother tongue. Elizabethan English was close enough to modern English that it would be comprehen-sible to us today. The main differences in pronunciation were in a few of the vowels: *weak*, for example, rhymed with *break*, and *take* sounded something like the modern-English *tack*. As in most modern North American accents, *r*'s were always pronounced. Overall, Elizabethan English would most resemble a modern Irish or provincial English accent; the pronunciation associated with Oxford and Cambridge, the BBC, and the royal family is a comparatively recent development. There was considerable difference in pronunciation from one place to another. The dialect of London was the most influential, but there was no official form of the language, and even a gentleman might still speak his local dialect: a biographer in the 1600s noted that Sir Walter Raleigh "spoke broad Devonshire to his dying day."[5]

Etiquette

In learning the language, the child would also learn the appropriate modes of address, which were more complex than they are today. For example, the word *thou* existed as an alternative to *you*. To us it sounds formal and archaic, but for the Elizabethans it was actually very informal, used to address a person's social inferiors and very close friends. You might call your son or daughter *thou*, but you would never use it with strangers (*thee* stood in the same relationship to *thou* as *me* to *I*—"Thou art a fine fellow," but "I like thee well").

The child would also have to learn the titles appropriate to different kinds of people. As a rule, superiors were addressed by their title and surname, inferiors by their given name. If you were speaking to someone of high rank or if you wished to address someone formally, you might call them *sir* or *madam*; you would certainly use these terms for anyone of the rank of knight or higher. As a title, *Sir* designated a knight (or sometimes a priest) and was used with the first name, as in Sir John.

More general terms of respect were *master* and *mistress*. These could be simply a polite form of address, but they were particularly used by servants speaking to their employers, or by anyone speaking to a gentleman or gentlewoman. They were also used as titles, Master Johnson being a name for a gentleman, Master William a polite way of referring to a commoner. Commoners might also be called *Goodman* or *Goodwife*, especially if they were at the head of a yeomanly household. Ordinary people, especially one's inferiors, might be called *man*, *fellow*, or *woman*. *Sirrah* was applied to inferiors and was sometimes used as an insult. A close friend might be called *friend*, *cousin*, or *coz*.

The child would have to learn the etiquette of actions as well as of words. Elizabethan manners were no less structured than our own, even if their provisions seem rather alien in some respects. The English commonly kissed each other as an ordinary form of greeting, although the practice declined in the first half of the 1600s. In greeting someone of higher social status, a person was expected to *make a leg*—performing a kind of bow—

and remove their hat; depending on the relative ranks of the two, the hat would stay off unless the higher-ranking person invited the other to put it back (the modern military salute derives from this practice of doffing the hat). Children were expected to show great respect to their parents. Even a grown man would kneel to receive his father's blessing and would stand mute and bareheaded before his parents. Status was also manifested in walking down the street: people of lower status were expected to *give the wall*—allowing others to walk closer to the buildings while they walked on the street side, closer to the gutters that ran down the middle of a street.

Naturally, learning to be polite also meant learning what was rude, and Elizabethan children could learn bad habits at this age as well as good ones. Making a fist with the thumb protruding through the fingers—a gesture sometimes called the fig of Spain—was the equivalent of giving someone the finger today. A similarly insulting gesture was biting the thumb, still seen in parts of Europe today.

Elizabethan English had a particularly rich vocabulary for expressing anger or contempt. The four-letter words of modern English were familiar, though used more as nouns and verbs than as exclamations. Strong language usually took the form of blasphemy, for example swearing by various attributes of God (sometimes abbreviated to 'Ods or 'S): *Ods bodkins* meant "God's little body"; the modern Londoner's *strewth* comes from "God's truth"; *gadzooks*, from "God's hooks [i.e., fingernails]." Those who had emotions to express but did not wish to cross the bounds of politeness or piety had plenty of milder options: *forsooth, i' faith* (in faith), *la*.

Elizabethan insults tell us much about the cultural values of the day. Common types of insulting terms related to bodily uncleanness or unhealthfulness (*dirty, poxy, lousy*), social inferiority (*peasant, churl, slave*), lack of intelligence (*fool, ninnyhammer, sot*), or subhuman status (*beast, cur, dog*).

Most of these insults would not have literal implications, but others could be taken more seriously. In 1586 a Salisbury woman was accused of having ranted at a wife of a former mayor of the town, calling her "Mistress Stinks, Mistress Fart . . . Mistress Jakes, Mistress Tosspot, and Mistress Drunkensoul."[6] The first three insults were merely offensive, but the last two amounted to accusations of drunkenness, and could lead to a lawsuit for defamation. Sexual insults could have even graver ramifications. Terms that implied that a woman was sexually incontinent (*whore, jade, quean*) had the potential to ruin her good reputation. For a man, one of the most serious insults was to imply unchastity on the part of his mother (*whoreson*) or wife (*cuckold*). Equally threatening were insults that accused a person of untruthfulness: to accuse a man of lying (called *giving him the lie*) was to invite potentially lethal conflict. Elizabethans had to learn from a young age that words had consequences: a serious insult could lead to legal action, or even to a duel.

Elizabethan children like their modern counterparts found it hard to resist the forbidden fruits of rude speech and conduct: a major responsibility of parents and teachers was to prevent rude conduct from becoming habitual, by beatings if necessary. Roger Ascham, who had been tutor to Queen Elizabeth when she was still a princess, was appalled by the laxity of some younger parents:

This last summer I was in a gentleman's house, where a young child, somewhat past four years old, could in no wise frame his tongue to say a little short grace; and yet he could roundly rap out so many ugly oaths, and those of the newest fashion, as some good man of fourscore years old hath never heard named before; and that which was most detestable of all, his father and mother would laugh at it. I much doubt, what comfort, another day, this child shall bring unto them. This child using much the company of serving men, and giving good ear to their talk, did easily learn, what he shall hardly forget all the days of his life hereafter.[7]

As Ascham suggests, children were expected to learn the rudiments of religion from a very young age. By law, the parish minister was required to provide religious instruction on alternate Sundays and on all holy days. All children over age 6 were required to attend, but most would already have received basic religious instruction at home. In particular, every child was expected to memorize the Ten Commandments, the Articles of Belief (also called the Creed—the basic statement of Christian belief), and the Lord's Prayer. The major component of the minister's instruction would be the catechism, a series of questions and answers regarding Christian belief. Parents who failed to send their children to receive this instruction might be prosecuted in the church courts, and children who could not recite the catechism might be required to do penance.

Play

Perhaps the most important part of the early learning process was play. Babies in wealthy families were given smoothly polished pieces of coral set in silver handles with bells attached: the sound of the bells pleased the baby, who could also suck or chew on the coral much as modern babies have pacifiers and teething rings. Cheaper versions were made with boar's teeth instead of coral. Whistles, rattles, and cloth or wooden dolls (called puppets or poppets) representing people or animals were also among the toys given to very small children. When toddlers were learning to walk, they might have a rolling walker that helped them along in the process.

As children grew, the range of toys and games grew with them. The stereotypical game for very young children was *put-pin*, which involved pushing pins across a table, trying to get them to cross over each other. Toys for older children included tops, hobby-horses, whirligigs, and cheap cast pewter miniatures. The miniatures might be in the shape of people, household furnishings, and arms and armor—there were even tiny toy guns of brass designed to fire gunpowder. Broken tobacco pipes were used with a soap mixture for blowing bubbles. In the autumn when nuts began to harden, children would play at Cob-Nut: nuts on strings were stuck against each other, the one whose nut broke first being the loser. Games played by older children included Tick (Tag), All-Hid (Hide and Seek), Hunting a Deer in My Lord's Park (akin to Duck-Duck-Goose), Leap-Frog, and Blind Man's Buff. Other children's pastimes included see-saws, swings, and mock military drill with toy drums, banners, and weapons.

Elementary Education

In spite of the vast social and economic differences that distinguished families from each other, the lives of very young children were remarkably uniform in many respects. At about age 6 this changed, as the social differentiations of class and gender began to play a real role. Girls remained in the world of women, wearing much the same clothing as they had when toddlers. Boys began to enter the world of men and abandoned their gowns in favor of the breeches worn by adult men. Both boys and girls began to be taught the skills appropriate to their rank in society.

For boys of privileged families, this meant going to school. Only a minority of Elizabethan children received formal schooling, although the num-

A 16th-century schoolroom. [Monroe]

ber was growing. There was no national system of education, but a range of independent and semi-independent educational institutions. Those children fortunate enough to have a formal education usually began at a *petty school*. Petty schools might be private enterprises or attached to a grammar school, but in many localities they were organized by the parish, and might be held by the parish minister in the porch of the church or in his own home. Petty schools were common—if there was none in a child's own parish, there was almost certainly at least one in an adjoining parish. Some children learned informally through private teaching, either from a family member, or from a neighbor, who might be paid to provide instruction.

The petty school typically taught the fundamentals of reading and writing, and perhaps *ciphering* (basic arithmetic with Arabic numerals). There was no set curriculum: a child might start at any age at which he was ready to learn, and many only stayed long enough to acquire rudimentary literacy.

The content of petty school education was strongly religious. The first stage was to learn the alphabet from a *hornbook*. This was a wooden tablet with a printed text pasted on it, covered with a thin layer of translucent horn to protect the paper: the text typically had the alphabet across the top, with the Lord's Prayer underneath. After learning the alphabet, the child would learn to read prayers and then move on to the catechism. Discipline was strict: schoolmasters had a free hand to use a birch rod to beat students for misbehavior or for academic failures. Most of the students were boys, but girls occasionally attended the petty schools. Masters at these schools were a mixed lot. Some were men of only small learning; some were women; some were in fact well-educated men—about a third of licensed petty school teachers may have been university graduates.

Literacy was expanding significantly during Elizabeth's reign, although it was still the exception rather than the rule. Some 20 percent of men and 5 percent of women may have had some degree of literacy at the time of Elizabeth's accession; by 1600 the figure may have risen to 30 percent for men and 10 percent for women. Literacy was generally higher among the privileged classes and townsfolk—perhaps 60 percent of London's craftsmen and tradesmen could read in the 1580s; and of a sample of London women in 1580, 16 percent could sign their names. Literacy was also more common among the more radical Protestants, and in the south and east. It tended to be lower among country folk and the poor, and in the north and west.[8]

What literacy means in an Elizabethan context could vary considerably. Not everyone who could read was good at it, and being able to read did not necessarily mean being able to write; nor did the ability to sign one's name mean that the person was a fluent writer. The diary of Lady Margaret Hoby, one of the few surviving texts from the hand of an Elizabethan woman, suggests that although she was a high-ranking gentlewoman

A LONDON SCHOOLBOY PREPARES FOR HIS DAY

Margaret the Maid Ho, Francis, rise, and get you to school! You shall be beaten, for it is past seven. Make yourself ready quickly, say your prayers, then you shall have your breakfast.

Francis the Schoolboy Margaret, give me my hosen; dispatch I pray you. Where is my doublet? Bring my garters, and my shoes: give me that shoeing horn.

Margaret Take first a clean shirt, for yours is foul...

Francis Where have you laid my girdle and my inkhorn? ... Where is my cap, my coat, my cloak, my cape, my gown, my gloves, my mittens ... my handkerchief, my points, my satchel, my penknife and my books? Where is all my gear? I have nothing ready: I will tell my father: I will cause you to be beaten. Peter, bring me some water to wash my hands and my face. ... Take the ewer, and pour upon my hands: pour high.

Peter the Servant Can you not wash in the basin? Shall you have always a servant at your tail?....

Margaret Have you saluted your father and your mother? ...

Francis Where is he?

Margaret He is in the shop.

Francis God give you good morrow, my father, and all your company. Father, give me your blessing if it please you....

Father God bless thee ... Now go, and have me recommended unto your master and mistress, and tell them that I pray them to come tomorrow to dinner with me: that will keep you from beating. Learn well, to the end that you may render unto me your lesson when you are come again from school.

Claudius Hollyband, *The French Schoolmaster* (London: Abrahame Veale, 1573), 62–66.

who read avidly and wrote daily, her spelling remained heavily phonetic compared to well educated men of her day.

Writing

The equipment used for writing was typically a goose-quill pen, an inkhorn, and paper. The quill was shaved of its feathers (contrary to our modern image), and a point or *nib* was cut into it. This was done with a small knife that folded into its own handle for safe transportation, to be brought out when the nib needed sharpening—the origin of the modern penknife. One of the first things children needed to learn was how to trim their own pens. The pen and its accessories were kept in a leather case called a penner. People who had to do a lot of calculating, such as shopkeepers, often used a slate, which could be written on and wiped clear afterward. Another form of temporary writing involved a wooden or metal stylus

A hornbook. [By permission of the Folger Shakespeare Library]

and a small thin board coated with colored wax, called a wax tablet. The writer would inscribe the letters into the wax with the stylus, which had a rounded end for rubbing out the letters afterward. Such tablets were typically bound in pairs (or even in books) to protect their faces, and were known as a "pair of tables."[9]

There were two principal types of handwriting used by the Elizabethans, known as secretary and italic. The secretary hand had evolved in the late Middle Ages as a quick and workaday version of "Gothic" script. In the Elizabethan period it retained its workaday character, and was often used for correspondence, accounts, and other practical uses, although to the modern eye it seems very difficult to read. The italic hand was similar to the style of letters known as italic today. It had been developed in Renaissance Italy, and is much more clear and elegant by modern standards; it was especially used by learned people in scholarly contexts.

The alphabet was essentially the same as we use today, with a few interesting exceptions. For a start, there were only 24 letters. The letters *i* and *j* were considered equivalent: *J* was often used as the capital form of *i*. The letters *u* and *v* were similarly equivalent, *u* commonly being used in the middle of a word and *v* at the beginning. Where we would write "I have an uncle," an Elizabethan might have written "J haue an vncle." Some

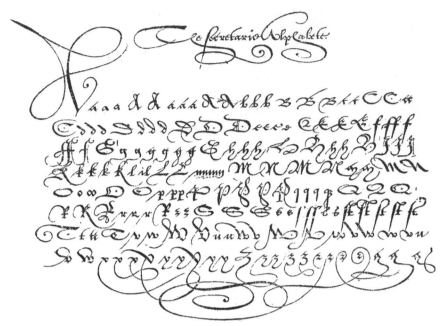

A secretary hand. [Beau-Chesne]

Elizabethan letters have since dropped out of use. The normal form of *s* was the long form, which today is often mistaken for an *f* (it is not actually identical: the crossbar on the long *s* extends only on the left side of the letter, where it goes right through on an *f*). The modern style of *s* was used as a capital or at the end of a word. There was also a special character to represent *th*, which looked like a *y*, but actually came from an ancient runic letter called *thorn*: when we see "Ye Olde Tea Shoppe," the *ye* should actually be pronounced *the.* Roman numerals were more frequently used than today, although reckoning was usually done with the more convenient Arabic numbers.

There were no dictionaries, so Elizabethan spelling was largely a matter of custom, and often just a matter of writing the words by ear. Still, the normal spelling of words was for the most part very similar to the spelling known today. The most obvious difference is that the Elizabethans often added a final *e* in words where we do not: *school*, for example, was likely to be written as *schoole.*

In printed books there were two principal typefaces: blackletter and Roman. Blackletter type, like the secretary hand, was derived from medieval writing; it resembled what is sometimes called Old English type today. Roman type, like the italic hand, was associated with the revival of classical learning during the Renaissance and eventually replaced the blackletter entirely: the standard type used today derives from Roman typeface. Italic type was also used, especially to set words apart from surrounding Roman text.

Grammar School

After petty school, if the family was rich or if the boy showed enough promise to earn a scholarship, he might go to a grammar school. This stage of schooling might last between 5 and 10 years, typically finishing by age 14 to 18. Some students might only remain for a year or two.

The grammar taught at a grammar school was Latin language and literature. For the first year or two the focus was on learning the elements of Latin grammar (*accidence*), after which the child was deemed ready to dive into Latin literature—in fact, older students were expected to speak Latin at all times and were punished for speaking English. Latin had long been Europe's international language of learning, and grammar-school students read a mixture of ancient authors like Caesar and Cicero, religious writings, and modern scholarship, particularly the work of Erasmus. Taken together, a student's grammar school readings would amount to a broad-based course of study that could include material on literature, history, theology, geography, and sciences. The school might also teach a bit of French, Greek, or Hebrew. Teaching was through a combination of reading and interpreting aloud, translation exercises, and class activities such as debates and plays. In addition to literary studies, the curriculum often included music, and there might even be provision for sports such as archery.

All students at the school sat in one room, without desks: they were grouped on benches, called *forms*, according to their level of schooling. Wolverhampton Grammar School in 1609 had 69 students, divided into an accidence class followed by six forms; students in the upper forms helped out in teaching the lower ones. The typical grammar school was headed by a master, usually a university graduate. The master might have one or more assistant teachers, called ushers, to assist him. At Wolverhampton, the master taught the top four forms, and the usher the lower two forms and the accidence class. The school often had a mix of paying students and poorer boys funded by scholarship. The Merchant Taylors' School in London, a leading grammar school founded in 1561, had 100 boys who paid 5s. a quarter, 50 partial scholars paying 2s. 2d., and 100 boys who paid no tuition, although all were required to pay a 12d. entrance fee to the cleaner hired to keep the school tidy.

It was rare for a girl to be admitted to a grammar school, and such an arrangement would only last from the age of 7 to 9 or thereabouts. However, there were also some specialized boarding schools for girls.

School hours were long. A typical school day would begin at 6 A.M., with a 15-minute break for breakfast at 9 A.M. or so. There would be another break for dinner at 11 A.M., with classes resuming at 1 P.M.; then a 30-minute break at 3 P.M. or so, with classes ending at 5 P.M. or so. Classes in the winter tended to begin an hour later and finish an hour earlier than in the summer. Depending on the school, the boys might be day students, boarders, or a mix of both. Day students generally went home for their meals; boarding students slept in common dormitories. Classes ran year-round, but students might have Thursday or Saturday afternoons off, as well as two-week holidays at Christmas and Easter.

In addition to these publicly available forms of schooling, wealthy families sometimes hired tutors for their children. A tutor might provide the child's entire education, especially for girls; in other cases, a tutor might cover subjects not included in the school curriculum. For example, if you wanted your child to learn modern languages, you might have to hire a tutor (except in larger towns, where there were often specialized schools for such purposes). This would be important for an upper-class family, whose children would be expected to learn at least some French, and perhaps Spanish or Italian as well. French had enjoyed a privileged place in English and European culture since the Middle Ages, and anyone of social pretensions was expected to be able to use it, while the cultural ascendancy of Italy during the Renaissance had given Italian a similar kind of cachet. Moreover, foreign languages were essential to Englishmen who were wealthy or important enough to travel abroad or have international connections, since few people outside of the British Isles bothered to learn England's provincial tongue.

Tutors were also hired to teach nonacademic subjects like dancing and music; a boy might also be taught fencing, riding, swimming, or archery. A girl's education was likely to focus on such skills and graces as would make her a desirable match, notably modern languages, needlework, and music. Book learning was not generally a high priority for girls, although plenty of parents ensured that their daughters had a good education—

**A GRAMMAR-SCHOOL TEACHER ON
THE EDUCATION OF GIRLS, 1581**

To learn to read is very common, where convenientness doth serve, and writing is not refused where opportunity will yield it. Reading if for nothing else . . . is very needful for religion, to read that which they must know and ought to perform . . . Music is much used, where it is to be had, to the parents' delight . . . I meddle not with needles nor yet with housewifery, though I think it and know it to be a principal commendation in a woman to be able to govern and direct her household, to look to her house and family, to provide and keep necessaries though the goodman pay, to know the force of her kitchen for sickness and health in herself and her charge.

Richard Mulcaster, *Positions* (London: Thomas Chare, 1581), 177–78.

Elizabeth herself was noted for her learning and was expert in both Greek and Latin. For some upper-class children, at least a part of this education might be acquired while living away in the household of a higher-ranking aristocrat.

Universities

After grammar school, a boy might pursue higher learning. University education in the Middle Ages had been almost exclusively the preserve of the clergy, but the 16th century witnessed a rising tide of secular students. Sons of the aristocracy came seeking the sophistication required of a Renaissance gentleman, and bright young men of lesser status came to prepare themselves for an intellectual career.

There were only two universities in England, Oxford and Cambridge, each subdivided into a number of semi-independent colleges that provided both lodging and teaching. The typical age of matriculation was 17 or 18; all students were boys. During the 1590s, Oxford took in around 360 new students each year.

The four-year course of study for a Bachelor of Arts included two terms of grammar (i.e., Latin grammar), four terms of rhetoric, and five terms of logic, or *dialectic*, as well as three terms of arithmetic and two of music. Candidates for the Master of Arts studied Greek, astronomy, geometry, philosophy (including natural philosophy, which we would call science), and metaphysics; the degree normally required another 3 years of study. Doctorates, which took 7 to 12 years, were available in divinity, civil law, and medicine. Degrees were awarded by the university, which offered lectures in the prescribed subjects and required graduating students to participate in disputations by way of a final exam. However, the bulk of the real teaching happened within the colleges under the tutor system. Each student was taken on by a *fellow* of the college, who guided the student's reading and met with the student periodically to discuss his studies.

However, not every student took a degree. Many of the attendees were the sons of gentry families looking to acquire a smattering of learning before moving on: in 1604 the young gentleman Thomas Wentworth was advised by his father, "All your sons would go to the university at 13 years old and stay there two or three years, then to the Inns of Court before 17 years of age, and be well kept to their study of the laws."[10]

Specialized Education

As the elder Wentworth suggested, university education was often only a prelude to study of the law at the Inns of Court. The Inns were residential institutions at the west end of London, close to Westminster, where young men could learn English law by attending lectures, observing actual legal and Parliamentary proceedings, and taking part in mock legal proceedings of their own. Closely associated were the Inns of Chancery, where young men might acquire a basic grounding in law, sometimes going on to study at the Inns of Court.

There were four main Inns of Court—Grays Inn, Lincolns Inn, Inner Temple, and Middle Temple—with subsidiary dependent Inns, housing over 1,000 students in all. Some of them were interested in legal careers and would remain for seven or eight years, eventually seeking to be licensed by the Inns to practice law (the Inns still perform this function today). Students at the Inns sat on benches, called *barrae* in Latin: once a student was deemed ready, his Inn summoned him to sit on the bench with the other practicing members of his Inn, and so become a barrister. A barrister was permitted to plead before the Common Law courts, with the exception of Common Pleas, to which a barrister had to be summoned after further practice, thereby becoming a Sergeant at Law. However, a person could provide legal counsel outside of the courtroom without becoming a barrister; such practitioners were called attorneys (in England today they are called solicitors).

Most students at the Inns stayed only long enough to acquire an acquaintance with the workings of the law; this knowledge could be of use to them as future landowners, justices of the peace, or holders of government office. The Inns also helped young men cultivate social skills and contacts to prepare them for a position in elite society.

A variety of other educational opportunities were available, particularly in London, which was sometimes called the third university of the kingdom. The Inns of Court had a Civil Law counterpart in Doctors' Commons, which offered a more practically oriented course of study in the subject than was available at the universities. The Royal College of Physicians sponsored lectures in medicine and surgery, and from 1596 the Royal Exchange hosted Gresham College, an endowed institution offering lectures in subjects including astronomy, geometry, music, medicine, and divinity. These were essentially continuing education courses aimed at London merchants and other urban elites: lecturers were hired from the universities, but enjoined to emphasize practical aspects of their subjects that would appeal to their audiences. In addition, London, Cambridge, Oxford, and other towns had small private academies and tutors offering instruction in subjects that included foreign languages, administration, and accounting.

Vocational Training

For those children not in school, age 6 was about the time for beginning the first steps toward work. Initially, children's work centered on the home and family. Young boys and girls performed light tasks about the house or helped out by minding their younger siblings. In the country, children were expected to work in the fields at harvest time, when the demand for labor was at its highest, binding and stacking the grain after the harvesters had cut it down. Children also helped their mothers by carding wool to be spun into thread, and they might be taught to knit to bring extra revenue into the home.

As they developed the physical and mental capacity, girls began to learn the skills they would need for running a household: cooking, brewing, spinning, dyeing, and basic medical skills. By the time she reached her teenage years, a girl would be capable of pretty much all the tasks that made up her mother's daily routine.

For boys the process was slower, especially in the countryside where the heaviest male labor was beyond the strength of a young teenager. At first a boy in the country might help with the lighter sorts of field work, such as chasing or shooting birds at sowing time to keep them from eating the seeds, or clearing stones from the fallow fields. Over time they would take on more challenging work, but they would be well into their teens before they could sustain heavy labor like ploughing. By the age of 12 or 14, a boy may not have been ready for the heaviest tasks, but he was still expected to be fully integrated into the working economy: the Statute of Artificers declared that any boy aged 12 or older could be compelled to work.

Many children left home during their teenage years to enter service in another household. In most households, only the eldest son had a future in the family farm or family business—his sisters and younger brothers would not inherit the land or business and needed to make their own way in the world. Service allowed them to earn their keep while starting to position themselves for long-term self-sufficiency.

For young people, employment as a servant was in many ways akin to the sorts of jobs available to teenagers today: it paid little, and required little in the way of prior skills, but offered an opportunity to build a record as an employee that could position them for better opportunities in the future. However, the Elizabethan servant lived in the employer's home, and the employer stood in the position of a parent. He was legally responsible for his servants as he would be for his own children, and so might discipline them as we would his own children, but he was also expected to look out for them as a parent. Service therefore offered a transitional stage between care by a parent and full independence.

Time spent in service allowed young people to accumulate some money, make useful social connections, and acquire polish in the ways of their social superiors. Even aristocratic youths might spend some time as pages, gentlemen-ushers, or ladies-in-waiting in a higher-ranking household. Many people spent significant years of their teens and twenties in service. Between the ages of 20 and 24, some 80 percent of men and 50 percent of women were servants; two-thirds of boys and three-quarters of girls went away from home in service from just before puberty until marriage, or a period of about 10 years.

THE ASTROLOGER SIMON FORMAN
RECALLS HIS BOYHOOD DAYS

Now Simon had put himself for an apprentice for ten years with Matthew Commin, with condition that he should be three years at the grammar school. Which his master performed not—which was a part of the cause why he went from his master afterwards. Simon at first, being the youngest apprentice of four, was put to all the worst, and being little and small of stature and young of years, everyone did triumph over him. Especially a kitchen-maid named Mary Roberts; oftentimes she would knock him that the blood should run about his ears . . . On a certain frosty morning his master and mistress were both gone to the garden and their kinswoman with them, leaving none at home but Simon and Mary, willing Mary to took into the shop and help, if occasion served. They being gone, so many customers came for ware that Simon could not attend them all. Whereupon he calls Mary to stand in the shop. She came forth, reviled him with many bitter words, and said she should anon have him by the ears, and so went her way again. Simon . . . made the best shift he could and rid them all away. He shut the shop door, took a yard [rod] and went into Mary, who so soon as she saw him, was ready to have him by the ears. But Simon struck her on the hands with his yard, and belaboured her so, ere he went, that he made her black and blue all over.

Simon Forman's Diary, in A. L. Rowse, *Sex and Society in Shakespeare's Age: Simon Forman the Astrologer* (New York: Scribner, 1974), 271–72.

An alternative path to service that shared some of its features was apprenticeship. Parents who had the necessary connections might find a tradesman to whom they could apprentice their child, signing a contract that bound the child to remain in service to the master for a term of years. According to typical terms from a London indenture of apprenticeship, the apprentice "his . . . master faithfully shall serve, his secrets keep, his lawful commands everywhere gladly do. He shall not commit fornication nor contract matrimony within the said term. He shall not play at cards, dice, tables, or any other unlawful games. He shall not haunt taverns nor playhouses, nor absent himself from the master's service day or night unlawfully." For his part, the master was expected to teach the apprentice his trade: "The said master his said apprentice shall teach and instruct or cause to be taught and instructed, finding unto his said apprentice meat, drink, apparel, lodging, and all other necessaries, according to the custom of the City of London."[11]

Apprenticeship often began in the late teens: most apprentices in London began around 18–20 years old, or a year younger among those who had been born in London. The duration of the apprenticeship was governed by the guild to which the tradesman belonged, but seven years was the most common figure, and the legal minimum by statute. More prestigious trades often required a longer period of apprenticeship—apprenticeships in London's Company of Grocers normally took eight or nine years.

An apprentice who completed the term successfully could become a journeyman and was allowed to take full employment in the trade. Those whose families had the necessary connections and resources could eventually seek admission to the guild as an independent master, setting up in business for themselves. The typical interval in London between completing apprenticeship and becoming an independent master was a bit over three years, although many took six years or more. Not all apprentices successfully completed their term—in London, the figure was only 41 percent, the rest either leaving or dying before completion of the apprenticeship.

Apprenticeship was a privileged position, and families paid to have their children taken on in this way. The apprenticeship was in many ways similar to service in establishing a kind of family relationship between apprentice and master, but unlike service, it offered the promise of learning a skill that the apprentice could use to improve his economic prospects in the long term. The overwhelming majority of apprentices were boys, though some positions were available to girls in trades like needlework.

Coming of Age

During the teenage years, several points of passage marked a young man or woman's integration into the adult world. By age 14, those children not of the privileged classes were expected to be full working participants in the economy. Fourteen was also the youngest age at which children could go through the ceremony of confirmation, which allowed them to receive communion at church; however, the ceremony was often put off until age 16 or even 18, and it was not widely regarded as an important ritual—Puritans generally rejected it altogether. Boys were subject to military service at age 16. Full legal majority came at age 21. According to Parliamentary law, the minimum age for finishing an urban apprenticeship was 24, while agricultural laborers were to be regarded as apprentices until age 21. However, the most important turning point in the life of both men and women was marriage.

Marriage

Marriage was the point at which an individual acquired full status in the society. For a man, to be married was to be a householder, and to be a householder was to be an independent person. Independent bachelors were extremely rare. Since marriage meant independence, it could not really take place until the couple were sufficiently established in the economy to support themselves.

A wedding in the early 1600s. [Ashton]

We tend to think of the Elizabethans marrying very young, an impression that has much to do with the 14-year-old Juliet of Shakespeare's play. Technically, church law permitted marriage at age 12 for girls and 14 for boys, although parental consent was required for anyone under the age of 21. In reality, such young marriages were almost unknown. The mean age of marriage was around 27 for men, 24 for women. The age was lower among the upper classes: 24 and 19 among the aristocracy, 27 and 22 among the gentry. Women in London also married a bit younger, the mean age being 22 to 24.

The first step on the path to marriage was finding a prospective match. How this worked depended on a person's station in life. The higher you were on the social ladder, the more control your family exerted over the process. For wealthy and prestigious families, the stakes were high: it was considered essential that the match was suitable to the family's interests. The children of such families were typically entrusted to the care of tutors, schools, relatives, and others who could be counted on to control the child's social environment, making them less likely to end up in an unauthorized match. This doesn't mean that the children had no say in choosing their partner—both church law and public sentiment insisted on consent from both partners—but it does mean that upper-class families tried to control the options and exert pressure so that the child would end up with what they considered a suitable partner. Only very rarely would an upper-class child slip through this network of family influence.

For most people, the stakes in marriage were much lower, and the level of family influence much more limited. Ordinary young people had extensive opportunities to meet those of the opposite sex: through their work, through family connections, at church services, at organized public festivities, and at informal entertainments like dancing or games on a Sunday afternoon. Two people who took an interest in each other might begin courting—exchanging gifts, letters, and visits, and spending time together as opportunities allowed. Lovers often exchanged other love tokens during courtship; typical courting-gifts included handkerchiefs, gloves, garters, locks of hair, foodstuffs such as fruits or spices (nutmeg and ginger were two favorites), and sometimes a coin broken in half.

At this stage, it was normal to involve the respective families, the man in particular visiting the woman's home so that her parents might have a chance to size him up. Although the parents' permission was not required unless the child was under 21, it was generally considered unwise and inappropriate to marry against the parents' wishes. For most young people, this was not a problem. While everyone regarded love and affection as indispensable components in the marriage equation, prudence was also a factor. Marriage in the 16th century was permanent, and both city and country were full of paupers who served as a constant reminder of the importance of choosing a spouse wisely and the potential consequences of an injudicious match.

Once the couple decided to marry, there might follow a process of negotiation between the families. If the families possessed any significant amount of property, they would be expected to contract to settle parts of it on the couple in various forms. The girl's family was expected to provide a dowry, property that the girl would bring with her into the marriage. There might also be an agreement on *jointure,* the part of the couple's property that the girl would have at her disposal to support her if she were widowed.

Once any practicalities were dealt with, the couple could become engaged or betrothed. Betrothal was taken very seriously: the promise to marry had to be made before witnesses, and it was considered a legally binding contract—those who reneged on a promise to marry could be prosecuted in the church courts, and they could be prevented from marrying anyone else until securing an agreement to dissolve the contract. If a promise to marry was followed by sexual consummation, the couple were regarded as married according to church law, although they might still be punished for fornication. The betrothal was often marked by a symbolic exchange of gifts, or the man would give the woman a gift—rings were a common choice, but gloves and bracelets were sometimes chosen.

Prior to the actual marriage, the *banns* were asked in the couple's respective parish churches on three successive Sundays. The banns were a form of marriage announcement; their main purpose was to provide an opportunity for people to reveal any impediments to the marriage. The marriage would have to be called off if the couple was closely related to each other or if there was a prior betrothal or marriage. Alternatively, the couple could pay the church authorities for a marriage license, which performed the same function as the banns—upper-class families generally preferred this rather private option.

On the wedding day, the couple dressed in their finest clothes—ideally new ones purchased for the occasion. Green was considered an especially suitable color, especially for the groom. There was no formalized outfit akin to the modern bridal attire, but the woman might wear knotted ribbons and wear a garland on her head: favored plants included flowers, ears of wheat (symbols of fertility), rosemary, myrtle and bay (all herbs that represented constancy, since they do not decay like most plants). The groom might also have ribbons and similar plants tied or pinned to his clothes. An especially common decoration was the *bride-lace,* a sprig of rosemary tied up in a lace to be worn on the left arm. Similar adornments could be worn by the wedding party and guests, and the site of the wedding feast might itself be similarly decorated. Once all was ready, the bride would be processed to the church. She might be attended by bridesmaids or children; the groom was accompanied by groomsmen.

The wedding itself was celebrated inside the couple's parish church, following the ritual that is still more or less used in the Anglican church today. Perhaps the greatest difference regards the wedding ring: the man placed a ring on the woman's ring finger, but there was no reciprocal exchange. It was also the practice for women to take their husbands' surname. The marriage was recorded in the parish register, which served the legal role of the modern marriage certificate.

Not every wedding followed these prescribed norms, and much of the work of church courts was in adjudicating cases of irregular marriages. Some marriages took place outside of churches—in private homes, in a barn, in a field, or even in alehouses. Some were performed without the proper banns or witnesses, or the officiating churchman turned out not to be an ordained minister. In some cases there was an impediment that failed to be discovered beforehand, such as a prior betrothal. Such marriages had to be sorted out on a case-by-case basis. A wedding celebrated outside of a church, without witnesses, or at night was illegal and punishable, but still valid. However, if the celebrant had not been ordained, this would generally nullify the marriage. Instances of prior betrothal could be complex, and the outcome often depended on the specific circumstances of the case.

Once married, the couple were legally required to live together. Separation was only permitted by order of a church court and only in such extreme circumstances as cruelty or adultery. In these cases, the separated couple were to remain celibate, and the wife could receive alimony. Divorce as such was not permitted, but annulment was possible if the marriage was proved to have been invalid—for example if the couple were within the forbidden degrees of family relationship, or if the man was discovered after the wedding to be permanently impotent.

Sexuality

Sexual activity outside of the marriage bond was punishable by law, although it was very much a part of daily life. It has been estimated that 1 child in 25 was born out of wedlock at the end of Elizabeth's reign. A large number of these illegitimate births arose from broken marriage contracts. Once a couple was betrothed, it was very common for them to become sexually active before the marriage. Statistics suggest that a quarter to a third of the first pregnancies of Elizabethan wives began before the wedding. Such premarital relations were punishable as fornication under church laws, but secular Elizabethan culture regarded it as a very minor misdeed, and such cases were rarely prosecuted. However, the situation could become complicated if the couple did not actually marry. Exploitative men looking to gain a woman's sexual favors might promise marriage—privately, if possible, so there would be no witnesses—and later deny that a promise had been made, or even leave the community, never to be seen again.

Elizabethan attitudes toward sex were complex and nuanced. Anyone who has read Shakespeare is aware of the Elizabethan penchant for bawdiness. The Elizabethans could be remarkably frank about sexuality—after all, their society allowed for comparatively little physical or social privacy, and therefore less isolation between people's sexual and public lives. However, it was essential for women of any standing not to compromise their reputation for sexual continence: for married women, any whiff of scandal could raise doubts about the paternity of their children, and for unmarried women, it could ruin their prospects of marriage. The standard for men was not quite as strict—to visit a brothel, for example, was considered immoral and disreputable, but it would not destroy a man's career.

Religious doctrine across the sectarian spectrum taught that sexuality within marriage was appropriate and beneficial, both for procreation and for mutual comfort, as long as it was not pursued with lascivious excess. Nonmarital sexuality (fornication and adultery) was punishable by the church courts, which could also impose child support on a man who fathered an illegitimate child. Nonprocreative sexuality might be classed as sodomy, punishable as a felony and subject to the death penalty.

Yet the realities of people's sexual lives could be complex. Single women who found themselves pregnant might turn to practitioners of folk medicine to supply herbs or even magic to abort the fetus—indeed it was widely felt that this was permissible until the *quickening* of the child, at about five months when its motion became detectable. Similar recipes might be used as contraceptives, although doubtless with unreliable results. Prostitution was illegal yet universally recognized as an established part of Elizabethan culture—everyone in London knew that you could easily find a prostitute in the Bankside district of Southwark, near the theaters (or even in them). Homosexual activity was classed as sodomy, but it was likewise widely recognized as present, at least among men (female homosexuality was virtually invisible both to contemporaries and in the historical record). Even pornography was available from London booksellers, smuggled across the Channel from Continental publishers.

Aging and Life Expectancy

A rapidly growing population and relatively high rates of mortality meant that the population of Elizabethan England was rather young. Still, a 40-year-old was not thought to be elderly. In fact, the forties and fifties were considered the prime of a man's life. If any age marked the beginning of old age, it was 60: the law allowed people to cease work after that age, nor was one liable for military service. It has been estimated that about 8 percent of the population were age 60 or older. Nonetheless, the prevalence of disease and the primitive level of medicine meant that illness could easily end a life long before its prime. Life expectancy at birth was only about 48 years, although anyone who made it through the first 30 years was likely to live for another 30. Life expectancy varied from place to place—it was particularly low in the cities, where crowded conditions and poor sanitation increased the dangers of disease.

For many people, living into old age must have been as frightening a prospect as not reaching it. Once a person was no longer able to work, they had to turn to other resources for support. Widows were especially at risk, since women had less earning power and fewer economic options than men: even a younger widow with a job could find herself in poverty if she did not secure a new husband who could support her.

The most fortunate of the elderly were those who had sufficient property to guarantee them an ongoing income. Parents who were past working age might pass on their land or business to their heirs in exchange for a guarantee of support for their remaining years. Guild members could look to their guild for assistance if they needed it. Those who had spent their working lives in the pay of others might look to their employers to support them, at least if the relationship had been one of long standing.

Many of the elderly had no such options. A few might find a place in a *hospital*: many large towns had endowed institutions that provided food and lodging for the elderly poor. These places imposed a quasi-monastic life of discipline on their residents, with uniform clothing, daily communal prayers, and strict codes of personal conduct, but they offered security in an uncertain age, and there were always more applicants than openings. Others were supported by the parish poor-rate, either through stipends or by lodging in a Poor House. Many people fell through the holes of this rudimentary safety net and were dependent on begging to scrape together enough money to feed themselves.

Death and Burial

People normally left the world as they had come into it and as they had conceived their own offspring: at home and in bed. When death was approaching, a person would be urged to make a will, if this had not yet been done (estates under £5 did not require a will). Moveable property could be disposed of by will, as could land held by burgage tenure or otherwise not subject to the customs of feudal or manorial inheritance. Among the upper classes and in open-field areas, feudal and manorial land was passed on by primogeniture, the eldest son inheriting all of it; this would prevent the landholding from being broken up into pieces too small to support the landholder's needs. Woodland regions were more likely to follow *partible inheritance,* whereby each of the sons was given a share of the land.

When a person was on their deathbed, the parish bell would toll. This was called the *passing bell,* and was a signal for all hearers to pray for the dying person. After the death, there would be one short peal; from its sound the hearers could tell whether the deceased was male or female. If the circumstances of the death were at all questionable, the county coroner would be brought in to inspect the body and determine whether there was a criminal matter that required investigation.

After death the body was stripped and washed, cleansing it of the sweat and other excretions that could come with the death throes. The corpse was then wrapped and bound in a winding-sheet, which might simply be a linen sheet from the bed in which the person had died. Flowers and herbs like rosemary were sometimes wrapped in the sheet with the corpse.

The body was now ready for burial, but preparations for the living might take longer. Depending on the status of the deceased, the funeral might be an elaborate affair to which many people would be invited, requiring time to make the necessary arrangements. However, if the ceremony was delayed too long, the corpse might begin to decay. Typically, the funeral would take place within a day or two, although if more time were needed, a wealthy family could pay for embalming or a lead-lined casket to circumvent the problem of putrefaction. In the mean time, the corpse was watched constantly. In very old-fashioned communities this watching might be celebrated as a full-fledged wake, and could be an occasion for the kind of drinking and carousing that met with stern disapproval from religious reformers.

THE WILL OF ELLEN GARNET OF SUTTON, DERBYSHIRE, 1592

In the name of God, Amen, the 27th day of April in the 34th year of the reign of our sovereign Lady Elizabeth, by the grace of God of England, France, and Ireland Queen, Defender of the Faith, etc. I Ellen Garnet of Sutton, late wife of James Garnet deceased, being sick in body but in perfect remembrance, God be thanked for it, make this my last will and testament in manner and form following, that is to say, first I give and bequeath my soul into the hands of almighty God, my maker and redeemer, and my body to be buried in the parish churchyard of Prescot, as near to my friends as the ground will permit and suffer, and my funeral expenses to be made of my whole goods. Item, I give and bequeath to my son John Tyccle one brass pan, one coffer standing in the house, and one old long bolster. . . . Item, I give to Margaret Tyccle, wife of the said John, my best hat. Item, I give my daughter Anne Turner all the rest of my clothes except one old red petticoat which I give to Margaret Houghton. Item, I give further to Margaret Houghton 3s. 4d. Item, I give to Anne Lyon my daughter 40s. . . . Item, I give to my son Thomas Garnet all the rest of my goods movable and unmoveable. . . . Item I constitute, ordain, and make Thomas Garnet my son my true and lawful executor to see this my last will and testament done and executed in manner and form aforesaid. In witness whereof I the said Ellen Garnet have set my hand and seal the day and year first above written.

Mary Presland, ed., *Angells to Yarwindles: The Wills and Inventories of Twenty-Six Elizabethan and Jacobean Women Living in the Area Now Called St. Helens* (St. Helens: St. Helens Association for Research into Local History, 1999), 11.

When it was time for the funeral, the corpse was laid in a casket, to be carried on a wooden bier; the bier was draped with a cloth called a pall. The parish normally provided the bier and casket, which were reused from one funeral to the next. Only the wealthy could afford to be buried in their own personal caskets; at most funerals, the corpse would be removed from the casket for burial. The bier was carried to the churchyard, where the priest met it at the gate to begin the religious ceremony of burial. Church bells would ring just before and after the ceremony.

The privileged would be buried inside the church under brass or stone markers bearing inscriptions of their names, and if they could afford it, some kind of inscribed portrait; the most expensive grave markers had fully carved effigies of the deceased in stone. Most people were buried in the churchyard in unmarked graves.

Funerals, like christenings and weddings, were important social occasions. For families that could afford it, the ceremony would be followed by a feast; food and alms were often distributed to the poor, while attendees would wear somber mourning clothes, often provided by the will of the deceased. Thomas Meade, a justice of the peace in Essex who died in 1585, made arrangements of this sort: "There shall be bestowed at my burial and funeral one hundred pounds at the least to buy black cloth and other things, and every one of my serving men shall have a black coat; and a gown of black cloth to my brethren and their wives, my wife's daughters and their husbands, my sister Swanne and her husband, my brother Turpyn and his wife, my aunt Bendyshe, and Elizabeth wife of John Wrighte."[12] In 1580, Essex gentleman Wistan Browne made provision that "at the day of my funerals dole be given to the poor people, viz. 6d. apiece to so many of them as will hold up their hands to take it, besides sufficient meat, bread, and drink to every of them."[13]

As baptism and marriage were recorded in the parish register, so too was burial, the ceremony of the third and final great passage of life.

NOTES

1. Sir Thomas Smith, *De Republica Anglorum* (London: Gregory Seton, 1584), 19.

2. Gamaliel Bradford, *Elizabethan Women* (Cambridge, MA: Houghton Mifflin, 1936), 60.

3. On infant mortality, see E. A. Wrigley and R. S. Schofield, *The Population History of England 1541–1871* (Cambridge, MA: Harvard University Press, 1981), 249.

4. Lu Pearson, *The Elizabethans at Home* (Stanford, CA: Stanford University Press, 1957), 100.

5. D. M. Palliser, *The Age of Elizabeth* (London and New York: Longman, 1992), 7. On Elizabethan English, see Charles Barber, *Early Modern English*. The Language Library (London: André Deutsch, 1976).

6. Martin Ingram, *Church Courts, Sex, and Marriage in England, 1570–1640* (Cambridge: Cambridge University Press, 1987), 300.

7. Roger Ascham, *The Scholemaster*, ed. Edward Arber (London: Constable, 1927), 57.

8. On literacy, see David Cressy, *Literacy and the Social Order* (Cambridge: Cambridge University Press, 1980), 175–76.

9. On writing, see Myrial St. Clare Byrne, *The Elizabethan Home* (London: Methuen, 1949), 20; Giles E. Dawson and Laetitia Kennedy-Shipton, *Elizabethan Handwriting 1500–1650* (New York: Norton, 1966); Sir Edward Thompson, "Handwriting," in *Shakespeare's England. An Account of the Life and Manners of His Age* (Oxford: Clarendon Press, 1916), 1.284–310.

10. Palliser, *Age of Elizabeth*, 426.

11. Steve Rappaport, *Worlds within Worlds: Structures of Life in Sixteenth-Century London* (Cambridge: Cambridge University Press, 1989), 234.

12. David Cressy, *Birth, Marriage, and Death. Ritual, Religion, and the Life-Cycle in Tudor and Stuart England* (Oxford: Oxford University Press, 1997), 440.

13. Cressy, *Birth, Marriage, and Death*, 444.

4

Cycles of Time

THE DAY

For most Elizabethans the day began just before dawn, at cockcrow—or, strictly speaking, third cockcrow, since cocks would crow first at midnight and again about halfway to dawn. Artificial light was expensive and generally feeble, so it was vital to make the most of daylight. This meant that the daily schedule varied from season to season, dawn being around 3:30 A.M. in the summer and 7 A.M. in the winter. According to law, from mid-September to mid-March laborers were supposed to begin work at dawn, and in other months at 5 A.M. Markets typically opened at dawn, and businesses at 7 A.M.

Domestic clocks and portable watches were available to the Elizabethans, but they were expensive. Most people marked time by the hourly ringing of church and civic bells; there were also public sundials and clock towers. In the towns, time was invariably reckoned by the hour of the clock: normally only the hour, half-hour, quarter-hour, and sometimes the eighth-hour were counted, rather than the hour and minute—in fact, clocks and watches had no minute hands. In the country, people were more likely to reckon time by natural phenomena—dawn, sunrise, midday, sunset, dusk, midnight, and the crowing of the cock.

Mornings were always cold. Fire was the only source of heat, and household fires were banked at night as a precaution against burning down the home. If there were servants in the house, they rose first and rekindled the fires before their employers left the warmth of their beds; the servants

AN ETIQUETTE BOOK FOR BOYS
DESCRIBES THE MORNING ROUTINE

At six of the clock, without delay,
　　use commonly to rise,
And give God thanks for thy good rest,
　　when thou openest thine eyes . . .
Ere from thy chamber thou do pass,
　　see thou purge thy nose clean,
And other filthy things like case—
　　thou knowest what I mean.
Brush thou and sponge thy clothes too,
　　that thou that day shalt wear,
In comely sort cast up your bed,
　　lose you none of your gear.
Make clean your shoes and comb your head,
　　and your clothes button or lace.
And see at no time you forget
　　to wash your hands and face.

Hugh Rhodes, *The Boke of Nurture* [1577], in *The Babees Book*, ed. F. J. Furnivall (London: Trübner, 1868), 72–73.

might even warm their employers' clothes. After rising, people would wash their face and hands. As there was no hot water available until someone heated it on the fire, most people had to wash with cold water (again, those who had servants could be spared this hardship). After washing, one was ready to get dressed—since people often slept in their shirts, this might just mean pulling on the overgarments. It was customary to say prayers before beginning the day, and children were expected to ask their parents' blessing: they knelt before their parents, who placed a hand on their heads and invoked God's favor.

Some people ate breakfast right away, while others did a bit of work first—a typical time for breakfast was around 6:30 A.M. The law allowed a half-hour break for breakfast for laboring people, and perhaps half an hour for a *drinking* later in the morning. Work was interrupted at midday for dinner, which took place around 11 A.M. or noon. By law, laborers were to be allowed an hour's break for this meal, probably their main meal of the day.

After dinner, people returned to work. In the heat of the summer afternoon, between mid-May and mid-August, country folk might nap for an hour or two; the law provided for a half-hour break for sleep for laborers at the same time of year. It also allowed a possible half-hour drinking in the afternoon. Work would continue until supper; according to law, laborers were to work until sundown in winter (around 5 P.M. on the shortest

A SERVANT'S DUTIES AT BEDTIME

When your master intendeth to bedward, see that you have fire and candle sufficient. You must have clean water at night and in the morning. If your master lie in fresh sheets, dry off the moistness by the fire. If he lie in a strange place, see his sheets be clean, then fold down his bed, and warm his night kerchief, and see his house of office be clean, help off his clothes, and draw the curtains, make sure the fire and candle, avoid [put out] the dogs, and shut all the doors. . . . In the morning if it be cold, make a fire, and have ready clean water, bring him his petticoat [vest] warm, with his doublet, and all his apparel clean brushed, and his shoes made clean, and help to array him, truss his points, strike up his hosen, and see all thing cleanly about him. Give him good attendance, and especially among strangers, for attendance doth please masters very well.

Hugh Rhodes, *The Boke of Nurture* [1577], in *The Babees Book*, ed. F. J. Furnivall (London: Trübner, 1868), 69–70.

day), 7 or 8 o'clock in the summer. For commoners, supper was generally a light meal relative to dinner.

Bedtime was typically around 9 P.M. in the winter, 10 P.M. in the summer. As in the morning, people would say prayers and children would ask their parents' blessing before bed. Candles were extinguished at bedtime, although wealthy people sometimes left a single candle lit as a *watch light* (the hearth was a good place for this). Household fires were banked: ashes from the hearth were raked over the burning coals, covering them just enough to keep them from burning themselves out, without allowing them to die entirely. As a result, nighttime tended to be very cold and dark—people usually kept a chamber pot next to the bed to minimize the discomfort of attending to nighttime needs! The wealthy often had special nightshirts, but commoners probably just slept in their underwear—shirts and breeches for men, smocks for women. A woman might wear a coif to keep her head warm, and a man might wear a nightcap.

Bedtime more or less corresponded to the hour of curfew, after which people were not supposed to be out on the streets. Both town and country streets tended to be very dark at night unless there was strong moonlight. Some towns had laws requiring householders to put lanterns outside their doors, although this would have had little effect on the dark of a moonless night. It was assumed that nobody who was outside at night had any honest business. Lone *bellmen* wandered the streets of the towns carrying a lantern, a bell to raise alarms, and a staff weapon for self-defense, keeping an eye open for possible fires or suspicious activity. They were supported by patrols of *watches*, civilian guards who could be summoned

A night watchman, called a *bellman* from the bell he carries. [*Shakespeare's England*]

to deal with problems and arrest anyone found on the streets without a good cause.

The exact structure of the day depended on one's position in society. The orderly schedule described above presupposes a working person. People in the upper classes had more diverse schedules. Some were highly disciplined, and would follow a course of daily activity as demanding as that of a laborer. Others might rise later, spend several hours at dinner, begin their evening meal at 5 P.M. or 6 P.M., and perhaps carouse late into the night.

THE WEEK

Elizabethans generally worked from Monday to Saturday, although many had Saturday afternoon off. Markets took place on regular days of the week—Wednesday and Saturday mornings were the commonest times. Wednesday, Friday, and Saturday were fasting days when no meat was to be eaten, except for fish. This requirement had been established for religious reasons by the medieval church, and was revived by Queen

DAILY ACTIVITIES FROM A PURITAN GENTLEWOMAN'S DIARY

Tuesday 28 [August 1599]

In the morning, after private prayer, I read of the Bible, and then wrought [embroidered] till 8 o'clock, and then I ate my breakfast; after which done, I walked into the fields till 10 o'clock, then I prayed, and not long after I went to dinner; and about one o'clock I gathered my apples till 4; then I came home, and wrought till almost 6, and then I went to private prayer and examination, in which it pleased the Lord to bless me; and beseeched the Lord, for Christ his sake, to increase the power of this spirit in me daily, Amen, Amen; till supper time I heard Mr. Rhodes read of [a book by the Puritan scholar Thomas] Cartwright, and soon after supper, I went to prayers, after which I wrote to Master Hoby, and so to bed.

The Lord's Day 18 [November 1599]

After private prayer I went to Church, and when I came home, I praised God for his mer[c]ies there offered me. After I dined, I went to church again and heard catechizing and sermon; then I talked and sang psalms with diverse that was with me, and after that I prayed privately and examined myself with what integrity I had spent the day, and then went to supper; after that, to public examination and prayers, and so to bed.

The Private Life of an Elizabethan Lady: The Diary of Lady Margaret Hoby 1599–1605, ed. Joanna Moody (Stroud: Sutton, 1998), 11–12, 38.

Elizabeth in order to foster the fishing fleet and by extension the navy; it does not appear to have been meticulously obeyed, especially on Wednesdays and Saturdays, but there were efforts at enforcement (especially supported by fishmongers). It was also possible to purchase exemptions.

Thursday afternoon was often a half-holiday for schoolchildren. Thursday and Sunday were the big nights for food—they were often occasions for roasts. Those who were paid weekly received wages on Saturday; Saturday afternoon was often a half-holiday for workers, and Saturday night was a favored time for carousing among common people since they did not have to work the next day. Saturday, coming at the end of the work week, was the typical day for weekly pay, as well as washing and laundry; if possible, people would wear clean clothes on Sunday morning for church.

Sunday was the Sabbath. Everyone was required by law to attend church services in the morning. On every second Sunday afternoon, the parish priest was required to offer religious instruction for the young people of the parish. After church, people were customarily allowed to indulge in games and pastimes; Sunday was the principal occasion for diversion and entertainment. However, Puritan-minded reformists felt that such activities violated the holiness of the Sabbath, so there was often vocal opposition to such entertainments. Church services were also supposed to be held on Wednesdays and Fridays, although attendance was not compulsory.

Men and women normally sat separately in church, although this was not a fast rule. The liturgy was laid down in the *Book of Common Prayer* issued shortly after Elizabeth's accession 1559 and remains the basis of services in the Anglican church today. During the course of the service, the parishioners would sing psalms and the priest would offer two biblical readings, one each from the Old and New Testaments, followed by the ceremony of communion and a sermon, and any baptisms that needed to be celebrated. Over the course of the year, the parishioners would go through the Psalms 12 times, the New Testament 48 times, and the Old Testament once. Other prominent features of the liturgy included recitation of the Ten Commandments, the Creed, and the Lord's Prayer.

The sermon was a major vehicle for public propaganda in both religious and political matters, and the priest was not allowed to preach a sermon of his own devising unless he had been specifically licensed to do so. Instead, the government published books of approved sermons that stressed religious conformity and political obedience, as well as the teachings of Christian doctrine.

Communion, the ceremony in which the parishioners received the sacred bread and wine, had always been a particularly important ritual in the Christian church. The Protestant Church of England taught that communion was a ceremony of commemoration, rather than the mystical transformation of bread and wine into the body and blood of Christ, as in the Catholic Church. In contrast with modern religious customs, people did not normally take communion every time they went to church, and the ceremony might even be omitted; it was only required on certain major holidays.

Most churches had been built in the Middle Ages, but the Protestant reformation brought about many important changes in the interior arrangement of the church. The Catholic crucifix above the altar was replaced by the royal coat of arms; religious paintings were covered over, statues were removed, and as stained-glass windows decayed they were replaced with plain ones. In Catholicism, the church was arranged so that the religious ceremonies, particularly that of communion, took place in a special holy space: the altar was located at the east end of the church, away from the parishioners, and was separated from them by a screen. The Protestants considered this arrangement superstitious; in an Elizabethan church the elaborate altar was exchanged for a simple communion table, which was placed in the center of the church right in front of the congregation, without any separation. Pews were arranged in the front of the seating area and could be rented by those who could afford them, while others sat on stools. Seating was sometimes a contentious issue, since a seat in front was considered a mark of high social rank. In some traditional communities, seats were assigned to particular landholdings, but in many places, this system had broken down, and there was a great deal of jockeying for the most prestigious positions.

THE ELIZABETHAN YEAR

The manner of reckoning dates in the year was similar to ours today, with a few important differences. To begin with, the number of the year did not change on New Year's Day. The English calendar had come down from the Romans, for whom January 1 was the first day of the year. Accordingly, this was called New Year's Day and was observed as an official holiday as the Feast of the Circumcision of Christ. However, the number of the year did not actually change until March 25, the Feast of the Annunciation. England differed from the Continent in this respect. The day that a 16th-century Frenchman (and a modern person) would consider January 1, 1589, would be called January 1, 1588, in 16th-century England. Educated Englishmen sometimes dealt with this problem by writing the date as 1 January 1588/9. On March 25 the year would be written as 1589, and England would be in line with the rest of Europe until January 1 came around again.

To make things even more confusing, England was using a slightly different calendar from most of Western Europe (the exceptions being the other Protestant countries and certain Italian city-states). This was the Julian Calendar, so named because it had been introduced by Julius Caesar. The Julian calendar had leap years, but this actually made the Julian year slightly longer than the actual solar year. The difference was slight, but over the centuries there had accumulated a 10-day discrepancy—so that, for example, the Spring Equinox, which should have fallen on March 21, fell on March 11. In 1582 Pope Gregory XIII established the Gregorian Calendar, which we still use today, by which three out of four years ending in -00 (e.g., 1900) are not leap years. This calendar was much more accurate, but English opposition to the papacy meant that England did not follow the pope's lead until 1752. As a result, whenever you crossed the English Channel to France, you jumped 10 days forward on the calendar, and you jumped 10 days backward on your return!

The seasons as they were known to the Elizabethans were naturally more like those in England today rather than those familiar to North Americans. Spring was reckoned to begin in February, when the ground thawed and planting began; this season was often equated with Lent, the six weeks before Easter, when Christians traditionally abstained from eating meat. Summer began in May, when the Lenten fast and the heavy work of spring was over and the warm weather of summer began. Autumn came when the harvest began in August (the season was also called Harvest, but not usually Fall). Winter arrived in November when the grass ceased growing and cattle had to be brought in from pasture.

In addition to the cycle of the seasons, the year was shaped by the festive and religious calendar of holy days, also called feasts. Every official holiday was ostensibly religious, with the exception of Accession Day (November 17), commemorating Elizabeth's accession to the throne. Nonetheless, holidays had their secular side as well: like modern-day Christmas and Easter, religious holidays had accumulated secular elements that sometimes overshadowed the religious component.

By law, everyone was obliged to attend church on holy days as well as Sundays, and to take communion three times a year, generally at Easter, Whitsun, and Christmas. This requirement was seen as a means of ensuring outward conformity and for rooting out Catholics and Separatists who might pose a threat to the country's religious unity. People did not necessarily observe this law rigidly, but most probably took communion at least at Easter.

The observance of any holy day began on the evening before, called the *eve* of the holy day—the principal surviving example is Christmas Eve. The eve of a major holy day was supposed to be observed by the same fast as on Fridays and in Lent.

The Protestant reformation in England had done away with many of the traditional saints' days and other religious holidays observed by the Catholic Church, and there continued to be pressures from Protestant reformers in the Church of England to take the process even further. Many of the traditional holiday celebrations were criticized as superstitious, rowdy, and inappropriate for occasions that were supposed to be religious observations. Over the course of Elizabeth's reign, the reformers were able to withdraw the church and civic support than many of the festivities had once enjoyed, and some of them began to fall out of use. However, in the more conservative parts of the country—the north and west, and in traditional-minded villages—customary rituals remained very much alive.

On the calendar following, the days listed in **boldface** were official holidays sanctioned by the Church of England. The remainder of the holy days listed were included in the church calendar but were not observed as holidays. In addition to the feasts listed below, many parishes observed the feast day of the patron saint of the parish church: the celebration was known as the Wake Day or Dedication Day and might be observed with the same sorts of activities as a village ale (see Whitsunday, under May). Finally, many towns had annual fairs appointed for a certain day of the year. Most fairs took place between May and November, although there were a few from December to April.

January

In this month the ground was too frozen to be worked, so the husbandman would be busy with maintenance jobs around the holding, such as trimming woods and hedges, repairing fences, and clearing ditches.

1 **The Circumcision of Christ** (*New Year's Day*). New Year's Day came in the midst of the Christmas season, which ran from Christmas Eve to Twelfth Day, and was generally a time for merrymaking and sociability. People often observed the day with by exchanging gifts: favored choices included apples, eggs, nutmegs, gloves, pins, and oranges studded with cloves. They would also drink the wassail, a spiced ale traditionally served in a wooden bowl; there were traditional wassail songs as part of the ritual.

6 **Epiphany** (*Twelfth Day*). The Twelfth Day of Christmas was the last day of the Christmas season. The evening before, called Twelfth Night, was traditionally the most riotous holiday of the year, an occasion for folk plays and merriment. One ritual was the serving of a spiced fruitcake with a dried bean and a dried pea inside. A man whose piece contained the bean would become the Lord of Misrule or King, and a woman who got the pea became the Queen; the two would preside together over the festivities. The wassail bowl was drunk as at New Year's.

—*Plow Monday* (*Rock Monday*). This fell on the first Monday after Epiphany. On this day plows were blessed, and in parts of England the plowmen drew a plow from door to door soliciting gifts of money. The day also commemorated the work of women, under the name Rock Monday (*rock* is another word for a distaff).

8 *St. Lucian*

13 *St. Hilary*

18 *St. Prisca*

19 *St. Wolfstan*

20 *St. Fabian*

21 *St. Agnes.* According to tradition, a woman who went to bed without supper on the eve of St. Agnes would dream of her future husband.

22 *St. Vincent*

25 *The Conversion of St. Paul.* Elizabethan country folk believed that the weather on St. Paul's Day would reveal the future of the year: a fair day boded a fair year, a windy day presaged wars, and a cloudy day foretold plague.

February

This was considered the first month of spring. In February the snows would melt, the ground would thaw, and the husbandman could begin preparing the fields designated for the spring or Lenten crop. He would spread manure on the fields and plow them, and then begin to sow his peas, beans, and oats.

2 **Feast of the Purification of Mary** (*Candlemas*). The name Candlemas derived from the tradition of bearing candles in a church procession on this day, although the custom was generally suppressed under the Protestant church.

3   *St. Blaise.* On this day the countrywomen traditionally went visiting each other and burned any distaffs they found in use.

5   *St. Agatha*

14 *St. Valentine.* In Elizabethan times as today, this day was a celebration of romantic love. Men and women drew one another's names by lot to determine who would be whose valentine, pinning the lots on their bosom or sleeve and perhaps exchanging gifts.

24 St. Matthias the Apostle

—*Shrove Tuesday (Shrovetide).* Shrovetide was the day before Ash Wednesday, falling between February 3 and March 9. This holiday was the last day before the fasting season of Lent. On the Continent this day was celebrated with wild abandon, reflected in the modern Mardi Gras. The English version was more subdued but still involved ritual feasting and violence. On this day it was traditional to eat fritters and pancakes. It was also a day for playing football (a game much rougher than any of its modern namesakes), and for the sport of *cockthrashing* or *cockshys.* In cockthrashing, the participants tied a cock to a stake and threw sticks at it: they paid the owner of the cock a few pence for each try, and a person who could knock down the cock and pick it up before the cock regained its feet won the cock as a prize. In towns, apprentices often chose this day to start riots. Their violence was often aimed against sexual transgressors: one of the favorite activities was destroying houses of prostitution. The two days before Shrovetide were sometimes called Shrove Sunday and Shrove Monday.

—*The First Day of Lent (Ash Wednesday).* Lent began on the Wednesday before the sixth Sunday before Easter (between February 4 and March 10). The medieval church had forbidden the eating of meat other than fish during Lent. Although the religious basis for this restriction was no longer a factor, Queen Elizabeth kept the restriction in place as a means of boosting England's fishing industry. The name Ash Wednesday was officially disapproved, as it smacked of Catholicism, but it was still commonly used. Lent was sometimes observed by setting up an effigy called a Jack-a-Lent and pelting it with sticks and stones: as this season was a season for fasting, the Jack-a-Lent symbolized all the hardships in the life of a commoner.

March

In March the husbandman would sow his barley, the last of the Lenten crops. This was also the time to begin work on the garden, a task that generally fell to the woman of the house. She might also do the spring cleaning in this month.

1   *St. David.* David was the patron saint of Wales, and Welshmen traditionally wore leeks in their hats on this day.

2   *St. Chad*

7   *St. Perpetua*

12 *St. Gregory*

18 *St. Edward*

21 *St. Benedict*

25 Feast of the Annunciation of Mary (*Lady Day in Lent*). The number of the year changed on this day.

—*Mid-Lent Sunday.* This was the Sunday three weeks before Easter (March 1 to April 4). Often called Mothering Sunday, it was traditional for people to visit their mothers on this day.

April

During this month, the woman of the house would continue work on the garden, as well as beginning work in the dairy, as the livestock had begun to produce their offspring and were therefore giving milk.

3 *St. Richard*

4 *St. Ambrose*

19 *St. Alphege*

23 *St. George.* George was the patron saint of England.

25 St. Mark the Evangelist

—**Palm Sunday.** This was one week before Easter Sunday, and it marked the beginning of the Easter Week. The ancient custom of bearing palm leaves or rushes into the church on this day had been suppressed by the Protestant church, although there may well have been conservative parishes where it was still observed.

—**Wednesday before Easter**

—**Thursday before Easter** (*Maundy Thursday*). This was traditionally a day for acts of charity.

—**Good Friday**

—**Easter Eve**

—**Easter.** Easter is a movable feast. It is based on the lunar Jewish calendar, which is why it does not always fall on the same day in the solar calendar we inherited from the Romans. Easter is the first Sunday after the first full moon on or after March 21; if the full moon is on a Sunday, Easter is the next Sunday. This places Easter between March 22 and April 25. Easter marked the end of Lent, and was an occasion for great feasting, as it was once again permissible to eat meat. Children might be given hard-boiled Easter eggs, possibly dyed like their modern counterparts, known as *paste eggs*.

—**Monday in Easter Week**

—**Tuesday in Easter Week**

—*Hocktide* (*Hock Monday* and *Hock Tuesday*). The second Monday and Tuesday after Easter. On Hock Monday the young women of the parish would go about the streets with ropes and capture passing men, who had to pay a small ransom to be released; the men would do the same on Hock Tuesday. The money raised would go to the parish funds.

May

May was the first month of summer. Now the hard work of spring eased somewhat: this was a prime season for festivals, before heavy work began again with haymaking at the end of June. In this month it was time to weed the winter crops and to plow the fallow fields in preparation for the next season. The woman of the house would sow flax and hemp.

1   **Sts. Philip and Jacob the Apostles** (*May Day*). This day was often celebrated as the first day of summer. Both villagers and townsfolk might travel to the forests and fields to bring back flowers and branches as decorations—and this was notoriously an opportunity for young men and women to engage in illicit sexual activity in the woods. There might even be a full-scale summer festival, such as was often celebrated on Whitsunday (see below).

3   *Feast of the Invention of the Cross (Crouchmass)*

6   *St. John the Evangelist*

10   *St. Gordian*

19   *St. Dunstan*

26   *St. Augustine of Canterbury*

—*Rogation Sunday.* This fell five weeks after Easter (April 26 to May 30). This holiday was the time for *beating the bounds*: the parishioners would gather with the local minister to walk around the boundary of the parish, reciting prayers and psalms, and asking God for forgiveness of sins and a blessing on the crops, which had by now all been sown. Religious processions had been banned in England's Protestant church, but this one was exempted since it helped preserve the knowledge of the traditional borders of the parish.

—**Ascension Day.** This was the Thursday after Rogation Sunday (April 30 to June 3). This was another popular occasion for summer festivals (see Whitsunday below).

—**Whitsunday** (*Pentecost*). Ten days after Ascension (May 10 to June 13). This was the favorite day for summer festivals, sometimes called *ales,* or *mayings* (even when they did not fall in May). Each locality had its own customs, but certain themes were common. There were often folk plays and dramatic rituals, especially ones involving Robin Hood or St. George. Another typical activity was morris dancing, a ritual dance in which the dancers—often just men—wore bells, ribbons, and outlandish attire. The dance sometimes involved other ritual figures: a hobby horse (a man dressed up with a mock horse to make him look like a rider), a Maid Marian (typically a man dressed as a woman), and a fool (a jester figure). The occasion might also be marked by displays of banners and by military demonstrations. The celebrants often elected a man and woman to preside over the festival under such names as Summer King and Queen, May King and Queen, or Whitsun Lord and Lady. Many towns and villages erected a maypole, brightly painted and adorned with garlands or flags, around which there might be a maypole dance.

Often a temporary hall or tent was erected where the parish would sell ale, the proceeds going to the parish church. Such traditional celebrations were strongly opposed by religious reformers, who saw them as occasions for drunkenness, superstition, and illicit sexual activity.

—Whitmonday

—Whitsun Tuesday. The two days after Whitsunday, as official holidays, often continued the Whitsun festival, and all three days together might be called Whitsuntide.

—Trinity Sunday. One week after Whitsunday (May 17 to June 20). This was another popular day for summer festivals, like those described for Whitsun.

June

June was the time to weed the Lenten crops and to wash and shear the sheep—sheepshearing time was often an occasion for rural festivities. At about Midsummer began the mowing season: the men would go out to the meadows, where the grass had been allowed to grow long, and cut it down with scythes in preparation for haymaking.

3   *St. Nichomede*

5   *St. Boniface*

11   *St. Barnabas the Apostle*

17   *St. Botolph*

20   *The Translation of St. Edward*

A PURITAN VIEW OF MAY CELEBRATIONS

Against *May, Whitsonday,* or other time, all the young men and maids, older men and wives, run gadding overnight to the woods, groves, hills, & mountains, where they spend all the night in pleasant pastimes; & in the morning they return, bringing with them birch & branches of trees, to deck their assemblies withal. . . . But the chiefest jewel they bring from thence is their May-pole. . . . they strew the ground round about, bind green boughs about it, set up summer halls, bowers, and arbors hard by it; And then fall they to dance about it, like as the heathen people did at the dedication of the Idols, whereof this is a perfect pattern, or rather the thing itself. I have heard it credibly reported . . . by men of great gravity and reputation, that of forty, threescore, or a hundred maids going to the wood overnight, there have scarcely the third part of them returned again undefiled.

Phillip Stubbes, *The Anatomie of Abuses* (London: Richard Jones, 1583), 94–95.

24 **St. John the Baptist** (*Midsummer*). This festival was an important civic occasion, marked by a variety of festivities and displays of communal identity. There was often a huge bonfire on St. John's Eve, and it was common to stay up late that night. Midsummer was an occasion for parades featuring giants, dragons, fireworks, drumming, military displays, and a march by the local watch and community officials.

29 **St. Peter the Apostle.** This holiday was sometimes observed with traditions similar to those on the feast of St. John.

30 *Commemoration of St. Paul*

July

During this month the mown grass was made into hay: it had to be laid out in the sun to dry, stacked, and then carted away for storage. It was crucial that the hay dry properly, as it would otherwise rot, and farmers earnestly hoped for sunny weather in July. Hay was vital to the rural economy, since it was fed to horses and cattle, especially during the winter when they could not graze. July was also a time for a second plowing of the fallow fields and for gathering hemp, flax, and beans from the garden.

1 *Visitation of Mary*
3 *Translation of St. Martin*
15 *St. Swithun*
20 *St. Margaret*
22 *St. Magdalene*
25 **St. James the Apostle**
26 *St. Anne*

August

August began the hardest time of a husbandman's year, with the harvest of the main crops. There was a great deal of work to be done in a short time, so the entire family was involved and temporary workers were often hired. The men went into the fields with sickles to harvest the grain. Then the harvested grain was bound into sheaves, often by the women and children. The sheaves were stacked and loaded onto carts to be taken away to shelter—as with the hay, it was essential to keep the grain dry lest it rot. The stalks of grain were cut toward the top, leaving the rest of the stalk to be harvested later with a scythe to make straw.

1 *Lammas*
6 *Transfiguration of Christ*
7 *Name of Jesus*
10 *St. Laurence*

Making hay while the sun shines. The man on the right has stripped to his shirt in the heat. [Hindley]

24 St. Bartholomew the Apostle (*Bartholomewtide*)

28 *St. Augustine of Hippo*

29 *The Beheading of St. John the Baptist*

September

At the end of harvest, the harvesters celebrated *harvest home,* or *hockey.* The last sheaf of grain would be brought into the barn with great ceremony, and seed cake was distributed. After the harvest was done, and on rainy days when harvesting was impossible, the husbandman threshed and winnowed. Threshing involved beating the grain with flails so that the husk would crack open, allowing the seed to come out. Then it was winnowed: the winnowers waved straw fans, blowing away the straw and the broken husks (called chaff). After harvest was over, the husbandman began work on the winter crop: the winter fields had to be plowed, and the husbandman would begin to sow rye. This was also the season for gathering fruit from the orchard.

1 *St. Giles*

7 *St. Enurchus the Bishop*

8 *Nativity of Mary* (*Lady Day in Harvest*)

**A GERMAN TRAVELER OBSERVES
A HARVEST HOME CELEBRATION**

As we were returning to our inn, we happened to meet some country people celebrating their harvest-home; their last load of corn they crown with flowers, having besides an image richly dressed, by which, perhaps, they would signify Ceres; this they keep moving about, while men and women, man- and maidservants, riding through the streets in the cart, shout as loud as they can till they arrive at the barn.

Paul Hentzner, *Paul Hentzner's Travels in England during the Reign of Queen Elizabeth* (London: Edward Jeffery, 1797), 55.

14 *Holy Cross Day* (*Holy Rood Day*). This was traditionally a day for *nutting,* or gathering nuts in the woods.

17 *St. Lambert*

21 St. Matthew the Apostle

26 *St. Cyprian*

29 St. Michael the Archangel (*Michaelmas*). This day marked the end of the agricultural year: all the harvests were in, and the annual accounts could be reckoned up. The day was often observed by eating a goose for dinner.

30 *St. Jerome*

October

October was the time to sow wheat, which had to be done by the end of the month. The end of the wheat sowing was often marked by a feast.

1 *St. Remigius*

6 *St. Faith*

9 *St. Dennis*

13 *Translation of St. Edward the Confessor*

17 *St. Ethelred*

18 St. Luke the Evangelist

25 *St. Crispin*

28 Sts. Simon and Jude the Apostles

31 *All Saints' Eve*

November

The dairy season ended during this month, and the cattle were brought in from pasture and put in stalls for the winter. This was the time to slaughter excess pigs in preparation for the winter—surplus meat was made into sausages or pickled. As the weather began to become too cold for agricultural work, the farmer took time to cleanse the privies, carrying the muck out to the fields as fertilizer; he might also clean the chimney before the chill of winter set in.

1   **All Saints** (*All Hallows, Hallowmas, Hallontide*)

2   *All Souls*

6   *St. Leonard*

11   *St. Martin.* This day was traditionally associated with the slaughter of pigs for the winter.

13   *St. Brice*

15   *St. Machutus*

16   *St. Edmund the Archbishop*

17   **Accession Day** (*Queen's Day, Coronation Day, St. Hugh*). This was the only truly secular holiday: it commemorated Queen Elizabeth's accession to the throne in 1558.

20   *St. Edmund King and Martyr*

22   *St. Cicely*

23   *St. Clement*

Warming up by the fire. [By permission of the Folger Shakespeare Library]

25   *St. Katharine*

30   St. Andrew the Apostle

—The season of Advent began on the nearest Sunday to the feast of St. Andrew (i.e., between November 27 and December 3). People were supposed to observe the same fast as in Lent, although few actually did.

December

This was one of the least demanding times of the husbandman's year, and one of the principal seasons for merrymaking and sociability, especially around Christmas. This was a good time for splitting wood; otherwise, relatively little outdoors work was suitable for this month, so it was a good time to sit at home maintaining and repairing tools in preparation for the next year. The winter snows arrived sometime in December.

6   *St. Nicholas*

8   *Conception of Mary*

13   *St. Lucy*

21   St. Thomas the Apostle

25   Christmas. Christmas, along with Easter and Whitsun, was one of the three most important holidays of the year. The Christmas season lasted from Christmas Eve to Twelfth Day (January 6); it was a time for dancing, singing, gymnastic feats, indoor games (especially cards), and folk plays. People often chose a Christmas Lord, Prince, or King to preside over the festivities. Elizabethan Christmas rituals in many respects resembled some of the traditions still in use today. People decorated their homes with rosemary, bay, holly, ivy, and mistletoe (Christmas trees were introduced from Germany much later); and they enjoyed the richest food they could afford. Nuts were a traditional food for Christmas, in addition to festive pies and cakes and *brawn*, a type of pickled pork. Warmth and light were an important part of the Christmas festivities, observed in the burning of a Yule log and the lighting of many candles. Christmas Eve was a highly festive occasion when people often drank the wassail (see its description under January 1).

26   St. Stephen the Martyr

27   St. John the Evangelist

28   The Holy Innocents' Day (*Childermas*)

29   *St. Thomas of Canterbury*

31   *St. Silvester the Bishop*

5

Material Culture

WORK, TECHNOLOGY, AND THE ECONOMY

Work in Elizabethan England was more personal than it is today. There was less distinction between people's work and their personal lives, or between work spaces and personal spaces. In many cases, employees were fed by their employer and often they lived in their employer's house. Specialized working facilities akin to modern offices, commercial buildings, and factories were rare. Work and business tended to be conducted in or around the home. Merchants, craftsmen, and shopkeepers all worked in their houses; in the country, women labored at home while the men were out in the fields.

Agriculture

England in the late 16th century was still predominantly rural, so for most people, work meant farmwork. The production of food was a vital necessity, and very labor-intensive since hardly any machinery was involved. This meant that a substantial proportion of the population was engaged in the growing of staple foods, especially grains. Yet contrary to what is sometimes imagined, the Elizabethan rural economy was already market-oriented. A country household produced some goods for its own use, notably foodstuffs, but it was not self-sufficient: farming families supported themselves by producing a surplus for sale, rather than subsisting on their own produce.

There were two general modes of agriculture: *champion* (or open field) and *woodland*. In general, champion agriculture was most common in the central part of the country, woodland around the periphery.

In champion areas all the fields around the village were open, divided into a few huge shared fields that might be hundreds of acres each, with each large field surrounded by a tall and thick hedge that served as a fence to control livestock. A landholding villager had multiple plots, each of a few acres or less, scattered among the large fields—the scattering of the plots ensured that no villager was stuck with all the worst land.

In addition to the fields for raising grains, the village also had meadows to produce hay and pasturage for livestock. Each villager's holding generally included meadows as well as fields and came with the right to pasture a stipulated number of oxen, horses, and sheep in the common pasture. There were also common rights over wastelands: forested areas were useful places for feeding pigs (they love acorns) and gathering firewood, and marshy lands could be used for pasturing livestock and gathering reeds. Administration of agricultural matters was handled by the manorial court.

The mode of life in woodland areas was more individualistic. There were no common lands, and each landholding was a compact unit separate from the others. Since there were no commons there was not the same need for the community to cooperate. Woodland areas were not actually wooded: each holding was bordered by its own hedges, which gave such regions a more wooded look.

Agricultural productivity was maximized by crop rotation, which in champion regions generally involved what is known today as the *three-field* system. By the early Middle Ages, it had been recognized that constant farming of land exhausts its ability to produce crops. However, certain kinds of crops helped refortify the land for producing wheat. In the three-field system, the village fields were divided into three large zones. In October–November, one of these three fields would be sown with a winter crop of rye and wheat (called a winter crop because it was planted in the winter). The second field would be sown the following spring with a spring crop of barley, oats or legumes (such as peas or beans). The remaining third would lie fallow, or unused, and would be plowed and fertilized during the spring and summer to help restore its strength. While the ground was lying inactive, villagers were allowed to pasture their animals there, feeding on the plants that naturally grew, and fertilizing the soil with their manure. All the crops were harvested in August and September, after which the fields were rotated: the fallow field would be planted with winter crops, the winter field would be planted in the spring, and the spring field would lie fallow.

The three-field system was predominant in the central part of England that produced the bulk of the country's grain. As well as maintaining fertility, it diversified the village economy and covered core dietary needs:

in terms of modern nutritional science, carbohydrates came from grains, proteins from legumes and livestock, calcium from dairy products.

However open-field farming had its drawbacks. The system required a high level of communal collaboration, and it was not well suited to innovation, since any change required the cooperation of all the village landholders. This made it difficult for the open-field village to take advantage of agricultural innovations that were appearing in the late 1500s. Dutch farmers were developing new systems of crop rotation that would further enhance productivity, and some Englishmen were beginning to experiment with these techniques. Enhancing the soil with marl or lime was another way to increase production. Landowners who wanted to implement these emerging technologies often turned to enclosure as described in chapter 2.

The staple grain of the Elizabethan diet was wheat. Its high gluten content means that wheat bread rises well, and wheat has a higher caloric content by volume than other grains. However, it does not grow well in marginal soils or poor weather. Rye and oats were better suited to the less fertile regions of England, although they produce coarser and heavier bread, and are less nourishing. Barley was grown chiefly for brewing ale. A major byproduct of grain production was straw, which was sometimes fed to the livestock (although they did not generally care for it), and had multiple other uses including making baskets, stuffing beds, thatching roofs, and strewing on the floor. Chaff, another grain by-product, could be fed to livestock or used for stuffing beds.

The most important livestock in the three-field system were cattle. Females were raised to become cows, providing offspring and milk. Males could be used in one of three ways. A few were allowed to grow up as breeding bulls. A larger number were gelded to become working oxen, useful for pulling plows and other heavy vehicles. The majority were destined to become beef: they were gelded while young and slaughtered once they were fully grown.

Other pasture animals included horses, sheep, and goats. Horses were the most common draft animals, since they could work faster and longer than oxen, though they were more expensive to feed and did less well plowing heavy soils; horses also served for riding. Sheep were raised for meat, milk, and wool; they were easier to graze than cattle in the highland zones in northern and western England. Goats were only a small part of the Elizabethan rural economy but did serve as a source of meat and milk for the very poor; they are hardy animals and could forage a living in some of the least fertile parts of the country.

Woolworking

Along with grains, sheep were the farmer's main source of cash. Woolen cloth accounted for 80 percent of the country's exports, while the production of woolen clothing for the domestic market was one of the principal engines of economic activity. There were nearly 11 million sheep in the country in 1558, almost four times the human population, and although sheep raising provided less employment per acre of land than agriculture, it did support a great deal of employment through the processes of converting the raw material into finished product.

Sheep were shorn once a year, during the summer. The fleeces were typically sold to entrepreneurial clothiers, who sent their agents, or *factors*, through the countryside to purchase the raw material and arrange for the various stages of processing. Much of the work was done as a cottage industry, with the factors bringing the material to rural households, who processed it and returned it to the factor ready for the next stage.

The first step was to wash the fleece, after which it had to be carded to make it ready for spinning. This involved stroking the wool between a pair of special brushes so that all the strands were running parallel, free of knots and tangles; this was a simple job that was often assigned to children.

The carded wool was then ready to be spun into thread. Spinning involved drawing out fibers from the carded mass and spinning them so that they would be tightly twisted. Wool fibers are covered with microscopic scales; when twisted, the scaly strands cling to each other, making it possible for them to form thread. Woolen thread could be spun with a drop spindle, essentially a weighted disk with a stick passing through the center. The spindle was suspended from the wool fibers and set spinning: the weight drew out the fibers, and the rotation twisted them into thread. Alternatively, wool might be spun with a hand-cranked spinning wheel— the treadle wheel was used only for spinning flax into linen thread. Spinning was proverbially the work of women, which is how unmarried women came to be known as *spinsters*.

After spinning, the thread was woven into cloth on a horizontal loom fitted with foot pedals that controlled the pattern of the weave. Weaving market-quality cloth required training and an expensive loom, and it was generally the preserve of professional male weavers, although like the female spinsters, they practiced their craft at home, receiving thread from the factor and returning the woven cloth.

Depending on the desired finish, the cloth might then be *fulled*, or washed, to shrink and felt it. This required beating the wet fabric and was often done in water-powered fulling mills. Fulling made the fibers join more tightly with each other, so that the fabric became stronger and denser, and therefore better at keeping out the English cold and rain.

Sometimes the wool would be left in its natural color, but usually it would be dyed. This might happen as the very last stage, but sometimes it was done before the wool was even spun—hence the expression "dyed in the wool." Once finished, the cloth was ready to go to the tailor who made it into clothing.

Ironworking

Ironworking employed far fewer people than agriculture or even wool, but since it provided a material that was essential to the tools of almost every other trade, it was a crucial determining factor in the economy and technology of Elizabethan England. It was also among the most complex and industrialized processes used by the Elizabethans, giving a good idea of the extent and limitations of Elizabethan technology.

Iron naturally occurs in ores where the metallic iron is chemically combined with oxygen and physically mixed with other impurities, especially silicon-based compounds, to make up the stony ore. Iron ores are abundant in England, but once mined from the ground, the metal still needs to be isolated from the oxygen and silicates, a complex chemical and physical process known as smelting.

Traditional smelting in Elizabethan England was done in small batches on a *bloomery* hearth. Fragments of iron-rich ore were piled inside a small clay oven along with charcoal (partially combusted wood, which is almost pure carbon), and a *flux* such as lime. The charcoal was ignited, and with the aid of a bellows was brought up to temperature. At about 800°C the oxygen in the ore would separate from the iron, combining with the car-

A smith at work. [Gilbert]

bon in the furnace to escape as carbon dioxide gas. At about 1,200°C the silicates would combine with the flux and melt, flowing out of the ore as glassy *slag* to leave relatively pure iron. Some of the slag would remain trapped amidst the iron, so the furnace was broken open and the red-hot mass (called a *bloom*) was beaten, or *wrought*, with heavy hammers to drive out as much of the slag as possible. Sometimes this was done with water-powered triphammers. The product was wrought iron, pure enough to be ductile, although always with some lingering slag in the metal.

In Elizabethan England, this traditional means of iron production was being displaced by the blast furnace. The blast furnace was a large continuous-production installation served around the clock by teams of workers. Water-powered bellows and a tall furnace stack allowed the blast furnace to reach higher temperatures than a bloomery hearth, while the addition of extra charcoal infused carbon into the iron to lower its melting point.

At the bottom of the furnace was a sand-covered work area. Molten high-carbon iron was released from the furnace into rows of troughs dug into the sand where the iron could cool and harden. The resulting cast-iron ingots were known as *pigs* or *pig-iron* from the resemblance of the troughs to a row of piglets suckling from their mother. This cast iron could be used to make such items as cookware, but it was too hard to be worked with a hammer; a secondary heating process known as *fining* could be used to reduce the carbon content to a point where the iron was malleable. Depending on the final carbon content, the resulting material might today be classed as steel (about 0.1% to 2% carbon) or wrought iron (under 0.1% carbon). Steel could be heat-treated for extra hardness, making it the ideal material for blades and other kinds of cutting tools; iron is softer but less likely to break.

Crafts and Trades

Blast furnaces and fulling mills presaged the industrialization that would begin in earnest within a century and a half of Elizabeth's death, but the bulk of the manufacturing in the 1500s was done by hand by individual craftsmen working from their homes. The independent craftsman combined the functions of employer, workman, merchant, and shopkeeper: he did his own work, and he marketed and sold his products from his own workshop. The craftsman's shop was usually the front ground-floor room of his home; he would live upstairs with his family, servants, and apprentices, and might hire additional workers, called journeymen, who would assist him during the day but live elsewhere.

Not all wares were sold by the craftsman who produced them. Certain kinds of products were usually sold through a retailer who purchased from multiple suppliers to provide customers with a range of goods. Grocers sold nonperishable consumables like dried fruits, sugar, spices, and soap; drapers offered a selection of cloth; mercers carried a variety of household wares like lace, pins, thread, ribbons, and buttons; stationers retailed writing supplies.

Crafts were highly specialized based on the materials and technology used by the craftsmen, as well as the products they manufactured. Woodworkers included carpenters, who worked with larger timbers and boards; turners, who shaped wooden utensils and furniture on lathes; and joiners, who built furniture with precisely fitted joints. Metalworkers included blacksmiths, who worked iron; braziers, who worked with copper alloys like brass; goldsmiths, who worked in precious metals; pewterers, who worked with pewter and related alloys; and plumbers, who worked with lead. Leather was worked at multiple stages by different specialists. The butcher slaughtered the animals and sold the skin to the tanner who treated it so that it would not decay—different types of tanners specialized in the skins of various types of animals. The processed leather then went to the currier who finished the surface. Finally it went on to the shoemakers, glovers, saddlers, and other craftsmen who made finished leather products.

Some of the materials used by Elizabethan craftsmen are no longer familiar today. The vast numbers of cattle slaughtered for the table yielded by-products that included bone and horn. Bone served as a cheap alternative to ivory. Horn is translucent, smooth, and watertight, and it can be molded when heated. It played a role similar to plastics today, being used for lantern panes, combs, inkhorns, drinking vessels, and spoons.

A large number of trades were involved in producing and retailing food—a particularly important function in the towns, where many people had limited cooking facilities at home. Among the most common were butchers, bakers, cooks, brewers, vintners (wine merchants), and itinerant vendors who sold fresh foodstuffs from hand-held baskets.

Elizabethan England's complex material culture required a well developed commercial network to distribute goods from the point of production to the various points of manufacture, and ultimately to the point of sale. At the top of the mercantile hierarchy were the merchants proper, who specialized in bulk trade over long distances, bringing English products to foreign markets, and importing materials and finished goods for which there was a demand at home. Fleets of water-going craft traversed the seas and plied England's coasts and waterways, manned by seamen and watermen who spent most of their days in a world apart from that of most Englishmen. On land, a network of commercial carriers was emerging that transported goods by wagon, in particular bringing the products needed to support London's massive and growing population. Some products carried themselves: drovers were employed to drive herds of meat animals from the countryside to the towns—much of London's diet walked to the city from as far afield as Wales.

The point of purchase varied depending on the locality and wares. The inhabitants of the larger towns had the best access, since there were plenty

Marketing. [Besant]

of street vendors, markets, and shops to choose from. Country folk might buy wares at home from chapmen, traveling salesmen who circulated from village to village with small household wares. Alternatively, the villager could visit the nearest market town—there was usually at least one within 12 miles of any village . Here the country family could find craftsmen and retailers, although fewer than in a large city. Market-town retailers were therefore less specialized than their big-city counterparts: a draper might carry not only cloth but mercery wares, groceries, and stationery. Since the town also had a weekly market, this could also be an opportunity for the household to sell some of its own produce.

Many goods were purchased used rather than new. Crafted items like furniture and clothing were fairly expensive, since so much labor went into producing them, but they were often more durable than their modern mass-produced equivalents. Second-hand dealers bought and sold used goods, sometimes refurbishing them to improve their resale value. The same dealers often doubled as pawnbrokers—Philip Henslowe, owner of the Rose Theater in London, traded as a broker in this way. The cost of materials also encouraged recycling, which was also a significant element in the economy: building materials, cloth, leather, and metal were all subject to reuse, and the paper industry relied wholly on recycled linen rags.

Money

It is difficult to compare Elizabethan to modern money, since the economic parameters were very different. Labor was relatively cheap, while manufactured goods were expensive—there was almost no mechanization, so the vastly increased hours of labor more than negated the lower rate of pay. Moreover, prices could fluctuate enormously according to time and place. Prices today tend to be fairly constant because we have a well-developed system of transportation and storage. Elizabethans did not have the same opportunities to shop around, nor could they stock up on perishable goods when they were cheap and plentiful. In particular, the price of grain could vary hugely from harvest to harvest, impacting the rest of the economy much as energy costs do today. Prices were very sensitive to the supply and demand at a particular time and place, and predictably they were higher in London than in the country.

Overall, the late 1500s were a period of unprecedented inflation, albeit modest by modern standards. Over the half-century of Elizabeth's reign, prices rose by about 100–150 percent. This was good news for some, bad for others. Substantial landholders whose production outweighed their expenditures profited: higher prices meant they could sell their surplus for more money. Small landholders, producing little or no surplus, were more at risk, since their income barely kept pace with their expenditures. Above all, wage earners suffered from inflation, as the real value of their wages was eaten up by rising costs. By the early 1600s, the real wages of agricultural laborers were only half of what they had been two centuries before. Contemporaries were largely unable to accept inflation as a natural economic phenomenon: people still adhered to the medieval notion that everything had a *just price,* and that rising prices were the result of individual greed rather than impersonal market forces.

Elizabethan money consisted of silver and gold coins; even the smallest, the halfpenny, was worth more than most coins today. There was a pressing need for smaller denominations, but the halfpenny was already so tiny (about half an inch across) that a smaller coin would have been unusable. The problem was not solved until Elizabeth's successor, James I, introduced brass coinage, although in the mean time some employers and tradesmen issued lead or copper tokens that could be accumulated and later redeemed from the issuer.

The typical Elizabethan coin bore an image of the Queen on one side and the royal coat of arms and a cross on the other. Its actual value was linked to the value of the gold or silver in it and was therefore susceptible to fluctuations in the prices of gold and silver, as well as to changes in the purity of the coins. When Elizabeth came to the throne, the value of English money had been undermined by repeated debasement of the coinage by her predecessors. Since the monarch could decide on the purity of the coin, it could be tempting for rulers to increase their short-term cash flow by reminting coinage at a lower purity, though this predictably led to

Elizabethan coins: halfpenny, penny, sixpence, shilling, and gold crown. [Ruding]

intense inflation and financial turmoil. One of Elizabeth's early measures was to restore English coinage to the *sterling* purity for which it had been known in the late Middle Ages.

The precious metal in the coinage was also a temptation to the unscrupulous. Coin clippers scraped tiny fragments off the edges of coins to accumulate the silver and gold (in later centuries coins would be milled with corrugated edges to make this kind of tampering easy to detect). Since compromised coins undermined faith in the value of the monarch's currency, clippers as well as forgers were subject to the death penalty if caught.

Some denominations were only *moneys of account,* used for reckoning but not actually minted as currency. Such was the mark, a large denomination used when dealing with substantial sums of money. The pound was also a money of account in that there were no pound coins, though there were coins that had the value of a pound. Other coins went in and out of production at various times: the farthing, worth a quarter of a penny, still existed under the earlier Tudors but was never minted during Elizabeth's reign; the groat was minted at the beginning of her reign, but was soon replaced by a threepenny piece.

There was no paper money, although it was possible to deposit money with a banker or merchant in exchange for a letter of credit. In fact, credit played a major role in the Elizabethan economy. Neighbors, friends, and associates regularly loaned money to one another or sold goods on credit to those whom they had reason to trust. Those who could not get an unsecured loan might turn to a pawnbroker if they needed to raise cash.

A tinker mends a pot. [Furnivall (1879)]

Table 5.1 offers some idea of the value of Elizabethan money. The table includes equivalents in modern US dollars, but these should be taken as rough magnitudes, not values. An Elizabethan halfpenny did not actually have the same purchasing power as a contemporary dollar, but it was more similar to a dollar than to a cent or to 10 dollars. The table also gives the Elizabethan abbreviations for various denominations—note that the normal abbreviation for a pound was *li.* (as opposed to the modern symbol £), which went after the number instead of before it.

A more meaningful idea of the value of these denominations can be obtained by comparing them with wages and incomes. Wages might be paid by the day, week, or year; the longer the term, the more likely that the wages included food and drink as well. In some cases, lodging was also part of the deal. Wages were regulated by law, although the theory was not always put into practice. The wages and incomes listed in Table 5.2 are only samples: actual wages and incomes varied according to time, place, and individual circumstances.[1]

Table 5.1.
Approximate Values of Elizabethan Money

	Denomination	Value	Purchase Value	Equivalent
Silver Coins	halfpenny (ob.)	½ of a penny	1 quart of ale	$1
	three-farthings	¾d.		$1.50
	penny (d.)	0.5 grams silver	1 loaf of bread	$2
	three-halfpence	1½d.	1 lb. of cheese	$3
	twopence (half-groat)	2d.		$4
	threepence	3d.	1 lb. of butter	$6
	fourpence (groat)	4d.	1 day's food	$8
	sixpence (tester)	6d.		$15
	shilling (s.)	12d.	1 day's earnings for a craftsman	$25
Gold Coins	half-crown	2s. 6d.	1 day's earnings for a gentleman	$60
	quarter angel	2s. 6d.		$60
	angelet	5s.		$100
	crown	5s.	1 week's earnings for a craftsman	$100
	angel	10s.	1 lb. of spice	$250
	sovereign (new standard)	20s. (1 li.)		$500
	sovereign (old standard)	30s.		$750
	German florin	3s. 4d.		$50
	Dutch florin	2s.		$50
	French crown	6s. 4d.		$150
	Spanish ducat	6s. 8d.		$150
Moneys of Account	farthing (q.)	¼ of a penny		$.50
	mark (marc.)	13s. 4d. (⅔ of 1 li.)		$350
	pound (li.)	20s.	1 cart horse	$500

Table 5.2.
Sample Wages and Incomes

Shepherd's Boy	2½d./day with food
Shepherd	6d./week with food
Unskilled Rural Laborer	2–3d./day with food
Plowman	1s./week with food
Skilled Rural Laborer	6d./day
Laborer	9d./day
	26s. 6d./year with food and drink
Craftsman	12d./day, 7d. with food and drink
	£4–10/year with food and drink
Yeoman	£2–6/year or more
Minor Parson	£10–30/year
Esquire	£500–1,000/year
Knight	£1,000–2,000/year
Nobleman	£2,500/year
30-acre landholder	£14, or a surplus of £3–5 after paying for foodstuffs
Soldier	5d./day
Sergeant, Drummer	8½d./day
Ensign	1s./day
Lieutenant	2s./day
Captain	4s./day

The real value of incomes can best be judged by comparing them to the prices of goods (see Table 5.3). Purchasing was much less straightforward than it is today. Measurements were not always uniform throughout the country, and different goods might be measured by different standards: woolen cloth was purchased by the yard, but linen by the ell (45″). Prices were also subject to negotiation: haggling was the rule rather than the exception, except in the case of basic staples such as bread and ale, which were closely regulated.

Levels of taxation were generally low compared to other parts of Europe. Taxes were mostly applied to imported goods, in the form of customs duty paid by the importing merchant, although towns might also impose taxes on transactions by traders who did not belong to the town. Tithes were paid to the parish church annually, but there was no equivalent taxation by the government under normal circumstances. In time of need, Parliament

Table 5.3.
Sample Prices of Goods and Services

Meal at an inn	4–6d.	Gentleman's meal in his room at an inn	2s.
Bed in an inn	1d.	Lodging a horse	12–18d.
Food for one day	4d.	Loaf of bread	1d.
Butter (1 lb.)	3d.	Cheese (1 lb.)	1½d.
Eggs (3)	1d.	Fresh salmon	13s. 4d.
Beef (1 lb.)	3d.	Cherries (1 lb.)	3d.
Sugar (1 lb.)	20s.	Cloves (1 lb.)	11s.
Pepper (1 lb.)	4s.	Wine (1 qt.)	1s.
Ale (1 qt.)	½d.	Tobacco	3s./ounce
Officer's canvas doublet	14s. 5d.	Officer's cassock	27s. 7d.
Shoes	1s.	White silk hose	25s.
Candles (48)	3s. 3d.	Soap (1 lb.)	4d.
Knives (2)	8d.	Bed	4s.
Spectacles (2 pr.)	6d.	Scissors	6d.
Bible	£2	Broadside ballad	1d.
Small book	6d.–2s.	Theater admission	1, 2, or 3d.
Tooth pulled	2s.	Portraits	62s. to £6
Horse	£1–2		
Hiring a horse	12d./day or 2½d./mile	Hiring a coach	10s./day

might vote a subsidy, a one-time tax of varying rates, assessed proportion-ally to property or income among those who had the means to pay—only a minority of households were expected to contribute. The ongoing cost of multifront wars during the 1590s, with repeated subsidies to cover the expense, was a significant factor in England's economic downturn during that decade.[2]

THE LIVING ENVIRONMENT

Villages

The overwhelming majority of the population lived in the country, typically in villages of about 200 to 500 people. The village in areas of open-field settlement consisted of a cluster of homes around one or more unpaved streets. The center of the village was also the site of the parish church, which was likely to be the oldest building in the village, and perhaps a village green. The central area might also have a manor hall and other manorial buildings grouped within a walled enclosure. These buildings might also be old, especially if there was no longer a resident manor lord; if the complex was currently inhabited, the hall was likely to have been rebuilt or at least renovated in recent years to accommodate current fashions in architecture.

There was necessarily a good source of water near the village center, whether a river or a well, and often both. Around the clustered homes were the village fields, pastures, and meadows, and beyond that were waste areas such as woods or marshes. Somewhere in the lands of the manor there would be a blacksmith, and at least one water-powered mill, or perhaps a windmill in the windblown parts of the country adjoining the North Sea.

The village was primarily a phenomenon of champion farmland. In areas of woodland agriculture, houses were likely to stand alone in the midst of their holdings, or in small clusters that were sometimes called hamlets.

Towns

Town location was heavily influenced by transportation. The most important towns were located on navigable rivers, usually at the site of one or more bridges, and all towns were hubs in the network of major roads. The larger towns were usually walled, and might also have a castle; walls and castles were among the oldest features in a town, often dating to the Middle Ages or even to Roman times. There were few other public structures in most towns. There might be a stone cross in the square where the market took place, or even a covered market building. If there was a municipal government, there would be some sort of town hall—sometimes no more than a large room above the market. Otherwise, the only public buildings were churches and their associated buildings, which often served secular as well as religious functions: meeting hall, courtroom, school, business place, muster hall, and armory. Specific crafts and trades tended to cluster in certain areas of the town, which facilitated guild administration.

Town streets had names, although houses were not numbered. Even London was rather small by modern standards, so it was possible to identify individual buildings by the name of their principal occupants or functions. Many buildings were named for an iconic sign that decorated the outside: the Swan, the Red Lion, the Green Dragon. Some city streets were surfaced with cobblestones, but many were unpaved and became difficult to use in wet weather when feet, hooves, and wheels churned them into a

The south end of London Bridge. [*Shakespeare's England*]

river of mud. A few streets were extremely broad, wide enough to be used as marketplaces or football fields.

Fire was a major hazard in urban environments. In spite of attempts to reduce the danger by passing laws against thatched or wooden roofs, fire remained an ever-present threat in an environment where buildings were crowded, most construction was of wood, and light and heat were provided by fire. There was no official fire department, but churches and

STREET LIFE IN LONDON

In every street, carts and coaches make such a thundering as if the world ran upon wheels; at every corner men, women and children meet in such shoals, that posts are set up of purpose to strengthen the houses, lest with jostling one another they should shoulder them down. Besides, hammers are beating in once place; tubs hooping in another; pots clinking in a third; water tankards running at tilt in a fourth. Here are porters sweating under burdens, their merchant's men bearing bags of money. Chapmen (as if they were at leapfrog) skip out of one shop into another. Tradesmen (as if they were dancing galliards) are lusty at legs and never stand still. All are as busy as country attorneys at an assizes.

Thomas Dekker, *Seven Deadly Sinnes of London* [1606], ed. H. F. B. Brett-Smith (Oxford: Blackwell, 1922), 37–38.

other public places often stocked fire-fighting equipment for residents to use in case of emergency. These included leather buckets for fetching water, and ladders and hooks with which to pull down burning buildings before the fire spread—the origin of the modern hook-and-ladder squad.

THE HOME

"A man's house is his castle," wrote the jurist Sir Edward Coke in the early 17th century. The sentiment still resonates today, yet the meaning of one's house for people in Coke's day was not the same as it is for us. Today the house is a place of refuge, the place for private life. Although these trends had roots in the Elizabethan period, the distinction between a person's private and public life was much less clear-cut than it is today. For the Elizabethan, the home was not just a private space: it was the focus of all aspects of life. People were born in their homes, they died in their homes, and often they worked in their homes too.

The nature of the home and its contents was changing during Elizabeth's reign. Overall, to a modern person, the material culture of the period would recall circumstances in the modern developing world. There was a

---

**A PARISH MINISTER REMARKS ON
RISING STANDARDS OF LIVING, 1577**

There are old men yet dwelling in the village where I remain which have noted three things to be marvellously altered in England within their sound remembrance. . . . One is the multitude of chimneys lately erected . . . The second is the great (although not general) amendment of lodging; for, said they, our fathers, yea and we ourselves also, have lain full oft upon straw pallets, on rough mats covered only with a sheet, under coverlets made of dagswain or hopharlots (I use their own terms), and a good round log under their heads instead of a bolster or pillow. If it were so that our fathers or the good man of the house had within seven years after his marriage purchased a mattress or flock bed, and thereto a stack of chaff to rest his head upon, he thought himself to be as well lodged as the lord of the town, that peradventure lay seldom in a bed of down or whole feathers, so well were they content, and with such base kind of furniture. . . . Pillows (said they) were thought meet only for women in childbed. As for servants, if they had any sheet above them, it was well, for seldom had they any under their bodies to keep them from the pricking straws that ran oft through the canvas of the pallet and rased their hardened hides. The third thing they tell of is the exchange of vessel, as of treen [wooden] platters into pewter, and wooden spoons into silver or tin.

William Harrison, *The Description of England,* ed. Georges Edelen (Ithaca, NY: Folger Shakespeare Library, 1968), 200–201.

vast difference between the lifestyles of the upper class and those of ordinary people; most houses were small and simply furnished, and personal property for most people was limited. But standards of living were on the rise: contemporaries remarked on the more comfortable furniture, finer tableware, and better constructed homes that were enjoyed by the middling sort, compared to circumstances a generation earlier.

Then as now, the nature of one's dwelling varied between the city and the country, as well as between social classes. There were also distinctive building traditions in each area of the country, as well as differences of design between any one house and another. The following pages will describe the technology of house construction, followed by the layout of three major types: the rural home, the gentleman's manor house, and the town house.

The Home

Most Elizabethan houses were based on jointed frames of oak: instead of nails, which would be too weak, the timbers were carved with tongues (tenons) and slots (mortices) so that the whole frame fit together, with the tenons secured in their mortices by thick wooden pegs. Ideally the frame would rest on a stone foundation, since prolonged contact with moisture in the ground would eventually cause the timbers to rot. However, the cheapest sorts of structures simply had their main posts sunk into the ground.

The basic frame carried the weight of the house, and it had to be filled in to make the walls. The typical means of filling was a technique known as *wattle and daub*. Wattling consisted of upright wooden stakes fixed at the top and bottom into the horizontal timbers of the house, with pliant sticks woven between them. The wattling served as a core for the wall, which was covered with daub—a mixture of clay, sand, and animal manure, with chopped straw or horsehair added for strength. Well-appointed homes might be plastered on the inside and outside, and the ceiling might also be plastered. These plasters were often more robust than the modern equivalent, mixed from lime, sand, and animal hair. In a very wealthy household, the interior walls and ceilings might be wainscoted with wooden paneling, often brightly painted or covered with tooled leather. Some interiors were surfaced with patterned woodblock wallpaper. The exterior of the building was usually coated with a limewash to prevent rain from damaging the water-soluble layers underneath. Limewash might also be used to coat interior surfaces, helping to preserve the surfaces, brighten the rooms, and deter insects.

Most English houses in this period were constructed in some version of this technique. In some places, lath and plaster took the place of wattle and daub: strips of wood were nailed to the upright stakes, serving as a base for a plaster covering. Those who had the money might use bricks to fill in the frame; this provided greater security against fire but it was much more costly. In areas where stone was plentiful, particularly the west and north, houses were often built of stone, but in other parts of the country stone was too expensive except for the very rich.

The commonest form of roofing was thatch, a very thick covering made with reeds or straw. A thatch roof was durable and an excellent insulator, although it could also be a haven for vermin, and it posed a serious fire risk as well. Alternatives were clay tiles, slate, or shingles. Tiles were expensive, as was slate (except in areas where it was naturally plentiful), while shingles were only readily available in regions with plenty of trees. Some wooden roofs were covered with lead to reduce the risk of fire, though again this increased the cost. The larger towns generally tried to forbid thatched roofs in favor of tile or wood covered with lead: a fire in the country might destroy only one house, but in the crowded conditions of the town it could lead to a major public disaster.

Doors were made of wood and might be secured with bolts, although it was not uncommon even for ordinary people to have locks. A well-to-do family would have glass windows, made of many small panes held together with lead. In poorer homes, there might be nothing more than the wooden shutters to close up the house at night, although cheap window filling could be made with thin layers of horn or oiled linen to let in light while keeping out the wind.

Important rooms would have a hearth for warmth or cooking. A poor home might have a simple smoke hood above; most houses had some form of chimney. This could be made of wattle and daub, but brick was preferred as it reduced the fire hazard. The hearth was lined with stones or bricks for the same reason.

Rural Homes

Only the very poorest country folk lived in a one-room cottage. Much more common was a two-room floor plan, which might measure around 30 by 15 feet. The front door led into an all-purpose hall, used for cooking, eating, and working. An inner door in the hall gave access to a parlor or chamber, which served as the sleeping-room for the householder and his wife; young children slept here too. Above these rooms would be a loft, providing storage and some additional sleeping space. A more prosperous home might have a full second story, with bedchambers above, in which case the parlor could be used for dining and entertaining visitors. There could also be additional side rooms for storage, food preparation, and similar tasks. Cellars were rare in country houses. In the simplest cottages, the floor might be no more than packed dirt, although those who could afford them had wooden floors. Access to upper levels was provided by ladders in simpler cottages or by permanent stairs in better cottages.

Rising standards of living for the yeoman class meant that many houses were being improved, usually by renovation, sometimes by rebuilding, making them larger and better appointed than they had been before. A contemporary writing of Cheshire farmhouses in the 1580s observed that "in building and furniture of their houses (till of late years) they used the old manner of the Saxons. For they had their fire in the midst of the house against a hob of clay, and their oxen also under the same roof. But within these 40 years it is altogether altered, so that they have builded chimneys, and furnished other parts of their houses accordingly."[3]

The Croft

The country home was located on a small plot of land called a *croft*. In addition to the house, the croft included outbuildings such as animal sheds and pens, storage buildings for tools and provisions, and—in the case of a more prosperous householder—perhaps a separate kitchen, brewhouse, dairy, or bakehouse. There might also be barns for threshing harvested grain and granaries for storing it. The croft also supported a small garden. Here the woman of the house might raise flax and hemp for linen and canvas, hops for brewing, and whatever other plants she needed for household use: trees for fruits and nuts, vegetables, herbs for cooking and for household medicines, and perhaps some flowers. Some crofts had cobblestone courtyards, and walkways might be covered with sawdust to prevent them from becoming too muddy.

Domestic fowl such as chickens, ducks, and geese were kept on the croft, providing the family with meat, eggs, and feathers. Dairy cows and pigs might also be kept here. The farming household typically also had at least one dog (providing some protection against human and animal intruders) and a cat (to keep down the mice and rats that were inevitably attracted to the farmer's grain). The smallest invited creatures in the country farm were the inhabitants of its straw beehives.

The Manor House

During this period the gap between the houses of the rich and the poor was increasing, as new and more elaborate styles of architecture evolved through which the wealthy could proclaim their social status. The medieval manor house, designed for defensibility, had given way in the 16th century to a more expansive and luxurious style that combined traditional medieval elements with new influences from Renaissance Italy. The stately Elizabethan home was typically based on an E or H shape, derived ultimately from the layout of medieval manor houses. The central section (the vertical part of the E or the horizontal part of the H) was a large hall, the principal public space of the house. It was flanked on one side by the family wing, which included the various private chambers of the family, and on the other by the service wing, which housed the kitchens, stores, and other working areas.

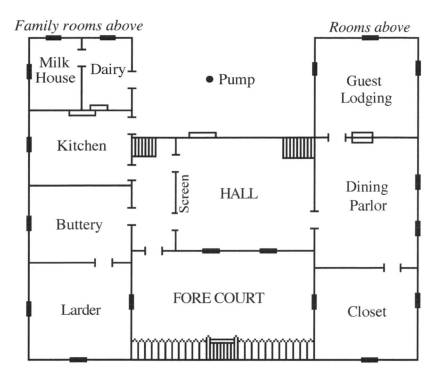

Design for an H-shaped country house for a prosperous commoner or a minor gentleman, after an early 17th-century design by Gervase Markham. The *closet* is a private room for the family, the larder is for storing food, and the buttery for drinks. Private meals would take place in the dining parlor, public ones in the hall. The screen is a wooden partition dividing the hall from the passageway to the main door, the service rooms, and the family's rooms above—it served to cut down on drafts. [Forgeng]

These houses were distinguished from their medieval predecessors by their open design. Aristocratic feuding and civil wars during the Middle Ages called for a compact structure surrounded by a stout wall, with the exterior walls of the house built to resist assault. By Elizabeth's time only a light wall enclosed the grounds, and the building itself abounded in windows. However, many people continued to live in houses of medieval origin—the aristocratic manor hall of the Middle Ages had been solidly built, so that plenty of them still stood in Elizabeth's day, although owners often attempted at least superficial alterations to adjust them to contemporary tastes.

The main residential building was surrounded by the facilities essential to the complex and cultured life of the aristocratic household. Kitchen gardens provided necessary herbs and vegetables for the household; these

47-8 FENCHURCH STREET   c. 1612

Reconstructed rear view of a block of London town houses on Fenchurch St., based on Ralph Treswell's survey of 1612. At left are three narrow tenements belonging to William Jennings, Anne Robinson, and John Yeoman. Around the courtyard at right are two small street-front tenements held by James Dyer and James Sutton, and a long tenement beside the courtyard belonging to Jacques de Bees. Access to the courtyard was through a passageway to the street. [Peter Jackson, by permission of Mrs. V. Jackson-Harris] were separate from the formal decorative gardens that were an expected feature of any aristocratic home. There would also be ancillary buildings such as bakehouses, brewhouses, barns, and stables. There might also be a dovecote: just before they learn to fly, the young of pigeons are easy to gather from the nest and are fat but unmuscled, making them perfect for the table—and the dung was used as an ingredient in gunpowder.

The Town House

The defining feature of the town house was a compact layout. Urban homes tended to be narrow, tall, and close together—they were often built as rows of connected structures. An ordinary home might be no more than 10 or 15 feet wide, although the plot of land might extend 50 feet or more back from the street, allowing for a garden in back and even space for keeping small livestock. Two or three stories were common, or even four; the upper floors might jut out into the street over the lower ones, creating additional floor space. There was likely to be a proper floor and a cellar.

If the owner of the town house was a tradesman or craftsman, the front of the ground floor might serve as a shop. The window shutter might swing downward into the street to create a kind of display counter, with a canopy overhead to protect against rain. The family slept above the main floor. Additional space in the upper floors might be occupied by servants or apprentices, or rented to laboring folk too poor to have a house of their own—taking on boarders was a common way for a family to supplement its income. Boarders, like servants and apprentices, were likely to eat with the family, as there were probably no separate kitchen arrangements.

At the top end of the urban housing scale was the courtyard residence of the wealthy household, with facilities similar to a rural manor house, but condensed into a four-square layout gathered around a courtyard. Stairs and galleries went around the courtyard frontage of the structures, with access to the street through a passageway in the street-side structure. Urban inns were also built on this plan, and some older courtyard residences had been broken up into multiple tenements, making something loosely analogous to a modern apartment block.

At the other end of urban architecture were the ramshackle homes of the poor at the margins of the town—particularly in the poorer areas of London. These buildings were built quickly and cheaply, often along lines similar to a poor peasant cottages.

Most urban neighborhoods were not segregated between wealthy and poor areas. Instead, expensive dwellings tended to be those that fronted on main streets, with cheaper ones off side streets or alleys, or located in the upper floors of a building. Many urban buildings were subdivided into multiple tenements, and there could be quite a few layers of leasing between the owner of the land and the actual inhabitants of the building that stood on it.

Living Spaces

The typical Elizabethan home allowed for very little privacy. Young children slept in their parents' bedchamber, and servants sometimes in the same room as their employers. Four family members living in a two-room cottage had little private time, and a family living in town might share its space with servants, apprentices, and boarders. Things were different for the wealthy and privileged, whose houses had many rooms and ample opportunities for private space. Even so, such houses always had a significant domestic staff; their responsibilities were both in the working areas of the house and in the private areas, where they served as personal servants to the householder and family.

Home Interiors

The floors in a commoner's house might be covered with straw or rushes; a slightly more expensive option was decoratively patterned rush mats. Fragrant herbs or flowers might also be strewn upon the floors—wormwood was sometimes included as a means of discouraging fleas. Carpets were used as coverings for furniture rather than the floor, and only in well-to-do households. For decoration and extra warmth, the walls were often adorned with tapestries (for the wealthy) or with painted cloths (for the rest). These might depict biblical or legendary scenes; a painted cloth might even be based on folkloric themes such as the legend of Robin Hood. Alternatively, such scenes might be painted directly onto the walls. Maps often adorned the walls in upper-class houses, and colored prints in all sorts of homes, while woodcut-illustrated ballads might be tacked to the walls of plebeian houses. Windows often had curtains, even in the houses of common folk.

Light and Heat

Although the average Elizabethan home was small and simple, it was not necessarily squalid. Even ordinary people took pains keep their houses in good order—in part because squalor invited vermin. The housewife used a broomstick (like the one now associated with witches) to keep the floor clean; if rushes or straw had been strewn, they were swept out periodically. When a goose died, the housewife saved the wing for dusting—the original feather duster!

The homes of the wealthy, lavishly endowed with windows, were airy and bright; but in poorer houses, where glass was too expensive, window-openings had to be few and small to conserve heat; such houses were dim even in the daytime. After dark, light was provided by beeswax or tallow candles. Wax burned more brightly and cleanly but was expensive. Tallow was a cheaper alternative, being derived from animal fats that were a natural by-product of food production.

Candles were not as simple to use as they are today. As the candle burned down, the wick remained long and the candle receded from the flame, which became progressively weaker. To keep the light strong, the wick had to be trimmed at least every half-hour or so. This was a tricky procedure, as trimming it too close would bring the flame too near the candle, melting the candle and wasting precious fuel; one could even put the flame out in the process (the wicks in modern candles are designed to curl as they burn, so the end is burned away and the candle trims itself).

Materials for candlesticks included silver, pewter, brass, clay, and wood. Other forms of light were the oil lamp, also fueled with animal fats, and the *rushlight*, an iron clip holding a rush that had been dried and soaked in grease. To provide light outdoors, people used torches (called *links*), or lanterns fitted with panes of horn. Artificial light was dim (as anyone who has tried to read by candlelight knows), and it cost money, so most people followed the schedule of the sun, the only source of light that was cheap and undeniably effective.

The late 16th century was a period of generally cool and wet weather, falling within what climatic historians call the Little Ice Age. Not only was the weather cold, but houses were drafty and poorly insulated—windows had no double glazing. Nor was there central heating: heat was provided by fireplaces burning wood or coal. Coal was cheaper but produced a foul smoke. Wood fuel was often in the form of bundles of smaller branches rather than heavy logs. Large trees were a valuable resource, so wood was often cultivated by techniques called coppicing and pollarding, cutting back trees at the stump or trunk to allow new shoots to emerge—this provided a renewable source of wood, although in small diameters. The best houses had fireplaces in as many rooms as possible, but most people were unlikely to have more than one or two. Hot coals from the fire might be placed in an earthen vessel to bring a source of warmth to other parts of the house, although this could run the risk of fire.

Starting a fire from scratch began with a flint and steel—a sharpened piece of flint could strike minute fragments from a U-shaped piece of steel held in the hand, heating them white-hot to create sparks. By catching the sparks in a readily combustible material such as tow (a by-product of linen making), a smoldering fire could be generated. This could ignite an actual flame with the help of a match, a sliver of cardboard coated in sulfur. This match would burn much like its modern equivalent (although with an intense acrid smell—the smell of *brimstone* that people associated with the fires of hell). People were naturally inclined to avoid this complex and sometimes frustrating process if they could—if there were no fires alight in the house, people visited a neighbor to ask for some hot coals to kindle their fire the quick way.

Furnishings

To the modern eye, an Elizabethan home would seem sparsely furnished. Much of our furniture today serves to store our personal possessions, and ordinary Elizabethans owned far fewer things—a person who has only two changes of clothing doesn't need a lot of wardrobe space. Furniture was mostly of oak and other hardwoods—pine had to be imported to Elizabethan England. Elizabethan furniture was quite durable, since old oak becomes almost as hard as metal.

Construction was of two general types. The cheapest furniture was *boarded,* consisting mostly of boards pegged together with wooden dowels. Quality furniture was *joined,* assembled with mortice and tenon joints. The wood might be carved or inlaid, and the surface was often painted in bright colors.

The Hall

The sparseness of furniture is illustrated by the inventory of a tanner in 1592, whose hall was furnished with a table, five joint stools, a chair, a bench, and painted cloths to hang on the walls.[4] Most people sat on stools or benches. Chairs (distinguished by having a back) were relatively rare: as in the tanner's hall, there was often just one, reserved for the head of the household or a privileged guest (for this reason the term *chair* is sometimes used today to designate a position of authority, as in *chairman*). The nicest chairs were upholstered, but this was a luxury seen only in wealthy homes; cushions were the more usual means of making a seat comfortable. In the Middle Ages, chairs always had arms as well as backs, but the 16th century saw the emergence of the *farthingale* chair: fashionable women wore large hoop-skirts (farthingales) that were too big to fit between the arms of a chair, so the farthingale chair was made without arms. There were also benches with backs, called *settles.*

The tanner's table mentioned above was probably a permanent and stationary piece of furniture, although in some houses they were still using medieval-style trestle tables—essentially a table-top mounted on two trestles that could be put up and taken down at will. This style was especially useful in small spaces and in large dining halls that sometimes had to be cleared for other uses.

In addition to the items listed in the tanner's inventory, the hall might have a cupboard or shelves for storing table gear. Open shelving was favored as a way to display the household's best tableware. In a small home the hall would also serve as a kitchen and would be equipped accordingly.

The Bedchamber

Like the hall, the typical bedchamber was sparsely furnished. The tanner's inventory listed a table, an old carpet (probably used to cover the

**POSTMORTEM INVENTORY OF HENRY BACKER
OF CHIPPING NORTON, OXFORDSHIRE, 1588**

In the Hall

2 long table boards and one frame, 3 short forms [benches], 10 joint stools, one bench with a chair, one cupboard, . . . an almain rivet [munitions-grade armor], one caliver [musket], and furnishings to the same, . . . one cleaver, one chopping knife, a toasting iron, a lantern, a pair of balances and weights, with other small implements, £1 6s. 8d.

In the Buttery

2 dozen of pewter vessels, 2 brass pots . . . one chafing-dish, 4 candlesticks, 3 salts [salt-cellars], 4 pottage dishes of pewter, 4 kettles, 2 pans, 6 barrels, . . . 2 broaches [spits], 2 pair of pot-hooks, gridiron, with other small implements, £3 7s. 8d.

In the Kitchen

A table board, a bench, one bedstead, one flock bed, a twill cloth, 2 little pillows, . . . a cheese press, one bushel [basket], with other implements, 13s. 4d.

In the Chamber

2 bedsteads, one feather bed, one flock bed, 2 bolsters, 2 pillows, 2 coverlets, 2 chests, one coffer, with other small implements £3. . . .
His apparel: 2 gowns, 3 coats, 3 doublets, one cloak, 3 pair of hose, a cap and a hat, 2 pair of stockings, 2 pair of shoes, 3 shirts, a purse, and a girdle, with 2s. 4d. in his purse, £3 6s. 8d.

M. A. Havinden, ed., *Household and Farm Inventories in Oxfordshire, 1550–1590* (London: HMSO, 1965), 259–60.

table), two joint stools, two chairs, a clothespress, two linen chests, three painted cloths to hang on the walls, a bed, a flock-bed, a featherbed, two bolsters, a pillow, four blankets, and a coverlet.

The tanner's clothespress was a kind of armoire, fitted with shelves for storing clothes—the chest of drawers was a later development. Otherwise, clothes would be kept in a chest, the commonest form of storage furniture. The simplest style was the boarded chest, consisting of boards nailed or pegged together. A more sophisticated design was the *paneled* chest, contrasted of a jointed frame filled in with thin panels. This was considerably lighter than a boarded chest and less subject to cracking—the panels were set in grooves in the frame so they could freely expand and contract with changes in temperature and humidity. A chest might have a small lockable box, or *till*, set inside at the top; otherwise, valuables could be stored in a small coffer.

The tanner's bed fittings were typical for a well-to-do tradesman. The bed mentioned in the inventory was probably his wooden bedstead, which would support the mattress on slats of wood, on heavy webbing-type cloth, or—most likely—on a woven lattice of rope topped with a straw mat. The bedstead would probably be of the four-poster type, designed to be draped about with a canopy and curtains. These could provide some privacy if there were children or servants sleeping in the same room. Most importantly, they kept out the night air, which was considered unhealthy—rightly so, since there was no heating in the room at night. Curtains reduced the likelihood of catching a chill.

The tanner's *flock-bed* would be made of ticking fabric stuffed with wool; if quilted, it might be called a mattress. This particular tanner was fairly prosperous, since on top of his flock-bed he had a featherbed, another mattress stuffed with feathers, which was much more comfortable than the flock-bed alone. Someone who lacked a featherbed might have a flock bed resting on a *pallet*, a bed stuffed with straw, or a *chaff bed*, filled with oat or wheat chaff. Poor people slept on the pallet or chaff bed by itself, which might lie directly on the ground. Ticking was of canvas or heavy linen, and was characteristically striped, as it has remained for centuries.

The tanner's bolsters were a kind of oversized pillow made like the flock-bed. A bolster went across the head of the bed, with the pillow (probably stuffed with feathers) on top. A person would sleep between two linen sheets covered by blankets or quilts, his back supported on the bolster and his head resting on the pillow. The bed was often covered with a decorative and protective coverlet. Because nights were so cold, people sometimes used a *warming pan*, a covered metal pan fitted with a handle and filled with warm coals, to heat up the bed before climbing in at night. A full bedstead might have a *trundle* or *truckle bed* underneath for a servant or children; this could be rolled underneath the main bed during the day. A bed might also be shared for reasons of space and economy—a pair of brothers or sisters often share a bed, and servants might likewise have to share their beds.

Water, Washing, and Waste

One major difference between Elizabethan home life and our own was the lack of running water. In the country, water was fetched from a stream or well. In larger towns, there were public fountains fed by water conduits; professional water carriers filled large containers at the fountains and brought water door to door for sale. Some very privileged families in London had pipes leading from the public conduits to their houses, providing a modest supply of running water—a typical *quill*, as it was called, might deliver three gallons in an hour. Most towns also had stream or river water, but townsfolk used it only for purposes like washing or laundering—water from inside the town was not healthy to drink. The house would have barrels or a cistern for storing water, from which the household could draw water as needed.

In the absence of faucets, people washed with a water-jug (called a *ewer*) and a basin. Those lucky enough to have servants could achieve the effect of running water by having it poured from the jug into the basin; otherwise you had to pour it yourself! Soap was a mixture of some sort of fat or oil with lye, an alkaline solution that the Elizabethans obtained by percolating water through wood ashes. Sometimes scents were added as well. After washing, people dried themselves with a linen towel. People were generally diligent about washing their face and hands, which they did every morning; they also washed their hands before a meal and after defecating.

Bathing the whole body was infrequent—this is hardly surprising considering the drafty rooms and very real danger of catching a chill, which could be deadly. When people did bathe, they used a wooden tub before the fire, allowing for warmth and a ready supply of hot water. Teeth were cleaned after meals with toothpicks. Some people occasionally used a linen tooth-cloth, and various recipes existed for liquids and powders to help in cleaning them.

The simplest Elizabethan equivalent of the modern toilet was the metal or clay chamber pot (commonly called a *jordan*), often stored next to the bed with a bit of water in the bottom of it. The chamber pot could be used when needed and emptied later into a cesspit. Slightly more elaborate was the close-stool, a small stool with a hole in the seat under which was placed a chamber pot. The close-stool was often built as a closed-in box to conceal the chamber pot within. The most substantial arrangement was the privy (also called a *jakes* or *house of office*); this was similar to a close-stool, but the seat was large, permanent, and set apart in a small room of its own (it was called a privy from the French word for *private*). Sometimes the privy would be built outdoors as an outhouse, with a cesspit underneath instead of a pot. Most rural homes had a privy of this sort, and many urban tenements had access to a similar privy at the base of their garden or in a shared courtyard, often with a stone-lined cesspit that facilitated cleaning. Large cities had public privies, though it was common for men to simply find a convenient wall to urinate against, and even in a house a man might urinate in the fireplace if a chamber pot was not readily accessible. The function of toilet paper could be served by some old straw or scrap paper, or a small piece of cloth, which could be washed.

The disposal of human waste could be a major problem, especially in the city. In the country, cesspits were cleaned out during the winter, the waste being used to fertilize the fields. Cesspits in the city needed emptying more often—this was the work of professional *gong-farmers*, who were required to remove the waste at night to minimize the unpleasantness for town residents. The absence of an effective means of collecting sewage and removing it from the crowded city environment were major factors in the poor health conditions and high rate of urban disease and mortality.

Other kinds of biodegradable waste might be dumped on a dunghill behind the house—the waste was allowed to decompose and could be used as garden fertilizer. Nonbiodegradable waste might be buried or dumped in a river or into the privy—the Thames today is a gold mine for diggers looking for the detritus of Elizabethan daily life. There were strict city ordinances against fouling the streets, but—as with many Elizabethan laws—they were not always effective. Town officials called *scavagers* were responsible for clearing the streets of refuse once or twice a week—probably hiring laborers to do the actual collection. Both street and cesspit waste was carted to dumping areas, called *laystalls,* outside the town.

Some kinds of waste had resale value. Itinerant buyers walked the streets calling for housewives to sell them old linen rags (used for paper), kitchen grease (usable for candles or lamps), or other refuse for which there was a secondary market.

Poor sanitation contributed to the breeding of vermin, a perennial problem in any Elizabethan home. Fleas, lice, and other insects were a constant pest, and housewives were expected to keep their homes as clean as possible to keep their populations in check. Mice and rats were also ubiquitous, and predators like foxes were the bane of a family's poultry. Most households kept at least one cat to control the rodent population. Mousetraps were another means of addressing the problem, and in the cities there were also professional rat catchers, equivalents of the modern exterminator who used a variety of tools, including poisons, ferrets, and terriers, to deal with infestations of pests.

SICKNESS AND MEDICINE

Poor sanitation, vermin, and urban overcrowding contributed to a high level of disease and low life expectancies. Common diseases included smallpox, measles, tuberculosis (known as *consumption*), stones, and venereal diseases (especially syphilis). Diseases such as influenza and malaria were also present but hard to diagnose today based on Elizabethan descriptions, which tended to label both as *fever* or *ague.* Typhus and dysentery were a frequent problem in crowded and unsanitary living conditions; they were rife in jails and among soldiers and sailors. Among sailors, scurvy was also common, due to the lack of fresh food onboard ship, and it could also affect people ashore during the months when fresh fruits and vegetables were hard to come by. A less serious but very common ailment was toothache: tooth care was poor, and dentistry was much less developed than medicine.[5] Mental illness was a well-recognized problem with minimal means of care: Bethlehem hospital in London specialized in the long-term care of the mentally ill, although for many of the residents the conditions were little better than a prison.

Diseases often came and went in cycles. At the beginning of Elizabeth's reign there was an epidemic of New Ague, perhaps a form of influenza, lasting from 1557 to 1559, which may have carried off over 1/10 of the population. There was a serious outbreak of smallpox in 1562, which, surprisingly, struck the upper classes hardest of all: Elizabeth herself almost died of the disease.

The most dreaded disease of all was the plague, or bubonic plague, which had arrived in Europe during the 1300s. The disease was declining in England relative to previous centuries, but outbreaks continued until the late 1600s (it is still found in some parts of the world today). The plague is carried by the flea *Xenopsylla cheopis*, which normally lives on rats. If plague-carrying fleas transfer to a human host, there is a possibility they will communicate the disease and cause an outbreak of bubonic plague, with a mortality rate of about 50 percent. If the plague enters a person's pulmonary system, it can become pneumonic plague, an even more virulent and deadly form of the disease. Pneumonic plague can be transmitted directly from person to person, and its mortality rate is near 100 percent.

The plague was largely an urban phenomenon and struck most severely in the summer. Epidemics commonly came from the Netherlands to London, whence they might spread to other towns, although occurrences in any given town were often independent of each other. London was visited by the plague in 1563, 1578–79, 1582, 1592–93, and 1603. The worst epidemics in London were those of 1563 and 1603, which may have killed almost a quarter of the city's residents; even worse was the outbreak in Norwich in 1578–79, which claimed nearly 30 percent of the town's population. Children and the poor were especially at risk.

Medical Practitioners

The problem of disease was aggravated by the inability of medical science to treat or even understand it. The medical profession in Elizabethan England was largely shaped by structures inherited from the Middle Ages. At the top of the hierarchy of practitioners was the physician, a university-trained theorist who specialized in diagnosis and prescription of medicines. These medicines were prepared by the apothecary, who was considered a tradesman and well below the status of the physician, although he belonged to one of the most privileged and prestigious trade guilds in England. Also ranking below the physician was the surgeon, another tradesman, who specialized in what we would call operations. Below the surgeon was the barber-surgeon, who performed similar procedures. Simple barbers also practiced basic forms of surgery, including teeth cleaning and dentistry.

In the latter part of Elizabeth's reign, there may have been one licensed medical practitioner for every 400 people in London, far fewer in the rest of the country. However, the official licensing system did not always restrict

A SURGEON DESCRIBES A SUCCESSFUL OPERATION

At the very beginning of this cure, I did shave or cut the hair away round about the wound, then with my finger I made further probation into the wound, and there I did manifestly feel a notable fraction or breach in the skull on the left side of his head upon the bone called *Os petrosum*, which . . . was depressed upon the panicle *Dura mater*. And for that the fracture of the skull was greater in length than the wound in the flesh, for that cause, without detracting of time, I made incision, and so followed the fracture, until all the rift or cracked bone was wholly discovered. When I did see and behold the full length of the fracture or breach in the skull and had raised up the flesh, then for that I could not at that present time proceed any further in this business, because of the great flux of blood, and the rather for that he had lost a great quantity of blood before he was brought home to his lodging— all which being considered, I filled the wound with pledgets and runlets [waddings] made of lint and very fine tow, wet in the whites of eggs being mixed with Galen's powder. Then after, with good bolstering and rolling, he remained thus until the next day.

William Clowes, *A Proved Practice for All Young Chirurgians* (London: Thomas Cadman, 1588), sig. P3r

the practice of medicine. Surgeons diagnosed illnesses and prescribed treatment for many who could not afford a physician or who lacked access to one. Outside of the formal medical hierarchy were the unlicensed practitioners, who typically practiced medicine only on a part-time basis. These included folk healers, midwives, and a fair number of outright quacks, as well as learned nonspecialists such as the mage-scientists John Dee and Simon Forman. Women also learned some basic home medicine as a part of their preparation for managing a household, and even an aristocratic lady might engage in charitable healing for her poorer neighbors. Indeed there was a substantial volume of medical literature coming from Elizabethan presses, providing households with voluminous advice on how to deal with a variety of medical situations.

If the structure of the medical profession was old-fashioned, its medical theories were even more so. By and large, there had been few major developments in medicine since the Middle Ages. Physiological theory was based on the ancient idea of the Four Humors, corresponding to the Four Elements, which were believed to make up all physical matter: Melancholy (cold and dry, like Earth), Blood (hot and moist, like Air), Phlegm (cold and moist, like Water), and Choler (hot and dry, like Fire). Physicians often attributed illness to an imbalance of these humors and treated it by prescribing foods and medicines whose properties were thought to be opposite to those of the excessive humor. Since the Galenic system identified correspondences between the humors, the zodiac, and the parts of the body, one of the most common medical procedures was bloodletting: it was believed that draining some blood from the appropriate part of the body could also help restore balance to the humors. (See Table 9.1 for the system of correspondences.)

Surgical practitioners may have been somewhat more effective, in part because the mechanics of the body were more readily understood than its chemistry, and many of the surgeons had experience in military service where they had ample opportunity to develop their skills by trial and error. Surgeons like William Clowes were able to provide meaningful treatment for serious injuries like fractured skulls and recognized the importance of cleansing wounds with compounds that included ingredients like wine or salt (both of which we now know have antibacterial properties). Nonetheless, rates of postoperative infection were high in a world that had not yet developed the concept of sterilization.

In spite of disease and nutritional shortcomings, our modern notion that people back then were smaller is an exaggeration. Average heights from London grave finds dating to the Elizabethan period are 5′ 7½″ for men, 5′ 2¼″ for women—less than 2″ below the 5′ 9″ and 5′ 3¾″ averages for Londoners today.

NOTES

1. For incomes and wages, see Sir John Harington, *Nugae Antiquae* (London: Vernor and Hood, 1804); William Harrison, *Description of England* [1587] (Ithaca, NY: Folger Shakespeare Library, 1968), bk. 2, chap. 5; Paul L. Hughes and James F. Larkin, *Tudor Royal Proclamations* (New Haven, CT: Yale University Press, 1964), 3.39–41; R. H. Tawney and Eileen Power, *Tudor Economic Documents* (London: Longmans, 1924); D. M. Palliser, *The Age of Elizabeth* (London and New York: Longman, 1992), 118; M. St. Clare Byrne, *Elizabethan Life in Town and Country* (London: Methuen, 1950), 115; Margaret Spufford, *Contrasting Communities* (Cambridge: Cambridge University Press, 1974), 52.

2. For prices, see Fynes Moryson, *An Itinerary* [1617], The English Experience 387 (Amsterdam and New York: Da Capo Press, Theatrum Orbis Terrarum, 1971), III.ii.62, III.iii.151; Harrison, *Description*, bk. 3, chap. 16; Hughes and Larkin, *Proclamations*, 3.21, 39–41; James E. Thorold Rogers, *A History of Agriculture and Prices in England* (Oxford: Clarendon Press, 1882); Percy Macquoid, "The Home," in *Shakespeare's England: An Account of the Life and Manners of His Age* (Oxford: Clarendon Press, 1916), 2.136–37, 141; Palliser, *Age of Elizabeth*, 134; Marjorie Plant, *The English Book Trade* (London: G. Allen and Unwin, 1939), 220, 241; Jo McMurtry, *Understanding Shakespeare's England* (Hamden, CT: Archon, 1989), 73. The daily cost of food given in this table is based on the amount of money allowed to workers for their daily food according to the official rates. The price of standard-quality bread was fixed; only the weight changed. Note that some of these were the officially decreed prices; the real prices could be rather higher, depending on the state of the economy.

3. Palliser, *Age of Elizabeth*, 129.

4. MacQuoid, "The Home," 2.120–22.

5. On medicine, see Margaret Pelling, "Medicine and Sanitation," in *William Shakespeare: His World, His Works, His Influence. Vol. 1: His World*, ed. John F. Andrews (New York: Scribner, 1985), 75–84; C. Webster, *Health, Medicine, and Mortality in Sixteenth-Century England* (Cambridge: Cambridge University Press, 1979); Alban H. G. Doran, "Medicine," in *Shakespeare's England. An Account of the Life and Manners of His Age* (Oxford: Clarendon Press, 1916), 1.413–43.

6

Clothing and Accoutrements

Of all aspects of Elizabethan culture, the most distinctive may well be its clothing. In a world of unprecedented physical and social mobility, clothing served as a crucial marker of status. The privileged classes used clothing to set them apart from ordinary people; the socially ambitious used it to help them stake a claim to status in the eyes of others. As fashion-conscious Elizabethans sought ever newer ways to stand out, clothing evolved a look that was elaborate, artificial, and striking. Moralists railed against the obsession with sumptuous apparel, rich accessories, and stylish coiffures. Government authorities issued decrees that regulated clothing, jewelry, and weaponry based on the wearer's rank. Such efforts at control were doomed, and ultimately even the lower ranks of society adopted scaled-back versions of the modish styles favored by the upper classes.

To the modern eye, Elizabethan clothing may look constrictive, hot, and uncomfortable. Clothing was indeed heavier in the 16th century than it is today. England has never had a very warm climate, and Elizabeth's reign fell within a period of particularly cold weather known today as the Little Ice Age. At the same time, the clothing we usually associate with the Elizabethan period is the most formal attire of the aristocracy, and formal clothes are typically more constrictive than everyday wear. The ordinary clothes of working people had to allow for more mobility and were considerably more comfortable by today's standards.

Most people owned little clothing—two changes of attire was typical for the majority, ensuring that they would have clean clothes to wear on Sunday. The wealthy had their garments tailor-made, but ordinary people

A royal hunting party.
[Ashdown]

purchased them off the rack, and many bought them used. Most Elizabethan clothing was robustly made, and would last much longer the modern
counterparts—only linen undergarments, which were subjected to regular
washing, and footwear were inclined to wear out quickly.

MATERIALS

The principal fibers used in Elizabethan clothing were linen and wool.
Linen derives from the flax plant; it is a very comfortable fabric, absorbent, easy to clean, and quick to dry. It was ideal for wearing next to the
skin in shirts, underwear, collars, cuffs, and hose: it could absorb sweat
and dirt and keep them from damaging the valuable outer garments. Its
absorbency made it less useful as an outer garment in England's rainy climate. Linen was also used for lining and interlining garments. Sometimes,
as an interlining, it was impregnated with gum (a sticky secretion derived
from certain plants) to make it stiffer, in which case it was called buckram. A certain amount of linen was produced domestically, although the
best linens were imported from the Continent, especially from northern
France and the Low Countries. Table linen might be had for 5d. an ell (45
inches). Holland could cost 1s. 6d. for the coarser varieties, 5s. for the finer
ones, and cambric could range from 2s. to 20s; both of these were finer

A PURITAN CRITIQUE OF FASHION

Now there is such a confused mingle-mangle of apparel in *Ailgna* [England], and such preposterous excess thereof, as every one is permitted to flaunt it out in what apparel he listeth [wishes] himself, or can get by any kind of means—so that it is very hard to know who is noble, who is worshipful, who is a gentleman, who is not. For you shall have those which are neither of the nobility, gentility, nor yeomanry, no, nor yet any magistrate or officer in the commonwealth, go daily in silks, velvets, satins, damasks, taffetas, and such like, notwithstanding that they be both base by birth, mean by estate, and servile by calling. . . . They have great and monstrous ruffs, made either of cambric, holland, lawn, or else of some other the finest cloth that can be got for money, wherefore some be a quarter of a yard deep. . . hanging out over their shoulder points instead of a sail. . . . Their doublets are no less monstrous than the rest, for now the fashion is to have them hang down to the middle of their thighs, or at least to their privy members, being so hard quilted, stuffed, bombasted, and sewed, as they can neither work nor yet play in them. . . . Every artificer's wife (almost) will not stick to go in her hat of velvet every day, every merchant's wife and mean gentlewoman in her French hood, and every poor cottager's daughter in her taffeta hat, or else of wool at the least.

Phillip Stubbes, *The Anatomie of Abuses* (London: Richard Jones, 1583), 10r, 22v, 25r, 34v.

linens often used for shirts. Lawn, an extremely fine linen used especially in neckwear and cuffs, cost 10s. and up.

Occasionally linen was used for outer garments such as breeches and doublets, particularly for reasons of economy. In such cases, it was generally of a heavier type than shirt-linen, such as linen canvas, which might range in price from 1s. to 3s. a yard. Canvas could also be made from hemp, the plant fiber used in making ropes. Canvas of this sort was very tough, suitable for such purposes as making sails and packing merchandise, but it might be used for clothing when economy or durability was more important than comfort. Hemp was also used to make lockram, a coarse fabric used in shirts.

Cotton was imported and most commonly found as a component of fustian, a fabric woven with a cotton weft and linen warp. Fustian cost 1s. for coarse stuff, 3–5s. for fine. Fustian was often used to give the appearance of silk and was also used for stuffing padded garments. Cotton fibers might also be used for stuffing or padding a garment. The term can be a source of confusion, since Elizabethans also used it as the name of a heavy woolen fabric.

By far the most common fabric for the outer layers of clothing was wool, which was one of the principal sources of England's wealth in Elizabeth's day. Wool is sturdy and versatile—it sheds water, keeps the wearer warm in cold weather, yet is remarkably cool in the summer. It accepts dye readily but does not absorb moisture (such as sweat) or wash well. One of the cheapest sorts was called frieze, which cost 6d. to 3s. a yard; 2s. to 4s. was a standard range for English wools. Woolen fabrics tended to be heavily felted, improving their resistance to cold, rain, and fraying. In fact, woolens might be so heavily felted that it was unnecessary to hem them, which made them especially suitable for outer garments, where hems can collect rainwater.

These heavily felted woolens had been made in England since the Middle Ages and were known as *old draperies*. Lighter woolens known as *new draperies* had become fashionable by Elizabeth's day: these were more elegant but less durable, similar to modern suiting fabric. The new draperies had originated in Italy, and the techniques for making them came to Elizabethan England with Flemish and French refugees.

The finest fabrics were made of silk and quite expensive. Satin was one of the cheaper luxury fabrics, ranging from 3s. to 14s. a yard; taffeta might cost 15s.; velvet, 31s.; and damask a princely £4, more than most people made in a year. Plain silk was used for fine shirts; satin and taffeta, for outer layers and for lining; velvet, for outer layers.

SHOPPING AT THE ROYAL EXCHANGE, LONDON

Atire-gain   *(the Shopkeeper's Maid)* Madam, what doth it please you to have? Would ye have any fair linen cloth? Mistress, see what I have, and I will show you the fairest linen cloth in London, if you do not like it, you may leave it, you shall bestow nothing but the looking on, the pain shall be ours to show them you.

Lady   . . . Have you any fair holland?

Atire-gain   Yes, forsooth, Madam, and the fairest lawn that ever you handled. . . . The cambric will cost you twenty shillings the ell.

Lady   Truly it lacketh no price. And if things be so much worth as those which sell them do make them to be, your cambric is very good, for you hold it at a good price. But yet I will not give so much though.

Atire-gain   How much will it please you to give then Madam?—to the end that I may have your custom.

Lady   I will give you fifteen shillings. If you will take my money make short, for I have other business than to tarry here.

Atire-gain   Truly Madam I would be very sorry to deny you if I could give it at that price, but in truth I cannot, unless I should lose by it.

Lady   I will give you sixteen, and not one halfpenny more. . . .

Sempster   Madam, I am content to lose in it, of the price that I sell it to others, in hope that you will buy of us when you shall have need.

Peter Erondell, *The French Garden* (1605), in M. St Clare Byrne, ed. *The Elizabethan Home* (London: Methuen, 1949), 57–59.

Leather was also an important element in the Elizabethan's clothing. It was used not only for gloves, belts, and shoes, but also for a variety of garments, especially among men, including hats, doublets, and even breeches. Leather garments were often adorned with slashing or tooling. Furs were also used to trim the edges of garments: cheap options included lambskin, rabbit, and fox; richer ones, mink, marten, and ermine.

DECORATION

The colors of Elizabethan fabrics were mostly based on natural dyes, the commonest being brown, grey, red, blue, yellow, and green. The various colors sometimes had specific associations, in many cases related to the expense of producing them. Brown and grey fabrics were inexpensive and were associated with the poor. There were two types of red fabric. One was dyed with the plant madder, which yields a russet color. Such fabric was also relatively inexpensive and was associated with honest plain folk. Bright red fabric, by contrast, had to be made with imported dyes and was expensive. Blue was fairly inexpensive and was often worn by servants and apprentices. The usual source for blue dye was the herb woad. Black was a difficult color to obtain with natural dyes and was consequently expensive: for this reason it was especially fashionable. Intense colors were difficult to produce, and natural dyes tend to fade quickly. Consequently, the colors of most Elizabethan clothing would have been rather muted.

Linen was generally undyed, although it was often bleached by exposing it to the sun. Sometimes it was block-printed or adorned with embroidery, particularly at visible points like the collar and cuffs. Clothes could be further ornamented by slashing or pinking (piercing) the outer layer to reveal a fine contrasting fabric underneath. Other adornments included *guarding* (ribbon trim, often used around the edge of a garment or to hide seams) and even gems or pearls on the most fancy outfits.

A distinctive feature of Elizabethan clothing was the extensive use of padding, known as *bombast,* to give the garments a fashionable shape. Bombast was especially common in men's clothes and typically consisted of raw wool, cotton, or horsehair, but oats or bran were sometimes used instead. To achieve the modish, highly shaped look of the fashionable torso garment, these were not only lined but also interlined with a stiffening fabric like buckram.

CLEANING

As a rule, only the inner layers of clothing (such as shirts and underwear) were actually washed; evidence suggests that ordinary people probably washed clothing on a weekly basis, donning a fresh shirt each Sunday. Detachable collars and cuffs might be changed more often. Washing was mostly for linen garments. They would be saturated in soap and hot water, beaten with paddles, rinsed, and then left out in the sun to

**FROM THE PRIVY COUNCIL'S PROCLAMATION
ENFORCING THE STATUTES OF APPAREL, 1562**

For the reformation of the use of the monstrous and outrageous greatness of
hose, crept of late into the realm to the great slander thereof, and the undo-
ing of a number using the same, being driven for the maintenance thereof to
seek such unlawful ways as by their own confession have brought them to
destruction, it is ordained . . . that no tailor, hosier, or other person . . . shall
put any more cloth in any one pair of hose . . . than one yard and a half, or
at the most one yard and three quarters of a yard of kersey or of any other
cloth, leather, or any other kind of stuff . . . and in the same hose to be put
only one kind of lining besides linen cloth; . . . the said lining not to lie loose
nor to be bolstered, but to lie just unto their legs as in ancient times was
accustomed. . . . Neither any man under the degree of a baron to wear within
his hose any velvet, satin or any other stuff above the estimation of sarcenet
or taffeta. . . .

   And whereas an usage is crept in, contrary to former orders, of wearing of
long swords and rapiers, sharpened in such sort as may appear the usage of
them cannot tend to defense (which ought to be the very meaning of wearing of weapons in times of peace), but to murder and evident death, . . . her
majesty's pleasure is that no man shall . . . wear any sword, rapier, or any
weapon . . . passing the length of one yard and half-a-quarter of blade at the
uttermost, neither any dagger above the length of twelve inches in blade,
neither any buckler with a sharp point, or with any point above two inches
of length.

Paul L. Hughes and James F. Larkin, *Tudor Royal Proclamations* (New Haven and
London: Yale University Press, 1969), 2.189–91.

dry and bleach, either in a field or on hedges (some thieves specialized in
snatching linens from hedges as they dried). They might then be pressed
with irons. Outer layers of clothing, most often made of wool or richer fabrics, did not wash well and were cleaned with a clothes-brush instead.

UNDERGARMENTS

   The principal undergarment for both men and women was the shirt,
which served as a comfortable, absorbent, and washable layer between
the body and the outer clothes. Shirts had long sleeves and were pulled
over the head. They were generally made of white linen, although the rich
favored silk. Shirts tended to be simple in cut, with straight seams, but
the fabric might be heavily gathered at the collar and cuffs. Fancy shirts
were sometimes decorated with lace or adorned with black, red, or gold

Laundresses at work. [Besant]

embroidery, especially about the collar, shoulders, and cuffs. Men's shirts typically reached to the crotch or thigh and were vented at the bottom of the side seams to allow for greater freedom of movement. Women's shirts, usually called *smocks*, were normally between knee- and ankle length. Triangular gores of fabric inserted into the side seams allowed extra mobility in these longer garments. The neckline of a woman's smock might be high or low. For many people the shirt also served as a nightgown, although wealthy people had nightshirts for this purpose.

The shirt was more truly an undergarment than it is today. People who were not manual laborers were almost never seen in their shirtsleeves, although gentlemen might strip to their shirts for respectable physical exertion (such as tennis). Working people were sometimes seen in their shirts when they had to perform heavy labor, but women would at least wear a sleeveless bodice on top.

In addition to the shirt, men often wore undershorts comparable to modern boxer shorts. These were generally called *breeches*, an ambiguous term since it could refer to an outer garment as well. Women did not normally wear breeches in England, although they had started to do so in Italy. Breeches were made of white linen and might be adorned with embroidery, especially about the cuffs.

WOMEN'S GARMENTS

On top of her smock, an Elizabethan woman might wear any of three general styles of attire, sometimes in combination with each other. The first was the *kirtle*, the second was a bodice and *petticoat* (skirt), and the third was a gown.

The kirtle was a long fitted garment reaching down to the feet, resembling a long close-fitting dress. It was a fairly simple style, derived from medieval garments, and was not generally worn by itself among fashionable women, although it might be worn under another garment.

The bodice, or *pair of bodies*, was a close-fitting garment for the upper body, normally made of wool. It kept the torso warm and was stiffened to mold the body into the fashionable shape. This shape was rather severe and masculine: flat, broad in the shoulders, and narrow in the waist. In effect, the bodice combined the functions of bra, girdle, and vest all in one. Its waistline was pointed in front. The neckline reflected the trends of fashion: it was low toward the beginning and end of Elizabeth's reign, high during the middle years. A low bodice might be worn with a high-neckline smock; the decolleté look was normal only with young unmarried women and in some fashionable circles. The bodice had no collar.

DRESSING A GENTLEWOMAN

Where be all my things? Go fetch my clothes: bring my petticoat bodies [bodice]: I mean my damask quilt bodies with whale bones. What lace do you give me here? This lace is too short, the tags are broken . . . Give me my petticoat of wrought crimson velvet with silver fringe. Why do you not give me my nightgown?—for I take cold. Where be my stockings? Give me some clean socks. I will have no worsted hosen, show me my carnation silk stockings. Where laid you last night my garters? . . . Put on my white pumps. Set them up, I will have none of them. Give me rather my Spanish leather shoes, for I will walk today. This shoeing-horn hurteth me . . . Tie the strings with a strong double knot, for fear they untie themselves. Jolie, come dress my head, set the table further from the fire, it is too near. Put my chair in his place. Why do you not set my great looking glass on the table? . . . Where is my ivory comb? . . . Take the key of my closet, and go fetch my long box where I set my jewels . . . Go to, Page, give me some water to wash. Where's my musk ball? Do you not see that I want my busk? What is become of the busk-point? . . . Let me see that ruff, How is it that the supporter is so soiled? . . . I believe that the meanest woman in this town hath her apparel in better order than I have. . . . Is there no small pins for my cuffs? Look in the pin-cushion. . . . Bring my mask and my fan; help me to put on my chain of pearls.

Peter Erondell, *The French Garden* (1605), in M. St Clare Byrne, ed. *The Elizabethan Home* (London: Methuen, 1949), 37–38.

The bodice could be sleeved or sleeveless. A sleeveless bodice was considered an adequate outer garment for women when they were doing heavy work, although they always wore a sleeved bodice or overgarment in less informal situations. Women of higher social status had no cause to be seen in their shirtsleeves, so a sleeveless bodice for them was solely an undergarment. A sleeved bodice might be worn on top of a sleeveless one. The sleeves were sometimes detachable, allowing for a change of sleeves to be laced or hooked in—a cheap way to change the look of the garment. If a sleeveless bodice was worn underneath, the outer bodice did not need to be as heavily stiffened. Bodices often had decorative tabs called *pickadills* about the waist; if worn on the outside, they might have rolls or wings of fabric around the armholes.

The degree of stiffening in the bodice depended on the wearer's station in life. Upper-class women wore stiffly shaped bodices, but ordinary women needed more freedom of movement to perform everyday tasks (such as churning butter, baking bread, or chasing children), so their garments had to be less constricting. Stiffening might be provided by whalebone (baleen), bundles of dried reeds, willowy wood, or even steel. A less fashionable bodice might be shaped with just a heavy buckram interlining. To get the fashionably flat look in front, a rigid piece of wood, bone, or ivory, called a *busk*, might be inserted and held in place by a ribbon at

A satirical print on women's fashions, ca. 1595. [Bibliothèque nationale de France]

the top; to this day women's undergarments often have a small bow in the midpoint of the chest, the last trace of the Elizabethan busk.

A bodice worn as an innermost garment took a fair bit of strain, so buttons would have been too weak a fastening. Instead, bodices were fastened with hooks and eyes, or else were laced up. Ordinary women's bodices usually laced up the front; side- and back-lacing bodices were worn by people who had servants to help them dress. The innermost bodice sometimes had holes around the bottom edge to which a farthingale, roll, or petticoat could be laced.

On top of a sleeveless bodice, women sometimes wore doublets similar to those worn by men. Unlike a bodice, the doublet had a collar and buttoned up the front.

Where the bodice served to flatten and narrow the upper body, Elizabethan fashion called for volume in the lower body. This was generally achieved either with a *farthingale* or a *roll,* or with a combination of the two. The farthingale had originated in Spain as a bell-shaped support for the skirts: it was essentially an underskirt with a series of wire, whalebone, or willow hoops sewn into it. During the course of Elizabeth's reign, the *wheel farthingale* was introduced. This stuck directly out at the hips and fell straight down, giving the skirts a cylindrical shape. The wheel farthingale was often worn with a padded roll about the hips. Sometimes the roll was worn by itself to give a somewhat softer version of the wheel farthingale look. This style was particularly common among ordinary people, for whom it served not only to imitate the fashionable shape but also to keep the skirts away from the legs for greater ease of movement.

Skirts were known as *petticoats.* Their shape was dictated by the shape of the undergarments. Bell-shaped farthingales required skirts of similar

Country women and a water carrier; detail from "Elizabeth I's Procession Arriving at Nonesuch Palace," 1582, by Joris Hoefnagel (1542–1600) [Private Collection/ The Bridgeman Art Library]

proportions, lightly gathered at the waist and made in several trapezoidal panels. Wheel farthingales required huge skirts, heavily gathered to the waist. Women who did not wear farthingales might wear many layers of petticoats to create volume (as well as warmth). The ordinary woman's outer petticoat was of wool; underpetticoats might be of linen and were sometimes richly embroidered. Often, hems were made of a different, more durable fabric that could be removed and replaced as they wore out.

The final main style of female garment was the gown, which was essentially a bodice and skirt sewn together, usually worn on top of a kirtle or petticoat. The gown was the richest form of garment, and it took many forms. The bodice was frequently adorned with false sleeves that hung down at the back, and often the skirt was open in front to reveal the contrasting skirts underneath.

MEN'S GARMENTS

Lower-body garments for men changed substantially during the course of Elizabeth's reign. In the early years, some people still wore the old-fashioned *long hose* and *codpiece*, a style that had changed little since the late Middle Ages. The hose were loose-fitting leggings roughly analogous to modern tights. They were often made of woven rather than knitted fabric. The fabric was usually wool (which is naturally somewhat elastic) and cut on the bias (i.e., diagonally) to allow them to stretch, but they still tended to bag, especially around the ankles. The codpiece was a padded covering for the crotch, originally introduced for the sake of propriety. It also served the function of a modern trouser-fly: it could be unbuttoned or untied when nature called.

This plain style of hose was already out of fashion by the time Elizabeth came to the throne. Well-dressed men had taken to wearing *trunkhose* over their long hose. These were an onion-shaped, stuffed garment that extended from the waist to the tops of the thighs. The trunkhose were often slashed vertically or constructed from multiple vertical panes, revealing a contrasting fabric underneath.

Later in the reign, a new fashion arose of attaching *canions* to these trunkhose. These were tight-fitting cylindrical extensions that reached from the bottom of the trunkhose to the wearer's knees. At the same time, the trunkhose themselves became fuller and longer, reaching to midthigh, and were more likely to be of a solid fabric rather than slashed or paned. Such trunkhose were increasingly likely to have pockets, and were worn with stockings rather than long hose.

Codpieces continued to be worn on the outside of trunkhose. They were sometimes quite elaborate and often in a shape that strikes the modern eye as downright obscene. Fashionable gentlemen occasionally had them made as pockets in which they could store candy and other knickknacks!

Codpieces became more subdued toward the latter part of the period and had fallen out of fashion by the end of the century.

During the latter part of Elizabeth's reign, a new style of lower-body garment appeared, known as *breeches*. They were sometimes called *Venetian breeches* or just *Venetians* to distinguish them from underwear. Venetian breeches were essentially knee-length trousers, originally cut rather close to the body but becoming more voluminous toward the end of the reign. They normally reached below the knee, although some styles stopped short of it. The commoner's Venetians were made of wool and might be lined with linen. Cheaper Venetians were made of linen canvas. Venetians were sometimes trimmed along the outseam and around the pockets. They could be fastened at the waist with buttons or with hooks and eyes. Venetians were not worn with codpieces; instead, they had a fly-opening that tied or buttoned. Like the later styles of trunkhose, they were worn with stockings.

Men's upper-body garments did not change nearly as much during the course of Elizabeth's reign. The characteristic upper-body garment was the doublet, a short, fitted jacket with a narrow waist. The doublet was

William Brooke, 10th Lord Cobham and his Family, 1567, by Master of the Countess of Warwick (fl.1567–69). [Longleat House, Wiltshire, UK/ The Bridgeman Art Library]

made of wool, canvas, or a fine fabric, or sometimes of leather. It might be padded and quilted, or decorated with slashes. It either buttoned, hooked, or laced up the front. It was often adorned with wings at the shoulders and pickadills about the waist. As with women's bodices, the doublet might have detachable sleeves that hooked or laced in. Early in the reign, the doublet was cut straight around the bottom edge, but in time it became fashionable for the front to dip downward in a sharp V shape. In the latter half of the period, doublets were cut with a distinctive *peascod belly,* a padded protruding flare at the front that imitated the design of military breastplates (on a breastplate this shape helped to deflect blows). An additional garment called a *jerkin* could be worn over the doublet when temperature or fashion demanded. The jerkin was essentially of the same design as a doublet, except that it might be sleeveless.

The doublet was worn by a very wide section of society, although the quality of the materials and the degree of tailoring and decoration varied enormously. People toward the lower end of the social scale might wear a coat instead. In its most elaborate form the coat resembled a plain doublet, except that it had long skirts. Fashionable men sometimes wore such coats over their doublets. The simplest form of coat was not fitted at all but dropped straight down from the shoulders; it might be belted at the waist.

OTHER GARMENTS

Stockings

Lower leg garments were called stockings, netherstocks, or hose; they were worn by all women, and by men to go with trunkhose or Venetians. At the beginning of the reign, stockings were typically made of woven cloth, but knitted stockings of silk or wool displaced them over the course of the reign.

Stockings might be white or colored; they were sometimes decorated with silk embroidery about the top and down the sides—colors included red, green, and black. In addition, people sometimes wore heavy colored overstockings outside comfortable white ones. Riders might wear protective overstockings of heavy linen, known as boothose. If a man wore breeches that stopped above the knee, the stockings could be pulled up over the breeches; otherwise they went underneath.

Neither cloth nor knitted stockings were able to stay up reliably without help, so both men and women held them in place with garters. Women gartered their stockings at the *gartering place,* the narrow spot between the knee and upper calf. Men's stockings gartered there or just above the knee, depending on the length of the breeches or trunkhose. Another style for men was *cross-gartering,* where the garter wrapped around the leg both above and below the knee, crossing behind it. Ordinary people's garters were made of woven or knit wool, or of leather straps with buckles. Fancier garters might be made of silk.

Shoes

Men's and women's shoes in the late 16th century were generally blunt-toed and flat: heeled shoes were not common until the 17th century. Most shoes were made of leather, although highly fashionable shoes for courtly use were sometimes made of fabrics such as velvet or silk. The shoe was secured on the foot with laces or a buckle. Decorations on fancy shoes included embroidery, cutwork, ribbon edging, pearls, gems, and slashes (sometimes puffed). Boots were generally worn only by men and only for riding, although working men sometimes wore low ankle-boots.

Collars and Cuffs

Early in Elizabeth's reign, both men's and women's shirts were heavily gathered at the neck; this had given rise to the practice of sewing a ruff into the neckband. Eventually, a new style emerged in which a separate ruff was tied around the neck. Both men and women wore ruffs, which became progressively larger and more intricate in fashionable circles. In 1565 starch was introduced to the laundry process. This method of stiffening enabled the ruff to grow even larger, requiring meticulous care to set it properly. By 1580–85 ruffs were so large that they needed the support of a wire framework to fan them around the head. Ruffs were made of fine linen, sometimes edged with lace. They were often worn with matching hand ruffs at the wrists. The starch was sometimes impregnated with a colorant that gave the ruff a tint—pink, yellow, mauve, or blue.

In the latter part of Elizabeth's reign, the *falling band* became fashionable among men. This had evolved from the neckband of the shirt; it was essentially a separate collar, which again tied around the neck. The simplest type was made of white linen of light to medium weight; fancier ones were adorned with lace or embroidery. Women did not wear falling bands, but they sometimes pinned a kerchief around their shoulders.

Outer and Inner Garments

Elizabethan England was generally a chilly place, so there existed a wide variety of garments for furnishing additional warmth; some of them were also crucial to the wearer's fashionable look. Between their shirt and outer garments, people sometimes wore a knitted undergarment called a *waistcoat*. Linen or knitted jackets were sometimes worn for extra warmth indoors. Loose gowns were a very common garment for both men and women. They were often open, reaching to the knee or ankle on men, to the ankle on women. Gowns of this sort might be adorned with false sleeves. Women were most likely to wear these indoors, whereas men, especially older men of the middle and upper classes, might wear them outside as well. They were typically made of very heavy fabric, often lined or trimmed with fur. Another warm garment was the cassock, a flaring coat especially favored by soldiers and sailors, but also worn by both men and women in general, particularly commoners. Among fashionable men, the circular or semicircular cape was especially favored: it might be long, or a merely decorative short cape reaching only to the waist.

Hair and Headgear

Men tended to wear their hair short in the early part of Elizabeth's reign, but longer hair became fashionable in the latter half. Although a few men were clean shaven, the overwhelming majority wore a moustache and beard, which might be handsomely trimmed to a point. Trimming the hair and beard was the work of a professional barber.

Men generally kept their heads covered—the main exception was when they doffed their hats or caps as a mark of respect before their social superiors. An exclusively masculine form of headgear was the brimless knitted cap, which resembled the modern toque. Men sometimes also wore toque-style linen caps indoors.

The flat caps that had dominated the first half of the century were still in use, although they became less fashionable as the reign progressed and eventually became the mark of the London citizen or apprentice. Common cap materials were wool, felt, or leather, and linen might be used to line the interior. Flat caps were either knit of woolen yarn or sewn of woven fabric. In an effort to support the cap-knitting industry, it was mandated by law in 1571 that male commoners wear knitted flat caps on Sundays and holidays; for this reason they came to be known as *statute caps*. The law was widely disobeyed and was repealed in 1597, but the flat cap was nonetheless one of the most common styles among ordinary men.

Hats might be made of wool, woolen felt, or leather; more expensive materials included velvet and silk. Some of the finest were made of felted animal fur, particularly beaver. Straw hats were especially common among country folk. Hats became increasingly fashionable as the flat cap became less so, and among men in the latter part of the reign, the height of fashion was represented by the high-crowned hats known as *copotains*. Another style of hat had a somewhat lower crown and a broad brim. Hats were often decorated with a hatband, which might be cut long such that a tail hung down at the back. The hatband might be adorned with a feather or a jeweled hat pin.

Elizabethan women wore their hair long, although they generally pinned it up. It was kept off the forehead and was not cut into bangs. A fashionable lady or a young unmarried woman might leave her hair uncovered, but most women wore at least a simple cap known as a *coif*.

The coif was typically of linen, and some were ornately embroidered. On top of the coif the woman might wear any one of a variety of head adornments. The simplest was the forehead cloth, a triangular piece of linen with ties, which went over the front of the head and tied at the nape of the neck. Another form of headgear was the French hood, a fabric bonnet shaped with interior wires; it was especially fashionable in the early part of the reign. Women also wore flat caps, and in the latter part of the reign, hats became increasingly common, in all the various styles worn by men.

Fasteners

The buttons of a commoner's clothes were often made of a wooden bead covered with fabric, or fabric scraps wrapped in a disk of fabric from the garment. The more expensive option was metal—pewter, brass, silver, or gold. Buttons were typically spherical and of the shank type, small and numerous, rather than large and widely spaced. In contrast with modern garments, they were generally sewn along the edge of the fabric rather than slightly in from the edge.

A characteristic feature of Elizabethan clothing was the *point*, a ribbon or lace made of leather or braided silk and fitted with metal tips (called *tags* or *aglets*). Points were used to attach the breeches to the doublet or the skirt to the bodice, to lace in a pair of sleeves, or to close up a doublet or jerkin. They were passed through matching pairs of holes in the garments and tied in a half-bow. Hooks and eyes were used for the same range of purposes. In addition, Elizabethans depended heavily on pins to hold their clothes together: a man's ruff or falling band was typically pinned in place, while a woman would use pins extensively for her headgear, neckwear, and other garments.

Belts, Knives, and Purses

The belt, known as a *girdle,* was an important part of people's attire, not for holding up garments but as a place from which to hang personal possessions. Gentlemen's girdles were thin, with a fixed buckle in the front, and a sliding buckle on the side to adjust for size, with hooks for a hanger to hold a rapier. Ladies were likely to have chain girdles or girdles made of fine fabric. Among ordinary people, thin leather girdles or girdles of woven tape were common. A girdle might support a knife in a leather sheath; often it held a leather purse, closing with a drawstring or a flap. Purses might hold one or more small knit or cloth pouches. Toward the end of the century, belt-purses became less important for men, as pockets became more common.

Gentlemen, and many of lower station, often carried swords on their girdles. The fashionable sword of the period was the rapier, which featured a blade about a yard long and weighed some 2½ to 3 pounds. Rapiers made in the latter part of Elizabeth's reign often had elaborately swept hilts to protect to the hand. The rapier was an Italian innovation; it contrasted with the more traditional English sword in that it was longer and thinner (although not much lighter), being designed for thrusting with the point whereas the sword relied more on blows with the edge. The rapier often came with a matching dagger, easily distinguishable from a civilian knife by its larger size and its crossguard. A dagger might also be worn by itself. Such weapons could be of actual use in a society where street fights and brawls were known to break out in broad daylight, but for gentlemen they served primarily as an expression of social status and were likely to be highly ornate.

Miscellaneous Accessories

Hand wear ranged from functional, heavy work gloves or mittens used by laborers to the heavily embroidered and perfumed gloves with tassels and gold beads worn by noble ladies. Gloves were particularly fashionable among the aristocracy, who were rarely without them. Both gloves and mittens tended to have long flaring cuffs.

Working women commonly wore long aprons made of linen, and fashionable women had aprons made of rich fabrics. Tradesmen also wore short aprons, and blacksmiths had leather ones. Handkerchiefs were used in this period; among the wealthy, they might be richly adorned. Travelers often wore canvas or leather satchels, and perhaps a small wooden cask or leather bottle for drink slung over the shoulder. Fashionable ladies owned fans, which had long, straight handles, and were often made of ostrich feathers. In 1590 folding fans were introduced as the latest fashion accessory from France. Mirrors were sometimes suspended from the belt, even by women of fairly ordinary station.

Spectacles of the pince-nez type were used in Elizabeth's day, although they were only for close-up activities like reading—they were fitted with magnifying lenses like modern reading glasses. Sometimes they were made more secure by strings that passed around each ear.

Men and women alike wore jewelry, including rings, earrings, bracelets, necklaces, and pendants. Miniatures (small portraits set in a frame) were fashionable, as were watches, usually suspended on a chain around the neck or incorporated into other pieces of jewelry.

Cosmetics were widely used among fashionable women, and sometimes even by men. The favored look for women called for a very pale face, often with a touch of red in the cheeks and perhaps a tinting of the eyelids. The makeup used to achieve the fashionable whiteness was rather toxic, being based on lead oxide. Fashionable men and women also used perfumes.

Bathing may have been rare, but grooming was frequent, at least among those who aspired to social respectability. Children were taught to clean their nails and comb their hair every morning. Combs were made of ivory,

horn, or wood and had two sides: one broad-toothed for preliminary combing of tangled hair, the other fine-toothed for combing out smaller knots
once the larger tangles were removed. Brushes were usually reserved for
cleaning clothes. The very fastidious even owned *ear-spoons*, small ivory
tools for getting rid of earwax. People of high social standing often carried
small grooming kits in *comb cases*. Mirrors, or *looking glasses*, were used in
wealthy households, but were still a relative luxury; they could be made
of glass with a metallic backing, or of polished steel. Most people rarely
saw their own faces.

CLOTHING PATTERNS

The instructions on the following pages will enable you to create a complete Elizabethan outfit, male or female, in a style appropriate to the latter
part of Elizabeth's reign. All the patterns are based as far as possible on
surviving originals. Of course, this approach has some disadvantages. The
survival of original pieces has been haphazard, and surviving pieces are not
always well documented in published sources. To make things even harder,
it is generally the unusual examples that have survived. Nonetheless, the
patterns here will allow you to make an ordinary Elizabethan outfit with a
degree of historical accuracy that is very rare in practical costuming books.

The instructions here presuppose a basic knowledge of sewing. You may
want to consult an experienced seamster for additional help. Another useful
source is *Singer Sewing Step-by-Step* (Minnetonka, MN: Cy de Cosse, 1990),
which has brilliant instructions and illustrations to assist the home sewer.

The first step in successful costuming is making the right choice of fabrics. The instructions here suggest the fabrics from which the garments
were most likely to be made. Even if you do not choose to use linen or
wool, you can still use them as a guide in choosing an alternative fabric.
You might also wish to line and/or interline overgarments. Lining would
normally be of linen, interlining of heavy linen, canvas, or buckram,
depending on the desired stiffness. Most garments made of wool could
also have been made of linen or canvas.

Unless specified otherwise, the patterns do not include a seam allowance: remember to add an extra ½" around the edges. Be sure to press
seams as you sew them.

With any of the more complex patterns, it can be helpful to make a
mock-up, or fitting, of cheap material first—muslin is ideal for this purpose. You can make the necessary adjustments to this fitting, and proceed
to the real fabric when you are satisfied with the fit.

Smock

This pattern is based on a Swedish man's shirt of the late 1560s, but it is
intended here as one of the easiest styles of women's shirts to reproduce.[1]

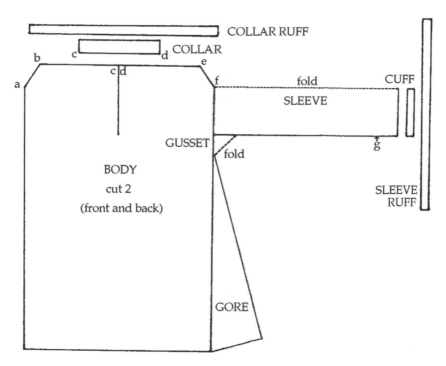

Pattern for a smock. The right side is as the left. [Hadfield/Forgeng]

The pattern has been altered by the addition of side-gores. This smock should require 3½ yds. of white linen; the ruffs might be of finer linen.

The exact measurements will depend on the wearer. The collar (**c-d**) should be about 2″ longer than your neck size (including seam allowance). The distance from the ends of the neck to the edge of the fabric (**a-b** and **e-f**) should be a bit longer than your shoulders. The length of the sleeve should equal the distance from your shoulder to your first knuckles, measured around your bent elbow. Adjust the overall length if desired—the smock should be fairly long, between knee-length and ankle-length. The neckline slash on the body is cut only on the front piece. Cut one each of the collar and collar ruff; two each of the body, gusset, sleeve, cuff, and sleeve ruff; and four of the gore.

Hem back the top and sides of the collar ruff. Hem back the side edges of the collar. Gather the collar ruff to the top of the collar (right sides together) and stitch in place. Press the seam allowances toward the collar so that the ruff stands up.

Hem back the front slit on the body front, and take in a small dart at the base of the slit. Sew the side gores to the body. Sew the body front to the body back at **a-b** and **e-f** (right sides together). Gather the top opening of the body (**c-b-e-d**) into the bottom of the collar (right sides together), matching **c** and **d** on the body to **c** and **d** on the collar. Stitch.

Treat the sleeve ruffs and cuffs as with the collar ruff and collar. Hem back the sleeve from **g** to the cuff edge. Gather the sleeve into the sleeve cuff (right sides together) and stitch. Stitch up the bottom edge of the sleeve from **g** to the beginning of the gusset, and stitch the gusset to the sleeve. Stitch the sleeve/gusset piece to the body. (For a more complete description of the gusset, see the pattern for the man's shirt below.)

Sew the outside edge of the side gores on each side together. Hem the bottom edge and add ties at the base of the cuff and collar.

Bodice

This design is based on a late-16th-century noblewoman's bodice.[2] A sleeveless bodice should require about 1 yd. of wool for the outer shell, 1 yd. of linen for a lining, and 1 yd. of canvas or buckram for an interlining. Add another 1 yd. of wool if you want sleeves (plus as much again for lining, if you want it).

The first step is to generate a pattern. Take a piece of denim-weight cloth and wrap your torso from armpit to hips, lifting your bust (it may help to wear a bra while doing this). Pin yourself in snugly, especially at bust and waist. Take the following measurements:

—Bust

—Waist

—Armpit to Waist

—Across Front (armpit to armpit)

Fold your fabric as shown and pin it in place. Rough-cut your pieces as shown—remember to allow ½" seam allowance. Note that the total measurement of the bottom of the back piece at the waistline (from point **d** to point **d** on the other side) is ⅕ of your waist measurement.

Cut the fore pieces from the back piece along a line midway between lines **a-b** and **c-d**. You will now have two fore pieces and one folded back piece. Pin line **a-b** to line **c-d**, and do the same with the other fore piece and the other side of the back piece. Remove all other pins, wrap the bodice around your torso, and pin the fore pieces together along CF line. Make sure each time you don the garment that you line up the waistline to your own waist.

Insert a new pin at CF waist to make the waist fit tightly. Measure the distance from the original CF waist pin to the new one, then remove this pin. Remove the bodice, and shift point **b** on each fore piece forward by this distance, so as to take in this amount at the side opening. On both sides, redraw the new line **a-b** and pin the new **a-b** to **c-d**.

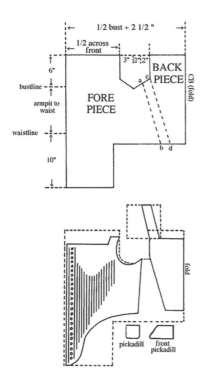

Pattern for a bodice. [Hadfield/For-geng]

Put the bodice on again. Redraw the armholes to fit your arms—they angle slightly from bottom front to upper back. Draw your neckline in front and back, and the bottom edge of your bodice as shown. Unpin CF and remove. Adjust your armholes, neckline, and bottom edge as needed to make them symmetrical. (The shaded area indicates the location of boning on the original—you can make this garment with boning if you choose.)

To design the shoulder straps, cut an 11x11" piece and pin it to the back piece as shown. Put the bodice on, then pin the shoulder piece to the front. Mark the desired shape for this strap—the outside edge should run along the edge of your shoulder.

At this point you have your patterns—you may want to make a paper copy in case you make another bodice in the future.

You can now cut your fabric. For the bodice, you will want a total of two fore pieces and one back piece cut of wool for the outer layer, two fore pieces and one back piece of linen for the lining, and two fore pieces and one back piece of canvas or buckram for the interlining (if you use boning, it will go between the lining and interlining). For the shoulder straps, you will want two straps of the wool, two of the lining, and two of the interlining. Remember to allow ½" for seams all around.

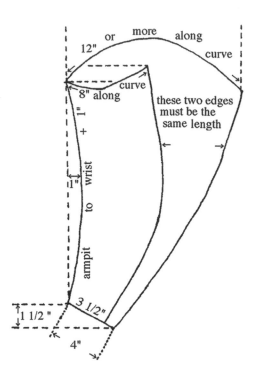

Pattern for a bodice sleeve.
[Hadfield/Forgeng]

You can now assemble the pieces. Pin the interlining pieces to their corresponding lining pieces, wrong sides together. Sew the lining/interlining
fore pieces to the back pieces along the line **a/c-b/d**, right sides together.
Sew the outer fore pieces to the outer back pieces in the same manner. Sew
the top and CF line of the outer layer to the top and CF line of the lining
layers, right side of the outer layer to the right side of the lining (leave the
armholes unsewn if you plan to add sleeves), *taking in a seam allowance of
1" at the CF line*—you will want to have the lacing holes pass through the
seam allowance, and this will also create a 1" gap at the front, giving you
some play when lacing up.

Of your outer fabric, cut two front pickadills and as many ordinary
pickadills as will be needed to reach around the bottom edge of the bodice
(the two front pickadills are mirror images of each other). Do the same
with the lining fabric. Pin each outer piece to its lining piece, right sides
together, and sew along the bottom and sides. Turn each pickadill right
side out. Pin the pickadills to the bottom edge of the outer layer of the
bodice, right sides together (the two front skirts flank the CF opening,
with the slanted side forward). Stitch. Turn in the bottom seam allowance
of the lining-interlining and finish.

For the shoulder straps, pin the lining pieces to the interlining pieces, wrong sides together. Then pin the lining/interlining pieces to the outer pieces, right side of the outer layer to the right side of the lining, and stitch along the ends and one long side. Turn right side out. Pin the straps to the place where they meet the back piece, with the raw edge facing outward. Put the bodice on, and pin the straps to the place where they meet the fore pieces. Remove the bodice, and sew the straps in place. If the bodice is sleeveless, press under the remaining seam allowance and sew shut.

Stitch lacing holes or apply grommets, at a spacing of about 1", at CF; lacing holes will work best if you stitch small rings onto the fabric around the holes. You might choose to insert rigilene boning on either side of the lacing holes, even if the rest of the bodice is not boned. (Rigilene boning is available from many sewing-supply stores.)

If the bodice will be worn as an outer layer, you may want a placket to cover the gap at CF. Cut a strip of the outer fabric 5" wide and as long as the front opening, plus 1" for seam allowances; cut a lining piece and an interlining piece of the same size. Sew these to each other along the long sides and one short side, right side of the outer fabric to the right side of the lining. Turn right side out, press, finish the open end, and sew it into the inside of the bodice to one side of the CF opening (behind the lacing holes, so that it doesn't get in the way of the lacing).

To make a sleeve, cut two pieces as shown (the two pieces are depicted one on top of the other: they share the same left edge). You can also cut lining pieces if you choose to have a lining. The actual length of the top curve on the larger piece will depend on how much gathering you choose to have; the total length of the top curve on the larger piece plus the top curve on the smaller piece must be at least 1" greater than the armhole it will be gathered into. Stitch the sleeve right sides together along both side edges. Gather the sleeve to the armhole, right sides together, lining up the front seam (the left one on the illustration) with the foremost point of the armhole. Stitch the sleeve to the armhole, finish the shoulder seams, and hem the cuff. The other sleeve is a mirror image of the first.

Roll

This pattern for a roll is based on visual evidence, as no originals are known to survive. Cut a piece of sturdy linen or light canvas **a-b-c-d** as shown above. Sides **a-b** and **c-d** will be equal to your hip measurement, **a-d** and **b-c** will be 12". Solidly hem sides **a-d** and **b-c**. Sew line **a-b** to line **d-c**, right sides together, creating a tube of fabric. Turn right side out. Pass a lace through the hems at the two ends. Tighten the lace and one end, gathering it shut, and stuff the roll with fabric scraps. Gather the other end shut, and use the laces to tie it on. It is worn slightly below the waist to accentuate the hips.

Pattern for a roll. [Hadfield/Forgeng]

Petticoat

This design for a woman's petticoat derives from an example of the early 17th century.[3] It should be ankle-length or toe-length, requiring about 8' of fabric: medium to heavy wool for an outer petticoat, linen or lighter wool for an underpetticoat. If you plan to wear a roll, make it first, as it will affect the design.

The easiest style to make is a drawstring petticoat. Cut the fabric crosswise into two panels as shown and sew them selvage to selvage (**c-d**). Sew the other selvages together (**a-b**), leaving the top 6" open. You now have a loop of fabric.

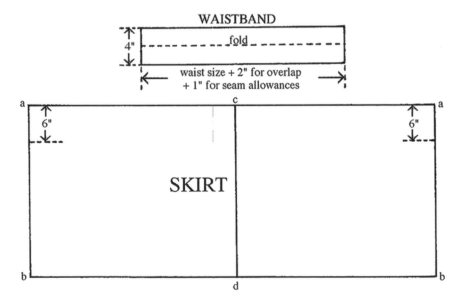

Pattern for a petticoat. [Hadfield/Forgeng]

If the overall circumference of this loop is greater than three times your waist measurement, you will need to trim the panels into trapezoids, until the measurement **a-c-a** is no greater than three times your waist (otherwise it will be too difficult to gather). This does not need to be done if the fabric will be pleated into a waistband, but it does need to be done if it is gathered to a waistband or drawstring.

Fold over 2" at the top of the loop and sew it down, creating a channel. Open a hole in the channel at the seam at point a, and thread a drawstring through. Put the roll on, put the skirt on, and draw the string tight, then have someone pin the bottom edge so that it reaches your ankle or toes. Remove and hem.

A more comfortable design in the long run (to which the drawstring petticoat can be converted) involves a waistband. Cut a strip of wool 4" wide and as long as your own waist size plus 2" for an overlap plus 1" for seam allowances. Fold the waistband as shown, right sides together, stitch up the ends, and turn right side out. Insert a strip of buckram or some other reinforcement. Gather or pleat the top edge of the petticoat to the seam allowance on the outside of the waistband, right sides together, leaving an extra 2" at one end of the waistband for the overlap. Stitch. Fold the waistband over, folding in the inside seam allowance, and stitch it closed. Use hooks to close the waistband—the petticoat can also be hooked or tied to the bodice to prevent gaping at the waist. You may add a placket to cover the opening in the petticoat.

Alternatively, you can use cartridge pleating, finishing the waistband first and sewing the pleats to it afterward.

Breeches

This design for a man's breeches is based on the photograph of a surviving Italian example of the late 16th century.[4] It will require 1 yd. of white linen.

Cutting: Cut two of each piece as shown.

—**a-b** = **a-f** = half waist measurement

—**b-c** = small of the back to midcrotch

—**d-e** = a bit more than half the circumference of the thigh

—**a-e** = hip to thigh (anywhere from midthigh to just above the knee)

—**f-c** = small of back to midcrotch

Sewing: Sew outseam of each leg (**a-e**), right side together. Sew inseam of each leg (**c-d**), right side together. Sew front and back seam (**f-c** and **b-c**), right sides together. Hem the cuffs. Fold over the top to make a channel for the drawstring: sew it down, open a hole at the front seam (at point **b**), and thread the drawstring through.

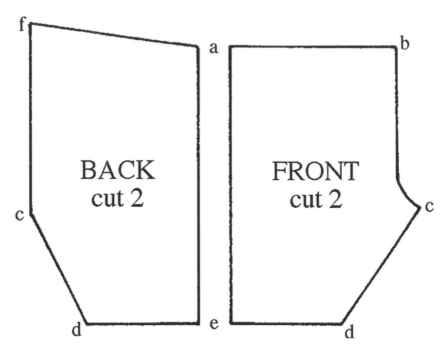

Pattern for a man's breeches. [Hadfield/Forgeng]

Shirt

This pattern is based on a man's shirt of the late 16th century.[5] It is shown without seam allowances. The shirt should require 3½ yds. of white linen.

Adjust the measurements as necessary. The collar should be 1" longer than your neck size (including seam allowance). The distance from the ends of the neck opening (**a**) to the sleeve should be a bit longer than your shoulders—narrow the neck opening if necessary. The length of the sleeve should equal the distance from your shoulder to your first knuckles, measured around your bent elbow.

Stitch the sleeve gusset to one side of the sleeve along **d-e.** Stitch the sleeve-gusset piece to the body. Do the same with the other sleeve. Fold the body-sleeve piece over crosswise and stitch up the sides (leaving open at the bottom as shown), stitching **f-g** on the gusset to **f-g** on the body. Stitch **g-e** on the gusset to **g-e** on the sleeve, and stitch up the rest of the sleeve from the gusset to the arrows. Do likewise with the other sleeve. Fold over ⅛" of the side reinforcements all around, and stitch to the point where the side seams end, as shown.

Hem back the open section of the sleeve seam. Fold the cuff along the dotted line, stitch up the ends, and turn right side out. Gather the cuff

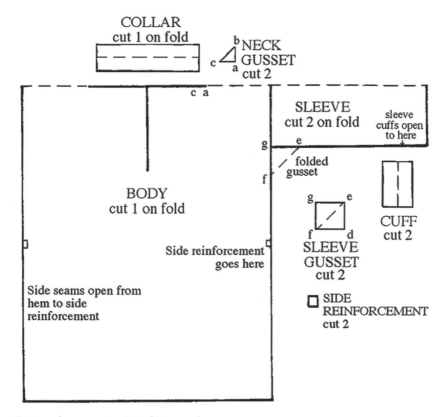

Pattern for a man's shirt. [Forgeng]

edge of the sleeve to the seam allowance on the outside of the cuff, right sides together. Stitch. Fold the cuff over, folding in the inside seam allowance, and stitch it closed.

Stitch the neck gussets into the ends of the neck openings, right sides together, matching points **a-b-c.** Hem back the front slit, and take in a small dart at the bottom. Fold over the collar and stitch as you did with the cuffs, and gather the neck opening into it as with the sleeves and the cuffs. Hem the bottom and the open edges of the sides, and add ties to the bottom edge of the collar and the sleeve edge of the cuffs. The original is heavily embroidered on the upper torso, collar, sleeves, and cuffs.

Venetian Breeches (Venetians)

This pattern for a man's Venetians is based on a pair from the early 17th century, probably of German origin.[6] The Venetians should require about 2–3 yds. of wool (and as much again for lining, if used) and a small amount of linen for the pockets (although these can be made of wool).

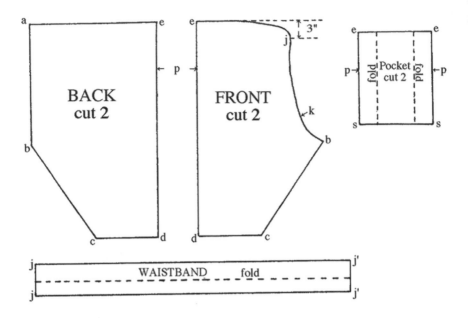

Pattern for Venetian breeches. [Hadfield/Forgeng]

Pattern: The easiest way to proceed is to don a pair of trousers and take a few measurements to draft a pattern based on the one shown here.

—**a-e** = **e-j** = ⅓ to ½ hip measurement, depending on how full you want them

—**a-b** = top rear of trousers to crotch

—**b-c** = crotch to 3″ below the knee along inseam

—**c-d** = ½ bottom cuff opening

—**e-d** = top of trousers to 3″ below the knee along outseam

—**j-i** = top front to crotch

—**j-k** = 7″

—**e-p** = 7″

—**j-j'** = waist size (remember to add seam allowances)

—**j-j** = **j'-j'** = 3″ (remember to add seam allowances)

—**e-s** = 16″

—**e-e** = **s-s** = 13″

Cutting: You will need two of each piece except the waistband.

Sewing: On the back and front pieces, sew point e to point e, and sew the outseam of each leg (**p-d**), leaving pocket slit open (**e-p**). On the pocket, sew point **e** to point **e** and **p-s** to p-s, leaving a slit from **e** to **p**. Fold the pocket along the dotted lines and sew across the bottom. Turn the pocket so the seam allowances are inside. Pin the slit of the pocket to the pocket slit in the outseam of the Venetians (**p-e**), right sides together and from the outside of the Venetians. Sew around the pocket slit, and turn the pocket in (you will have to sew the ends of the slit by hand).

Sew the inseam of each leg (**b-c**). Sew center back seam (**a-b**). Sew center front seam from **b** to **k**.

Fold the waistband on the dotted line, sew up the ends, and turn right side out. Gather the top of the breeches to the seam allowance on the outside of the waistband, right sides together, with the top end of the pockets caught into the waistband (the pockets are not gathered), and matching the ends of the waistband to points **j** and **j'** on the Venetians. Stitch. Fold the waistband over, folding in the inside seam allowance, and stitch it closed.

Finish the fly (**j-k**) and cuffs, add three buttons and buttonholes to the fly opening, and attach hooks and eyes to fasten the waistband. You may also use hooks and eyes to attach the waistband to the bottom of the doublet, and at the cuffs to make them fit your leg more tightly (this works best if you leave open a few inches of the inseam or outseam at the bottom). A placket can also be added at the fly.

Doublet

The design given here is based primarily on an Italian doublet of the 1570s.[7] You should need about 3 yds. of wool for a man, 2 to 2½ for a woman (and as much linen for lining, if used). It may be advisable to use a fairly stiff fabric or to reinforce it with a stiff lining, perhaps including an interlining. Use a medium weight wool and a sturdy lining fabric for best results. The same basic design can be used for a sleeveless jerkin.

Pattern: The surest means of making a doublet fit properly is to make the pattern from an old fitted shirt.

—Cut off the collar of the shirt.

—Cut off the bottom of the shirt to shape of the doublet as shown. Point **c** is 4" below the waist; **b** is at the waist.

—Cut the shirt in two down the middle of the back.

—Cut off the sleeves at the armhole seams.

—Cut the sleeve down the seam to give the sleeve pattern.

—Cut the shoulder seam of the shirt body (this is normally at the front of the shoulder panel on the shirt).

—Cut the underarm side seam of the shirt to give the fore and back pieces.

—The length of the collar will be equal to the distance around the neckline, plus 1" for seam allowances.

—The wings and pickadills are optional.

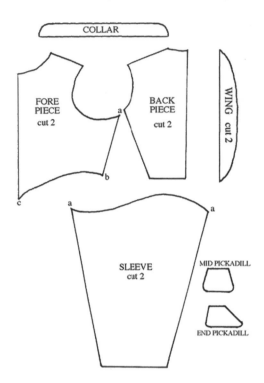

Pattern for a doublet. [Forgeng]

Cutting: Cut two each of the fore, back, and sleeve pieces (omit the sleeve pieces for a sleeveless jerkin). If you want a lining, cut two each of the fore, back, and sleeve pieces. If you use an interlining, cut two each of the fore and back pieces. If there is no lining, allow a 1″ seam allowance at the front opening to support the buttons and buttonholes.

For wings, cut four of the outer fabric. Cut two of the interlining (without seam allowances) if you have it.

For pickadills, you will need two end pickadills to go on each side of the front opening, and as many mid pickadills as are needed (measure the total bottom edge of the body, subtract 4″ for the two end pickadills, and divide by 3). For each pickadill, cut one of the outer fabric and one of the lining fabric. The end pickadills are mirror images of each other.

For the collar, cut one of the outer fabric and one of the lining. Cut one of the interlining (without seam allowances) if you have it.

Sewing: Sew the front pieces to the back piece at the shoulder seam, right sides together. Sew the sleeves to the armholes of the body, matching point **a.**

If you want wings, you will need to insert them *before* sewing the sleeves to the armholes. To make a wing, sew two outer pieces along the curved side, right sides together, and turn right side out. Insert the interlining if you have it. When you pin the sleeves to the body, insert the wing between the right side of the body and the right side of the sleeve, lining up the raw edges of all three pieces together and making sure the midpoint of the wing lies at the shoulder seam. When you sew the sleeve to the armhole, you will also be sewing the wing in place.

Sew up the sleeve and side seams.

If you have a lining, assemble it as you did the outer layer (it will not have wings). Sew it to the outer piece along the CF, right sides together. Turn right side out, and push the lining sleeves through the outer sleeves.

For the collar, sew the outer fabric piece to the lining piece, right sides together, leaving the bottom edge open. Turn right side out. Insert the interlining, if you have it. Sew the neckline of the body to the outer seam allowance of the collar, right sides together, matching the raw edges. Fold the collar over, folding the inner seam allowance in, and stitch it shut. If you have a lining, you will stitch the lining of the collar to the lining of the body.

If you want pickadills, see the instructions for them under the bodice pattern. Otherwise fold over the bottom seam allowance and finish. Fold over the cuff seam allowance and finish.

The doublet normally buttons up the CF; buttonholes would be 1" to 1¾" apart (depending on button size). You may also add hooks around the waist to support eyes to hold up the breeches; if you are ambitious, you could consider matching rows of paired eyelets in the doublet and in the waistband of the Venetians for points. The sleeves could also be attached with hooks and eyes or laces to make them removable.

Coif

The original on which this coif is based is said to have belonged to Queen Elizabeth; it is made of white linen and is heavily adorned with embroidery.[8] The piece measures 17" by 8¾". After cutting, hem the entire coif. Fold on the dotted line, and sew **a-c** to **a-c.** Thread a small string through the top from **c** to **c,** gather, and secure the ends of the string. Gather the

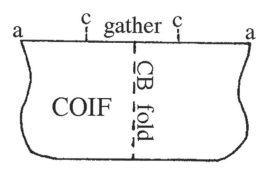

Pattern for a coif. [Hadfield/ Forgeng]

bottom edge in the same manner, or use a lace, the ends of which can be used to hold the coif on your head.

Flat Cap

The flat cap is the easiest type of male Elizabethan headgear to reproduce. It might also be worn by women over a coif. Use wool for the outer layer, with linen for a lining if you want one, and sturdy canvas or buckram to stiffen the brim. The design is based on an Italian man's flat cap of the 1560s.[9]

The diameter of the hole in the brim piece is such that it will fit snugly over the head—probably around 6″. The brim should be about 1½″. The diameter of the crown piece will be the diameter of the brim piece plus twice the width of the brim. Cut two brim pieces and one crown piece; cut another crown piece of lining fabric if you want lining. Sew the outside edges of the brim pieces together, right sides together, and turn right side out to make the brim. You may wish to insert a third brim piece of stiffer fabric to make the cap less floppy—canvas or buckram are two possibilities. Then gather the outside edge of the crown piece into the inside edge of the upper brim piece to make the crown. Finish the edges, and the cap will be complete.

Netherstocks and Garters

Woolen socks that reach the knee are available for cross-country skiing and mountain climbing. For knitters, patterns are also available.[10] If you

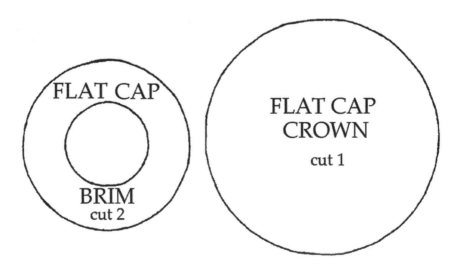

Pattern for a flat cap. [Hadfield/Forgeng]

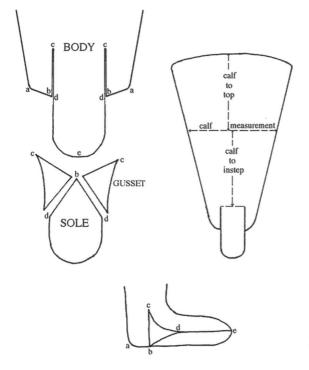

Pattern for cloth hose.
[Hadfield/Forgeng]

choose to make hose of a woven fabric, the weave should be loose and cut on the bias to allow for a snug fit. The following design is based on a number of surviving examples.[11] They can be made with 2 yds. of fabric (1½ yds. for a woman). Wool will give the best fit; linen is also possible, although it will not have the same stretch.

Draft your hose as follows:

—**a-a** = the measurement around heel and instep

—**c-c** = **d-d** = half the measurement around the broad part of your foot

—line **a-b** is drawn at a slight angle

—**b-c** = **c-d** = half the distance from anklebone to anklebone measured under the sole

—lines **b-e** and **d-d** on the sole intersect at the broadest point of the foot (measure its distance from the toe)

—**b-e** = the distance from heel to toe less **a-b**

—**d-e-d** on the body is the same as **d-e-d** on the sole

—the measurements on the gussets are the same as the measurements on the body and sole

Extend the body upward as follows:

The distance from the calf line to the top is the distance from the thick of the calf to the knee + 6".

When cutting, do not worry about the lack of a seam allowance in the slashes on the body: just stitch them close to the edge.

Using zigzag stitch to prevent breakage of the thread, sew up the stocking, right sides together:

—Sew around the slashes, close to the edges, to prevent raveling.

—Sew the gussets to the sole.

—Sew the gussets to the slashes on the body.

—Sew the foot of the body to the sole.

—Sew up the heel and body, curving the seam around the heel.

Try the stockings on the opposite feet, still inside out. Repin seams (primarily the long heel-leg seam) to fit them as closely to your leg as you can without making it impossible to pull the stockings on and off. Remove, and restitch, using the new seam lines. Cut away the excess seam allowance, and finish seams and top. Don't worry about the tendency for these stockings to bag at the ankle and twist around the leg: cloth stockings by nature did not fit as snugly as knitted ones.

Garters are strongly recommended, as they can save the aggravation of having your stockings slide down your legs. They can be made of strips of fabric at least 39" long and 1–4" broad. If the fabric is springy, so much the better, as it will allow a better fit. This can be achieved by cutting a woven fabric on the bias; a quick and easy route is to use bias tape. Alternatively, you could knit a strip of wool about 1–2" wide and at least 2' long, alternating knit and purl stitches in both directions. Cross-garters, which wrap

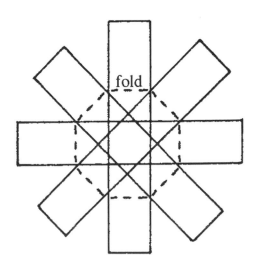

Pattern for a shoe rosette.
[Hadfield/Forgeng]

around the legs twice, once above the knee and once below, will have to be considerably longer.

Shoes

Shoes are much harder to make, but certain styles of bedroom slipper strongly resemble the plainer style of Elizabethan shoe. Tai-chi shoes are an alternative, with or without the strap: the design is again similar to that of Elizabethan shoes, although they would normally have been of leather instead of cloth.

Your shoes can be given a more distinctively Elizabethan look by adding rosettes, which can be made with four ribbons (preferably two each of two contrasting colors) roughly 7"x ¾". Sew them together in the middle as illustrated. Fold the ends over so that they overlap each other in the center back, and sew them in place. Then attach them to the shoe.

Falling Band

This design for a man's falling band derives from visual evidence and surviving examples from the early 17th century.[12] The band should be of linen. The collar piece is 25" long, 4¾" deep at the ends, and 3¾" deep in the middle. The neckband is 4" deep before folding, and as long as your neck measurement (remember to add ½" at each end for the seam allowance).

The eight pleats on the collar piece are evenly spaced and deep enough to make the curved edge equal to your neck measurement. The first pleat on each end is ¼ of your neck measurement away from the edge, so that it lies over the midpoint of your shoulder. Pin the pleats up and press: each

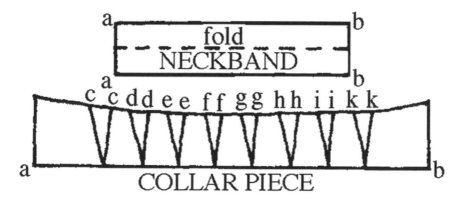

Pattern for a falling band. [Hadfield/Forgeng]

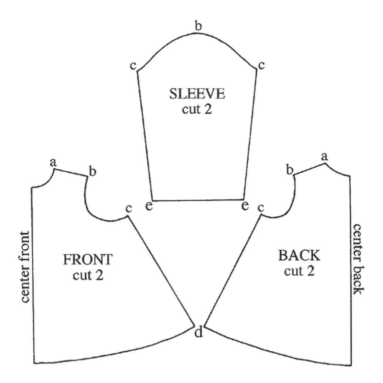

Pattern for a cassock. [Hadfield/Forgeng]

pleat folds forward, so that the opening faces the back of the neck (the pleats lie on the underside of the collar). Hem the bottom and sides of the collar piece by ⅛″. Sew the pleats shut on top with a hemming stitch.

Fold the neckband along the dotted line, and sew up the sides. Turn right side out. Sew the collar piece to the outside seam allowance of the neckband, right sides together. Fold the neckband over, fold back the inside seam allowance, and stitch shut. Attach flexible ties, about 5″ long, to the top of the fore-edge of the neck piece.

The collar should be pinned to the doublet and folded down over the doublet collar. Cuffs can be constructed in the same manner as the falling band.

Cassock

The cassock is a good warm garment for both men and women. The design given here is based on a mid-17th-century Swedish example, adjusted to make it closer to 16th-century illustrations.[13] The cassock should require 2 yds. of wool. Two of each piece will be needed. Sew the back pieces together at the CB seam. Sew the fore pieces to the back at the shoulder seams. Sew the sleeve to the armhole, and stitch up the sides and sleeve seam. Hem the neckline and cuffs; if the wool is sufficiently felted, you will not need to hem the bottom edge.

The cassock can fasten with buttons all the way down the front, or just a few at the top, with the remainder of the front sewn up. The side seams can be sewn shut, left open, or fastened with buttons or ties. The sleeves could be omitted. If you decide to add a lining, remember not to sew the lower edge of the garment to the lining: this will attract rainwater.

Buttons

Button-making kits are an easy means of reproducing the look of Elizabethan cloth-covered buttons, although the originals would have been more round. Try to get small ones—Elizabethan buttons tended to be under ¾" in diameter. When choosing a button kit, try to be sure that the shank comes attached to the face rather than to the back plate; buttons of the latter type are less sturdy. You can also make an Elizabethan button entirely of cloth: cut a 1½" diameter circle, then sew a 1" diameter gathering stitch around it. Gather the stitch, stuffing the edge of the circle into the center as you do, and sew it up. Buttons were generally sewn to the edge of the garment, rather than slightly in from the edge as is usual today.[14]

NOTES

1. A. M. Nylen, "Stureskjortorna," *Livrustkammaren* 4 (1948): 8–9, 217–76.

2. Janet Arnold, *Patterns of Fashion: The Cut and Construction of Clothes for Men and Women c.1560–1620* (New York: Drama Books, 1985), 112–13 [#46].

3. Arnold, *Patterns*, 116–17 [#51].

4. Millia Davenport, *The Book of Costume* (New York: Crown, 1948), 633.

5. Janet Arnold, "Elizabethan and Jacobean Smocks and Shirts," *Waffen- und Kostümkunde* 19 (1977): 102.

6. Arnold, *Patterns*, 86–87 [#21].

7. Arnold, *Patterns*, 55–56 [#3]. For the wings and pickadills and an example of a jerkin, compare 70–71 [#9].

8. Davenport, *Costume*, 445.

9. Arnold, *Patterns*, 55–56 [#22].

10. For a pattern, see Weaver's Guild of Boston, *17th Century Knitting Patterns as Adapted for Plimoth Plantation* (Boston: n. p., 1990), 18–24.

11. This design is based on one given by Richard Rutt, *A History of Hand Knitting* (Loveland, CO: Interweave Press, 1987), 74.

12. M. Channing Linthicum, *Costume in the Drama of Shakespeare and His Contemporaries* (Oxford: Clarendon Press, 1936), 160; Davenport, *Costume*, 636; Norah Waugh, *The Cut of Men's Clothes 1600–1900* (London: Faber and Faber, 1964), 25.

13. Waugh, *Men's Clothes*, 31, pl. 5.

14. For examples of various types of buttons, see the various garments analyzed in Arnold, *Patterns*.

7
Food and Drink

Food ranks among the most important of human needs, a fact of which the Elizabethans were more acutely aware than is sometimes true today. By Renaissance standards, the Elizabethans were well fed. Travelers from the Continent were often impressed by the Englishman's hearty diet: even the husbandman ate reasonably well compared to the Continental peasant. Yet in England as elsewhere during the 16th century, food production was a laborious and precarious endeavor. Agriculture was back-breaking work, which by modern standards yielded only low returns in produce. Worse, it was extremely susceptible to natural misfortunes: mysterious illnesses could devastate livestock, and a summer that was too dry or too wet would lead to poor harvests, skyrocketing food prices, and famine. The harvests of Elizabeth's reign were relatively good, but severe shortages in 1586–88 and 1594–98 led to widespread hunger and mortality. Even in a good year, poverty and malnutrition were never wholly out of sight of those who had steady sources of income: the poor were always highly visible in Elizabethan England. Not surprisingly, there seems to have been less waste of food: when an aristocratic family finished eating, the leftovers were given to the servants; when the servants were done, the remains were brought to the door for distribution to the poor.

MEALS

The first meal of the day was breakfast, which was generally an informal bite on the run rather than a sit-down meal. Many people did not take

An Elizabethan meal. [By permission of the Folger Shakespeare Library]

breakfast at all but waited until dinner in the late morning. Those who did have breakfast might eat right after rising or up to several hours later. A simple breakfast might consist of a pottage (porridge or stew) or leftovers from previous meals. A more hearty breakfast could include bread with butter or cheese, ale or wine, fruit, and some sort of meat—beef, mutton, or chicken.

The real meals were dinner, served around 11 A.M. or noon, and supper in the evening, somewhere from 6 P.M. to 9 P.M. For ordinary people, the midday dinner was probably the largest meal of the day, while the privileged classes often had their principal meal in the evening. A simple meal might be served all at once, but in wealthy households—or on special occasions like holy days—a meal might consist of several courses, each containing multiple dishes, with cheese and fruits at the end of the meal. Sweet dishes would be included in each course, rather than served at the end. One contemporary cookbook offers the following sample menu:

The First Course: Pottage or stewed broth; boiled meat or stewed meat, chickens and bacon, powdered [salted] beef, pies, goose, pig, roasted beef, roasted veal, custard.

 The Second Course: Roasted lamb, roasted capons, roasted conies [rabbits], chickens, peahens, baked venison, tart.[1]

DINNER AT A TOWNSMAN'S HOME

Wife Go cause the folk to sit which are in the hall, and I go to the kitchen to cause to serve the board.

Father Make speed then, I pray you, for truly I am hungry. Masters, you be all welcome: I am sorry that I make you tarry so long.

Guests No force, sir, we do warm us in the mean while. Come near the fire, come warm you.

Father Truly I am more hungry than a cold. Go to, let us wash hands . . .

James What is your pleasure mother?

Wife Where are you? Why went you not to meet your father, and your uncle? I will tell your master: I will cause you to be beaten. Go quickly, say grace, and take your sister by the hand. Take off your cap, and make curtsey.

James Well mother, I go thither. You are welcome father, and all your company . . .

Wife Joan, is the children's table covered?

Joan Not yet mistress.

Wife Bring their round table: and make them dine there at the board's end. Read a chapter or two of the New Testament, whilst they make ready your table. . . . Husband, I pray you pull in pieces that capon, and help your neighbour: truly he eateth nothing.

Father Tarry a little wife, I have not yet tasted of these cabbages.

Wife You cannot eat of them, for they be too much peppered and salted.

Father Ah, what pity is that? It is the meat that I love best, and it is marred: they say commonly in England that God sendeth us meat, and the Devil cooks.

Claudius Hollyband, *The French Schoolmaster* (London: Abrahame Veale, 1573), 86–102.

These formal meals were not the only times people ate. Those who felt hungry during the day might have a bit of bread or cold food, and perhaps a bit of ale. During haymaking and harvesting seasons, rural folk took their food into the fields; common harvesting fare included bottled beer, apple pasties (a sturdy, hand-sized pastry), bread, cheese, and butter. At the other end of the social scale, an aristocratic hunting party might bring along cold meats, pies, and sausages.

DIET

Bread, a prominent feature of everyone's diet, was always present at meals, although contemporaries agreed that it was less important in England than on the Continent. Wheat was the favored grain for bread, and whiter breads were preferred to dark ones, although even the whit-

---

REGULATIONS ON FOOD AND MEASURES

Innholders, cooks, and victualers are not only by the laws and ancient good orders of this realm forbidden to bake, seethe, or roast any fish or flesh twice, or sell and utter unto the subjects any manner of corruptible victuals, which may be to the hurt and infection of man's body; but also that they shall not utter and sell their ale and beer within or without their houses by retail or otherwise unto any the Queen's Majesty's subjects, with any false or unsealed measures, lesser than the standard beforementioned . . . Item, if any butcher, fishmonger, innholder, victualer, baker, poulter, or any other whatsoever, which shall sell any victuals unto the subjects at any excessive price or prices otherwise than the plenty or scarcity of the time, and the distance of carriage of the same considered, shall accord with equity and good conscience, then mayors, bailiffs, and other chief officers of cities, boroughs, and towns corporate shall have full power and authority to enquire and examine all such offenses and defaults therein done and committed, and to inflict punishment on the offenders.

The Assize of Bread (London: John Windet, 1600), sig. F1r-v.

---

est Elizabethan bread was almost as brown as a modern whole-wheat loaf. The finest bread was the small hand-loaf called a *manchet.* Commercial manchets typically weighed 8 oz. when they went into the oven and 6 oz. when they came out—the price of a loaf of bread was fixed by law, but the weights were allowed to change according to the current price of grain. The next highest grade was called *cheat,* which was less refined; a cheat loaf weighed 18 oz. going into the oven and 16 oz. when it came out. Poorer people often made do with rye, barley, or mixed-grain bread; beans, peas, oats, tares, and lentils were used in times of dearth. Breads were not baked in pans, so they were low and round rather than tall. Bread would go stale after a few days, since there were no preservatives to keep it fresh. However, nothing was wasted: stale bread could be used to make bread puddings, and bread crumbs served to thicken soups, stews, and sauces. An alternative to bread was biscuit, which kept longer and was especially useful aboard ships. Unground oats and barley were used in pottages and stews, as was imported rice.

Contemporaries agreed that just as bread was less prominent in the English diet than it was on the Continent, meat was correspondingly more so—according to the Elizabethan traveler Fynes Moryson, England was particularly noted for the quality of its roast meats. A greater variety of meat was consumed in the 16th century than is common today. Red meats included beef, mutton, veal, lamb, kid, and pork. For poultry there were chickens, ducks, geese, and even pigeons. Game meats included deer, rabbit, and an enormous variety of wildfowl—for example, larks, sparrows, pheasants, partridge, quail, crane, plovers, and woodcocks. Another distinctive feature of Elizabethan cuisine was that very little of the animal went to waste: cookbooks for prosperous households include recipes for pigs' and calves' feet, lamb's head, and tripe.

Seafood was another important source of protein—in fact, fish were a much larger part of the Elizabethan diet than is generally the case today. English fishermen exported a great deal of cod and herring, the coasts abounded in oysters and mussels, and the rivers supplied freshwater fish and eels. Popular seafood included flounder, mackerel, carp, pike, salmon, trout, shrimp, crab, and even the occasional porpoise or seal. During the season of Lent, people were supposed to abstain from eating meat, relying on fish instead: this was no longer a religious requirement, as England was a Protestant country, but the ban was reinstated by Elizabeth as a means of supporting English fisheries (and thereby English sea power in general). The same rule applied on Wednesdays, Fridays, and Saturdays, as well as throughout Advent and on the eves of certain holy days; in total, it accounted for over a third of the year. This fasting was not rigorously observed by Elizabeth's subjects—one could purchase an exemption, and the Queen herself refused to be bound by the decree, although she saw to it that everyone else at her court was served no meat on fast days. Nevertheless, seafood was a handy staple: it was relatively cheap, it was available fresh in much of the country, and it could be preserved by salting, drying, or pickling.

The truly poor probably derived most of their protein from what was termed *white meat*: milk, eggs, butter, and cheese. Cheese featured in the aristocratic diet too, being commonly served at the end of a meal. Nuts were another source of protein: chestnuts, walnuts, and hazelnuts were all common.

Vegetables probably played a larger part in the Elizabethan diet than is sometimes supposed today. Houses normally had gardens, even in the middle of London; these provided a variety of vegetables for the household, including artichokes, asparagus, cucumbers, endive, radish, spinach, lettuce, beans, cabbage, carrots, leeks, parsnips, peas, and turnips. Fruits were also a regular part of the diet: they were used to flavor dishes and were often served at the end of a meal. Domestically produced fruit included apricots, grapes, figs, strawberries, raspberries, apples, pears, plums, currants, mulberries, and cherries. England also imported certain fruits, especially oranges and lemons from the Mediterranean.

Fruits were probably the principal source of sugar for most people. Honey, although not cheap, was a common sweetener. Refined sugar was expensive—about a shilling a pound—although still within the reach of people of means. People at the top of the social scale liked to indulge in a variety of sweet foods, including gingerbreads and cakes, candies, marzipan, conserves, and marmalade—ordinary people probably had such foods only on special occasions, such as holy days.

Spices, like sugar, were expensive. Then as now, they were mainly imported from Asia, but their transport was much more difficult, dangerous, and time-consuming than it is today. Consequently, the use of spices was a good way to demonstrate one's social position. Elizabethan recipes call for a distinctive range of spices, particularly cinnamon, nutmeg, cloves, mace, saffron, ginger, and pepper. Other imported flavoring agents were capers, olives, and lemons.

Ordinary people relied more on the seasonings that grew in their household gardens, such as cress, fennel, mint, onions, scallions, marjoram, parsley, rosemary, sage, savory, thyme, and tarragon. Mustard was a particular favorite, especially in sauces for dressing meats. Vinegar and oil were popular, as was *verjuice*, the sour juice of the crabapple. Salt was the commonest flavoring agent of all; it appears in many Elizabethan recipes, and it was always set out on the table at mealtimes. One last additive worth noting is flowers, which provided both flavor and coloring: marigolds, primroses, and violets were commonly used in this way.

Some staples of the modern table were either rare or wholly unavailable in Elizabethan England. This is especially true of New World plants such as coffee, vanilla, and cocoa. Tomatoes had arrived in southern Europe but not yet in England. Potatoes were first imported to England during Elizabeth's reign: they were an extremely expensive delicacy!

The content of a meal depended very much on the season, since many kinds of food did not keep or transport well. In November, people at the low end of the economic scale would slaughter any excess pigs they planned to eat during the winter. The meats were preserved by smoking or salting; bacon, ham, and sausage were all familiar winter fare. Fish were likewise smoked, dried, or salted. Salted meats were soaked before cooking to remove some of the excess salt, but they tended to be fairly salty nonetheless. Butter and cheese were essentially ways to preserve milk by reducing its water content, and they were also preserved by salting. Another means of preservation was pickling, especially for seafoods and vegetables. Fruits, peas and beans could be preserved by drying; fruits were also made into preserves.

THE KITCHEN

At all levels of society, the conditions under which a meal was prepared would be beyond the skills of most modern cooks. All cooking involved an actual fire, requiring a fair bit of attention to control the cooking temperature. There were three principal ways of cooking a main dish: boiling, roasting, or baking. Of these, boiling was the easiest and probably the most common. It involved placing the food in a pot over hot coals or an open flame. Many pots had legs so they could be set directly in the fire, and fireplaces typically had chains and hooks for suspending pots; sometimes a ratchet allowed the pot to be moved up or down to adjust the temperature. Once the food was set to boil it needed relatively little attention, so boiled soups, pottages (stews), and meats were convenient dishes for busy housewives. Frying similarly involved laying the pan on a gridiron over the fire.

Roasts were turned on a spit next to the fire, with a dripping-pan below to catch the grease—a by-product that might be used in other recipes or in providing domestic lighting. Roasting was a laborious procedure, since the spit had to be turned constantly. Some kitchens had automatic devices for this job, powered by the rising heat of the fire, but usually it was done by hand, often by the children of the house or the lowest-ranking kitchen servants.

Baking involved an enclosed clay or brick oven, sometimes built as a separate structure outside the home to reduce the risk of fire. A fire was lit inside the oven and allowed to burn until the interior was sufficiently hot, at which point the coals were raked out, the baking surface wiped with a damp rag-mop called a *malkin*, and the food slid inside with a *pell* (a flat long-handled wooden shovel) to bake in the residual heat. Those who could not afford a proper oven might bake under a crock turned upside down and covered with coals. Probably the commonest form of baked dish was the pie, which might stuffed with meat, poultry, fish, shellfish, fruit, or vegetables. The crust or *coffin* was often a heavy paste that served merely to seal up the food—it was not actually eaten.

Cooking utensils were typically made of clay, iron, copper, or brass. Because copper and its alloys (such as bronze and brass) are less susceptible than iron to rust and can transmit heat very quickly, they are good for heating water. Iron, on the other hand, transmits heat more slowly but spreads it more evenly, and after long use, it acquires an oily coating that keeps food from sticking to it. For these reasons, iron was the better material for cooking food. Clay pots were also useful for cooking, since they could be placed very close to the fire and conduct heat quite evenly.

A well-appointed kitchen would also have a wooden kneading-trough for making bread and a mortar and pestle for grinding. To protect the flour from vermin, it was kept in legged wooden bins called *meal arks*. Spices and dried fruits might be stored in small boxes or clay pots; vinegar, oil, and other liquids in leather, earthenware, or glass bottles. Additional storage was provided by baskets and linen and canvas bags and sacks. Spices were normally stored whole, to be ground as needed. Salt was kept in special salt boxes. The kitchen would be provided with cupboards and shelves for storing all of these utensils and provisions.

DRINKS

Water was not a particularly healthy drink in Elizabethan England due to poor sanitation in the cities and natural impurities in country water. Under the circumstances, fermented drinks were actually the healthier choice, since the brewing process and alcoholic content tended to inhibit bacteria. The traditional English beverage was ale, made of water, malted barley, herbs and spices; it lacked hops, so it tasted little like what we call ale today, and its shelf life was short. The closest modern equivalents in flavor are the spiced ales of Belgium and northern France. Beer—similar to ale but brewed with hops—had come to be favored in the cities. Beer was lighter and clearer than ale; the hops also made it keep longer, which made it cheaper. The best beer was one to two years old, but usually it was consumed after just a month of aging.

Ale varied greatly in strength, from the watery small ales to *double ale*, or even the rather expensive *double-double*, sometimes known by such evocative names as Mad Dog, Huffcap, Father Whoreson, and Dragons' Milk. Ale was the staple drink of Elizabethan England, having nutritional properties as well as being a source of water for the body. As a daily staple it was generally consumed in forms with very low alcohol content: children drank it as well as adults, and people would drink it when they breakfasted and throughout the working day. A gallon a day seems to have been a normal ration for a grown man.

Wine in Elizabethan England was invariably imported, since English grapes were unsuitable for winemaking. What the Elizabethans called French wine came from the north of France; wines from southern France, such as the modern Bordeaux, were known to the Elizabethans as Gascon wine or *claret*. Rhenish wines, both red and white, were also enjoyed in England; other wines came from Italy and even Greece. The favorite imports appear to have been the sweet fortified wines of the Iberian peninsula, especially *sack*, imported from Jerez (whence its modern name, *sherry*), and *madeira* and *canary*, respectively, from the Madeira and Canary Islands off the northwest coast of Africa. The English liked their wines sweet and would often sugar them heavily. Because it was imported, wine was quite expensive—typically 12 times the cost of ale—so it was primarily a drink for the privileged. For reasons of health (and perhaps expense), many people would add water to their wine.

Although English grapes were not used for winemaking, other English fruits yielded a range of alternative drinks. These included cider from apples, perry from pears, and *raspie* from raspberries. Other fruits used in winemaking included gooseberries, cherries, blackberries, and elderberries. Mead and metheglin, made with honey, were common in Wales and were also known in England. Distilled liquors were also in use, albeit mostly for medicinal purposes: the commonest was known as aqua vitae. There were also mixed drinks, notably posset, an ale drink vaguely comparable to eggnog, and syllabub, a similar concoction soured with cider or vinegar. Both wine and beer might be seasoned with herbs and spices—spiced wine was often called *hippocras*. Milk was not normally consumed plain, but whey, the watery part of milk that remains after coagulated curds are removed, was sometimes drunk by children, the poor, and the infirm.

The Elizabethans closely associated drink with tobacco, which was served along with beer in alehouses. In fact, it was common to speak of *drinking* tobacco smoke. Tobacco was first brought to England from the New World during Elizabeth's reign, and it quickly became widely popular. Some, like King James of Scotland (soon to be king of England as well), reviled the new weed, but most authorities believed it had great medicinal powers. In the words of one contemporary author, "Our age has discovered nothing from the New World which will be numbered among the remedies more valuable and efficacious than this plant for sores, wounds, affections of the throat and chest, and the fever of the plague."[2]

Elizabethan tobacco was considerably stronger and more narcotic than modern commercial versions. A Swiss visitor to England in 1599 was struck by the English fondness for the tobacco-pipe:

The habit is so common with them, that they always carry the instrument on them, and light up on all occasions, at the play, in the taverns or elsewhere, drinking as well as smoking together, as we sit over wine, and it makes them riotous and merry, and rather drowsy, just as if they were drunk, though the effect soon passes. And they use it so abundantly because of the pleasure it gives, that their preachers cry out on them for their self-destruction, and I am told the inside of one man's veins after death was found to be covered in soot just like a chimney.[3]

TABLEWARE

In the Middle Ages the dining table had most often been a temporary board set upon trestles, but by the late 16th century the trestle table had generally been supplanted by the permanent *table dormant*. At mealtimes this table was covered with a white linen tablecloth. A typical place setting consisted of a drinking vessel, a knife and spoon, a trencher (wooden plate), a bowl, and a linen napkin.

Elizabethan drinking vessels were quite varied. Some were plain beakers of ceramic, horn, or pewter; others were fine goblets of glass, silver, or gold. Very poor folk might drink from a wooden bowl (a custom observed by many at Christmastime when drinking the wassail, or spiced ale). One of the most distinctive Elizabethan drinking vessels was the *black jack*, a mug made of leather and sealed with pitch. Drinks were poured from jugs, which were made of the same range of materials as the drinking vessels themselves. The jug might sit in a vat of water to keep the drink cool.

The least expensive spoons were made of horn or wood; finer spoons were cast in metals such as pewter or silver. The characteristic spoon of the period had a thin handle, round in cross-section, and a large fig-shaped bowl. The handle of a metal spoon sometimes had a decorative ending called a *knop*. Designs for knops included various sorts of balls, acorns, and even human figures: one form was the Apostle Spoon, which had a knop in the figure of one of the Twelve Apostles. Pewter and silver spoons

A SERVANT'S DUTIES AT TABLE

When your master will go to his meat, take a towel about your neck, then take a cupboard cloth, a basin, ewer, and a towel, to array your cupboard; cover your table, set on bread, salt, and trenchers, the salt before the bread, and trenchers before the salt. Set your napkins and spoons on the cupboard ready, and lay every man a trencher, a napkin, and a spoon. . . . See ye have voider [clearing-platter] ready for to avoid [remove] the morsels that they do leave on their trenchers. Then with your trencher knife take off such fragments and put them in your voider, and set them down clean again. All your sovereign's trenchers or bread, void them once or twice, especially when they are wet, or give them clean.

Hugh Rhodes, *The Book of Nurture* [1577], in *The Babees Book*, ed. F. J. Furnivall (London: Trübner, 1868), 66–67.

were among the commonest luxuries in ordinary households and were frequently given as gifts at weddings and christenings.

The ordinary form of plate was the trencher, a square piece of wood with a large depression hollowed out for the food and a smaller one in the upper right-hand corner for salt; fancier round plates might be made of pewter or silver. The trencher was smaller than a modern dinner plate, more like a modern salad plate. Ordinary bowls were made of wood or ceramic. In addition to the plates for the diners, empty plates called *voiders* were often set out to receive bones, shells, and other scraps.

Missing from the typical place setting was the fork, which was not a feature of the Elizabethan table at all. The Italians were using forks in this period, but in England, the fork was exclusively a kitchen utensil. Food was cut on either the cook's bench or the serving platter, so by the time the food hit the trencher, it did not need to be held down and cut.

In some cases, diners would provide their own knives, since many people carried these as part of their ordinary attire. The Elizabethan knife was invariably pointed—the blunt form of modern table knives was introduced during the 17th century to reduce the danger of mealtime brawling. The blade was of carbon steel; unlike modern stainless steels, it had to be kept dry and oiled to prevent rust. The handle might be of wood, horn, bone, or ivory.

Salt was put out in saltcellars, and the diners transferred it with their knives to the salt-depression on the trencher. Silver saltcellars were a common luxury, pewter being a cheaper alternative. Condiments (such as mustard) and sauces were also set out for the diners. Valuable tableware was one of the likeliest luxuries for a person to own, as it could be brought

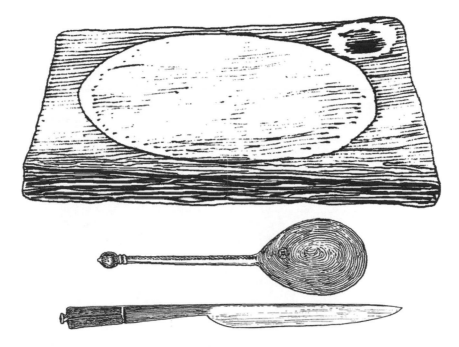

A trencher, knife, and pewter spoon. [Hoornstra/Forgeng]

out to impress guests: a poor man might well invest in some pewter, and a man of limited means might own some silver or glass.

ETIQUETTE

Eating and drinking are among the most ritualized aspects of daily life, and this was as true in Elizabethan England as in other societies. It was customary to begin the meal by washing hands—a particularly important ritual in an age when people used their fingers in eating much more than we do today. This generally involved one of the servants or children passing among the guests with a pitcher of water, a basin, and a towel. When everyone had washed, someone would recite a prayer, after which the meal would begin.

Adult men generally kept their hats on at the table, unless one of their fellow diners was clearly higher in social status; women wore their coifs, while boys and menservants were bareheaded out of respect for their superiors. In large and wealthy households there might be a substantial number of servants to bring the food to the table and clear it away, as well to pour drinks when they were called for. In the best households, drinks

MEALTIME PRAYERS FROM A DEVOTIONAL BOOK OF 1566

A Prayer to Be Said before Meat

All things depend upon thy providence, O Lord, to receive at thy hands due sustenance in time convenient. Thou givest to them, and they gather it: thou openest thy hand, and they are satisfied with all good things.

O heavenly Father, which art the fountain and full treasure of all goodness, we beseech thee to shew thy mercies upon us thy children, and sanctify these gifts which we receive of thy merciful liberality, granting us grace to use them soberly and purely, according to thy blessed will: so that hereby we may acknowledge thee to be the author and giver of all good things, and above all that we may remember continually to seek the spiritual food of thy word, wherewith our souls may be nourished everlastingly, through our Saviour Christ, who is the true bread of life, which came down from heaven, of whom whosoever eateth shall live for ever, and reign with Him in glory, world without end. So be it.

A Thanksgiving after Meals

Glory, praise, and honour be unto thee, most merciful and omnipotent Father, who of thine infinite goodness hast created man to thine own image and similitude; who also hast fed and daily feedest of thy most bountiful hand all living creatures: grant unto us, that as thou hast nourished these our mortal bodies with corporal food, so thou wouldest replenish our souls with the perfect knowledge of the lively word of thy beloved Son Jesus Christ; to whom be praise, glory, and honour, for ever. So be it.

Henry Bull, *Christian Prayers* (New York: Johnson Reprint Co., 1968), 54–55, 58.

did not sit on the table but on a sideboard: a thirsty diner would summon a servant to provide him with a cup, which was taken away once he had drunk from it. The bond created by sharing of food and drink was emphasized by the custom of toasting and pledging with one's drink. In humbler homes, it was common for children to serve their parents before sitting down to eat, and they were likewise expected to clear away the food at the end of the meal.

Men draped their napkins across one shoulder, while women kept their napkins on their laps. Manners books warned children not to smack their lips or gnaw on bones, to keep their fingers clean with their napkins, and to wipe their mouths before drinking. Once the meal was over, it was customary to recite another prayer and to wash hands again. People might clean their teeth at this point with a toothpick made of wood or ivory, turning away from the company and covering the mouth with a napkin while doing so.

EATING OUT

When not at home, Elizabethan folk could get food and drink at taverns, inns, alehouses, and *ordinaries*. An inn was primarily a place for lodging, but also offered food, ale, beer, and wine. The tavern generally provided respectable lodging, and served wine but not food; its clientele was largely middle to upper class. The alehouse offered ale and beer, and sometimes simple food and lodging on the side. The alehouse was by far the most common sort of establishment, and the only one at which ordinary folk could be sure of a welcome. It was often recognizable by the *ale-stake* displayed over the door: either a pole with a bush attached at the end, or a broom, such as was used to sweep the yeast from the top during brewing—when a batch of ale was ready, the broom was set out to alert passersby. Many rural households opened temporary alehouses when a batch of ale came ready, although they could be fined if they failed to secure a license from the local justice of the peace. An establishment that primarily served food was called an *ordinary*, so named because it served fixed fare at a standard price. According to the Swiss tourist Thomas Platter, women were as likely to frequent taverns and alehouses as men: one might even invite another man's wife to such an establishment, in which case she would bring several other female friends and the husband would thank the other man for his courtesy afterward.

Many urban residents lacked full kitchen facilities, so they often purchased meals from one of these establishments, or bought "carry-out"

A bakehouse. [Besant]

from a baker, pie maker, or other food retailer. Even a household with a full kitchen might not have a bakeoven: some people would prepare the food at home, then bring it to a baker to be cooked.

RECIPES

The following recipes are all based on original sources: Gervase Markham's *The English Housewife*, first published in 1615; Thomas Dawson's *The Good Huswifes Jewell* and *The Second Part of the Good Huswifes Jewell*, first printed in the 1580s; and the anonymous *The Good Huswifes Handmaide for the Kitchin* (ed. Stuart Peachey), printed in 1594. In each case the original text is given in italics (with spelling modernized), followed by an interpretation for the modern cook.

Bread

Of baking manchets [small loaves of fine flour].

First your meal, being ground upon the black stones if it be possible, which make the whitest flour, and bolted through the finest bolting cloth, you shall put it into a clean kimnel [kneading trough], *and, opening the flour hollow in the midst, put into it of the best ale barm the quantity of three pints to a bushel of meal, with some salt to season it with: then put in your liquor reasonable warm and knead it very well together both with your hands and through the brake* [a board with one end of a rolling pin hinged to it]; *or for want thereof, fold it in a cloth, and with your feet tread it a good space together, then, letting it lie an hour or thereabouts to swell, take it forth and mould it into manchets, round, and flat; scotch about the waist to give it leave to rise, and prick it with your knife in the top, and so put it into the oven, and bake it with a gentle heat. . . .*

And thus . . . you may bake any bread leavened or unleavened whatsoever, whether it be simple corn, as wheat or rye of itself, or compound grain as wheat and rye, or wheat and barley, or rye and barley, or any other mixed white corn; only, because rye is a little stronger than wheat, it shall be good for you to put to your water a little hotter than you did to your wheat. [Markham, chap. 9, nos. 15–17]

Sift **3 cups unbleached flour;** use white flour for manchets, whole wheat for a household loaf, or any combination of wheat, rye, and barley as Markham suggests. Dissolve **1 teaspoon active dry yeast** in **1 cup lukewarm water or beer** and stir in **1 teaspoon salt.** Make a well in the flour and pour the yeast mixture into it. Mix and knead for 5 minutes. Since the wheat can vary in initial moisture, you might have to add water or flour to ensure that it is moist to the touch but not sticky. Let the dough rise in a warm place for about an hour. The loaf should be round and flat, and pricked on top with a knife. Let it rise until it has doubled in volume, about 45 minutes to an hour. Preheat the oven to 500 degrees F. When the dough has risen, put it in the oven and reduce heat to 350 degrees F. After about 20 minutes the bread should be golden brown and ready to remove from the oven.

Pottage

To make the best ordinary pottage, you shall take a rack of mutton cut into pieces, or a leg of mutton cut into pieces; for this meat and these joints are the best, although any other joint or any fresh beef will likewise make good pottage: and, having washed your meat well, put it into a clean pot with fair water, & set it on the fire; then take violet leaves, endive, succory [a salad herb, closely related to endive], *strawberry leaves, spinach, langdebeef* [oxtongue], *marigold flowers, scallions, and a little parsley, and chop them very small together; then take half so much oatmeal well beaten as there is herbs, and mix it with the herbs, and chop all very well together: then when the pot is ready to boil, scum it very well, and then put in your herbs, and so let it boil with a quick fire, stirring the meat oft in the pot, till the meat be boiled enough, and then the herbs and water are mixed together without any separation, which will be after the consumption of more than a third part: then season them with salt, and serve them up with the meat either with sippets* [a small slice of bread, toasted or fried, used to sop up gravy or broth] *or without.* [Markham, chap. 2, no. 74]

Cut **1½ lb. mutton** into 1-inch cubes. Add **6 cups water.** Bring to a boil. Chop together **1 cup endive, 1½ cup spinach, 1½ cup scallions, 1 cup parsley,** and **2 cups rolled oats** (if you can find yourself the violet leaves, succory, strawberry leaves, oxtongue, and marigold flowers, then so much the better). Stir the herbs and oatmeal into the liquid, cover and simmer gently for about 1 hour or until meat is tender, stirring periodically. Add **salt** to taste. Makes 4–6 servings.

This dish is fairly representative of the ordinary fare of the Elizabethan commoner, relying on mutton and domestically grown grain and herbs.

Roast Chicken

Preheat oven to 450 degrees F. Clean one 4–5 lb. chicken or capon. Stuff with 1 recipe stuffing (see below), truss up the legs, and sew the body cavity shut. Place the bird on a roasting pan in the oven and reduce temperature to 350 degrees F. Baste frequently with the juices from the bird; you may begin the process by basting with 2 teaspoons salt dissolved in 1 cup water. Roast for about 20 minutes a pound (the bird will be done when its juices run clear and there is no redness left in the meat). Pour 1 recipe capon sauce (see below) on the bird just before serving.

Stuffing

To farse all things. Take a good handful of thyme, hyssop, parsley, and three or four yolks of eggs hard roasted, and chop them with herbs small, then take white bread grated and raw eggs with sweet butter, a few small raisins, or barberries, seasoning it with pepper, cloves, mace, cinnamon, and ginger, working it all together as paste, and then may you stuff with it what you will. [Dawson, *The second part*, p. 10]

Take the yolk of **1 hard-boiled egg,** and chop it up with ½ **teaspoon thyme** and **2 tablespoons parsley.** Work together in a bowl with **2 cups** bread crumbs, 2 raw eggs, 2 tablespoons unsalted butter, 2 tablespoons raisins, ⅛ teaspoon pepper, ⅛ teaspoon cloves, ⅛ teaspoon mace, ⅛ teaspoon cinnamon, and ¼ teaspoon ground ginger.

Capon Sauce

To make an excellent sauce for a roast capon, you shall take onions, and, having sliced and peeled them, boil them in fair water with pepper, salt, and a few bread crumbs: then put unto it a spoonful or two of claret wine, the juice of an orange, and three or four slices of a lemon peel; all these shred together, and so pour it upon the capon being broke up. [Markham, chap. 2, no. 79]

Peel and dice **1 small onion.** Add to **1¾ cups boiling water,** along with **¼ teaspoon pepper, ½ cup bread crumbs,** and **salt** to taste. Boil for 5 minutes, then remove from heat, and add **1 tablespoon red wine, 3 tablespoons freshly squeezed orange juice,** and **1 teaspoon grated lemon rind.** Pour it on the roast and serve.

Salads and Vegetables

Your simple sallats are chibols [wild onion] *peeled, washed clean, and half of the green tops cut clean away, so served on a fruit dish; or chives, scallions, radish roots, boiled carrots, skirrets* [a species of water parsnip], *and turnips, with such like served up simply; also, all young lettuce, cabbage lettuce, purslane* [the herb Pastalaca oleracea], *and divers other herbs which may be served simply without anything but a little vinegar, salad oil and sugar; onions boiled, and stripped from their rind and served up with vinegar, oil and pepper is a good simple salad; so is samphire* [the herb Crithmum maritimum], *bean cods, asparagus, and cucumbers, served in likewise with oil, vinegar, and pepper, with a world of others, too tedious to nominate. Your compound salads are first young buds and knots of all manner of wholesome herbs at their first springing, as red sage, mints, lettuce, violets, marigolds, spinach, and many other mixed together, and then served up to the table with vinegar, salad oil and sugar.* [Markham, chap. 2, no. 11]

The term *salad* as used by Markham covers a range of vegetable dishes. His description suggests several possibilities, of which two are offered here.

(1) Chop **3 carrots, 2 parsnips,** and **1 turnip** into 1-inch cubes. Bring **4 cups water** to a brisk boil and add the chopped vegetables. Chop together **1 tablespoon chives, 2 radishes,** and **1 tablespoon scallions.** When the vegetables are tender, drain them, mix them with the chives, radishes, and scallions, and serve.

(2) Wash and tear up **½ head leaf lettuce** and an **equal quantity of spinach.** Add **3 tablespoons mint leaves** and, if possible, **3 tablespoons violets** and **3 tablespoons marigolds.** Mix **3 tablespoons olive oil** and **3 tablespoons vinegar** with **½ teaspoon sugar** to make a salad dressing. This salad can be varied with the addition of **sliced cucumber, endive, radishes, spin-**

ach, or **mint.** The salad oil could be made with ¼ **teaspoon pepper** instead of the **sugar.**

Pies

Pie Crust

Your rye paste would be kneaded only with hot water and a little butter, or sweet seam [animal fat] and rye flour very finely sifted, and it would be made tough and stiff that it may stand well in the rising, for the coffin thereof must ever be very deep: your coarse wheat crust would be kneaded with hot water, or mutton broth and good store of butter, and the paste made stiff and tough because that coffin must be deep also; your fine wheat crust must be kneaded with as much butter as water, and the paste made reasonable lithe and gentle, into which you must put three or four eggs or more according to the quantity you blend together, for they will give it a sufficient stiffening. [Markham, chap. 2, no. 109]

Sift together **2 cups unbleached white flour** with **1 cup whole wheat flour.** Make a well in the flour, and shave ½ **cup butter** into it. Mix into a finely crumbling consistency. Work **2 eggs** into it, then work ½ **cup water** into it bit by bit (you may need slightly less or more water—the dough should be just elastic enough to be worked). Divide the dough in half, and roll it out into two circles for a pie shell and a lid. Pour the **1 recipe fruit or spinach filling** (see below) into the pie shell, and cover with the lid.

Fruit Filling

To make all manner of fruit tarts: You must boil your fruit, whether it be apple, cherry, peach, damson [plum], pear, mulberry, or codling [a kind of apple], in fair water, and when they be boiled enough, put them into a bowl and bruise them with a ladle, and when they be cold, strain them, and put in red wine or claret wine, and so season it with sugar, cinnamon, and ginger. [Dawson, The Good Huswifes Jewell, p. 18].

Preheat oven to 450 degrees F. Cut **6 peaches** into eighths, removing the pits, stems, and skins. Bring **4 cups water** to a boil, add the peaches, and boil for 5–10 minutes or until tender. Remove the mixture from the heat and crush the peaches with a ladle. Let the mixture cool, and strain it to remove excess water. Add ½ **cup red wine,** ½ **cup sugar, 1 teaspoon ground cinnamon,** and **1 teaspoon ground ginger.** Place in pie shell and cover. Bake at 450 degrees F for 10 minutes, then reduce to 350 degrees F and take it out when the crust is golden brown, which should be approximately 45 minutes later.

Spinach Filling

To make a tart of spinach: Boil your eggs and your cream together, and then put them into a bowl, and then boil your spinach, and when they are boiled, take them out of the water and strain them into your stuff before you strain your cream, boil your stuff and then strain them all again, and season them with sugar and salt. [Dawson, *The Good Huswifes Jewell*, pp. 20–21]

Preheat oven to 375 degrees F. Stir **4 eggs** into **1½ cups cream,** bring to a boil, and remove from the heat. Boil **6 cups spinach** in **4 cups water** for 1 minute. Strain the spinach, add it to the egg and cream mixture, boil, and season with **½ tablespoon sugar** and **salt** to taste. (Other recipes replace the salt with cinnamon and ginger—you can use a teaspoon of each.) Place in pie shell and cover. Bake at 375 degrees F for 35–40 minutes, and take it out when the crust is golden brown.

This dish is essentially an Elizabethan quiche.

Spiced Cake with Currants

To make a very good Banbury cake, take four pounds of currants, & wash and pick them very clean, and dry them in a cloth: then take three eggs and put away one yolk, and beat them, and strain them with barm [froth from ale making], *putting thereto cloves, mace, cinnamon, and nutmegs; then take a pint of cream, and as much morning's milk and set it on the fire till the cold be taken away; then take flour and put in good store of cold butter and sugar, then put in your eggs, barm, and meal and work them all together an hour or more; then save a part of the paste, & the rest break in pieces and work in your currants; which done, mould your cake of what quantity you please; and then with that paste which hath not any currants cover it very thin both underneath and aloft. And so bake it according to the bigness.* [Markham, chap. 2, no. 172]

Preheat oven to 350 degrees F. Dissolve **1 teaspoon dry active yeast** in **¼ cup lukewarm water or beer,** and allow to sit for 10 minutes. Add **1 beaten egg,** **¼ teaspoon cloves,** **¼ teaspoon mace,** **½ teaspoon cinnamon,** and **¼ teaspoon nutmeg.** Warm **¾ cup half and half,** and stir it into the yeast mixture. Mix **2 cups sifted unbleached flour** with **¾ cup sugar,** and work in **½ cup butter.** Work the yeast mixture into the flour mixture. Work in **1 cup dried currants.** Bake in a greased bread pan for about 1 hour; when the cake is done, the surface will be golden brown and a knife stuck into it will come out dry.

An Elizabethan cake, like bread, was leavened with yeast, since baking soda had not yet been introduced.

Spiced Beer

Take three pints of beer, put five yolks of eggs to it, strain them together, and set it in a pewter pot to the fire, and put to it half a pound of sugar, one pennyworth of nutmegs beaten, one pennyworth of cloves beaten, and a halfpennyworth of ginger beaten, and when it is all in, take another pewter pot and draw them together, and set it to the fire again, and when it is ready to boil, take it from the fire, and put a dish of sweet butter into it, and brew them together out of one pot into another. [*The Good Husewifes Handmaide for the Kitchin*, p. 62]

Add **1 egg yolk** to **1 pint of beer,** and warm. Stir in ¼ **cup sugar** and **a pinch each of ground nutmeg, ground cloves,** and **ground ginger.** When it is on the verge of boiling, remove it from the stove, add **a spoonful of butter**, and stir.

This sort of drink was often consumed as part of the festivities of the Christmas season.

Hippocras

Take a gallon of wine, an ounce of cinnamon, two ounces of ginger, one pound of sugar, twenty cloves bruised, and twenty corns of pepper big beaten, let all these soak together one night, and then let it run through a bag, and it will be good hippocras. [The Good Huse-wifes Handmaide for the Kitchin, p. 54]

Take **1 bottle red wine;** add ¼ **teaspoon ground cinnamon,** ½ **teaspoon ground ginger,** and **5 crushed whole cloves, 5 peppercorns,** and **1 cup sugar.** Stop up and let it sit overnight, then the next day strain it through a coffee filter.

Mulled wine was also consumed during the Christmas season, but hippocras was drunk cold at any time of the year. It was considered medicinal; its name derived from the ancient Greek physician Hippocrates.

NOTES

1. Thomas Dawson, *The Good Huswifes Jewell* [1596], ed. Susan J. Evans (Albany, NY: Falconwood Press, 1988), 1.

2. Joel Hurstfield and Alan G. R. Smith, *Elizabethan People: State and Society* (New York: St. Martin's Press, 1972), 101.

3. P. Razzell, ed., *The Journals of Two Travellers in Elizabethan and Early Stuart England* (London: Caliban Books, 1995), 32.

8

Entertainments

Leisure, no less than work, played an important part in the lives of Elizabethans. The landowning classes were not obliged to work at all. Many of them did work quite hard, whether in government, estate management, or some other aristocratic calling; but all of them had plentiful opportunity to pursue leisure activities. Ordinary people had much harder schedules, laboring from dawn to dusk most days of the week, yet they eagerly pursued entertainments in such free time as was allowed them. For such people, the principal leisure time was after church on Sundays and holidays, although religious reformers increasingly objected to Sunday games as a violation of the Sabbath.

The Elizabethan traveler Fynes Moryson commented on his countrymen's devotion to their pastimes:

It is a singularity in the nature of the English, that they are strangely addicted to all kinds of pleasure above all other nations. . . . The English, from the lords to the very husbandmen, have generally more fair and more large Gardens and Orchards, than any other nation. All Cities, Towns, and villages swarm with companies of musicians and fiddlers, which are rare in other kingdoms. The City of London alone hath four or five companies of players with their particular theaters capable of many thousands, wherein they all play every day in the week but Sunday. . . . Not to speak of frequent spectacles in London exhibited to the people by fencers, by walkers on ropes, and like men of activity, nor of frequent companies of archers shooting in all the fields, nor of Saints' days, which the people not keeping (at least most of them, or with any devotion) for church service, yet keep for recreation of walking and gaming. What shall I say of dancing with curious and rural

"A Fete at Bermondsey," ca.1570, by Joris Hoefnagel (1542–1600). [Hatfield House, Hertfordshire, UK/ The Bridgeman Art Library]

music, frequently used by the better sort, and upon all holidays by country people dancing about the Maypoles with bagpipes or other fiddlers, besides the jollities of certain seasons of the year, of setting up maypoles, dancing the morris with hobby horses, bringing home the lady of the harvest, and like plebeian sports, in all which vanities no nation cometh anything near the English. What shall I say of playing at cards and dice, frequently used by all sorts, rather as a trade than as recreation. . . . As the English are by nature amorous, so do they above other nations assert and follow the pleasant study of poetry. . . . To conclude with hawking and hunting, no nation so frequently useth these sports as the English.[1]

THEATER

The Elizabethan period witnessed the true emergence of an entertainment industry, particularly in the theaters of London. At the beginning of Elizabeth's reign, theatrical performances took place in the courtyards of large inns. In 1576 London's first successful public theater was built—outside the city limits, to escape the stringent regulations imposed by hostile city authorities. Called simply the Theatre, this structure was the model that gave rise to a series of similar facilities constructed over the following decades: the Curtain in 1577, the Rose in 1587, the Swan in 1595, the

---

THE CITY FATHERS OF LONDON COMPLAIN TO THE PRIVY COUNCIL ABOUT THE EVILS OF STAGE-PLAYS, 1597

Stage-plays . . . are a special cause of corrupting their youth, containing nothing but unchaste matters, lascivious devices, shifts of cozenage, and other lewd and ungodly practices, being so as that they impress the very quality and corruption of manners which they represent. . . . They are the ordinary places for vagrant persons, masterless men, thieves, horse-stealers, whoremongers, cozeners, coney-catchers, contrivers of treason and other idle and dangerous persons to meet together . . . which cannot be prevented nor discovered by the governors of the city for that they are out of the city's jurisdiction. They maintain idleness in such persons as have no vocation, and draw apprentices and other servants from their ordinary works and all sort of people from the resort unto sermons and other Christian exercises, to the great hindrance of trades and profanation of religion . . . In the time of sickness it is found by experience that many having sores and yet not heart-sick take occasion hereby to walk abroad and to recreate themselves by hearing a play, whereby others are infected.

John Dover Wilson, *Life in Shakespeare's England* (Harmondsworth: Pelican, 1951), 231.

Fortune in 1600. In 1598–99 the Theatre was dismantled and moved to the emerging theater district in Southwark, on the south bank of the Thames, where it reopened as the Globe.

These early theaters resembled the innyards from which they had evolved. They were built around courtyards, with three-story galleries on three sides, facing a stage that projected out into the yard. People sat in the galleries, while the less privileged stood on the ground; a few ostentatious young gentlemen might sit on the stage itself. The plays were attended by all manner of people. Aristocrats were often to be found in the galleries, while standing room on the ground was certainly within the means of most people. General admission cost only a penny, the price of two quarts of beer—the price of going to the theater was analogous to going to the cinema today, although the low wages of working people meant they could not do it very often. The Swiss visitor Thomas Platter in 1599 described the experience of a London theater:

The playhouses are so constructed that they play on a raised platform, so that everyone has a good view. There are different galleries and places, however, where the seating is better and more comfortable and therefore more expensive. For whoever cares to stand below only pays one English penny, but if he wishes to sit he enters by another door, and pays another penny; while if he desires to sit in the most comfortable seats which are cushioned where he not only sees everything well, but can also be seen, then he pays yet another English penny at another door.

The Swan Theater in 1596.
[*Shakespeare's England*]

And during the performance food and drink are carried round the audience, so that for what one cares to pay one may also have refreshment. The actors are most expensively and elaborately costumed; for it is the English usage for eminent lords or knights at their decease to bequeath and leave almost the best of their clothes to their serving men, which it is unseemly for the latter to wear, so that they offer them for sale for a small sum to the actors.[2]

Plays had to be licensed, and government authorities were always wary of the overcrowding, plague, and disorder associated with play going. In fact, laws against vagrants were often used against actors and other performers, who lived wandering lives, unattached to any employer or household. In response, theatrical companies placed themselves under the patronage of the great noblemen of England, which allowed players to avoid punishment by becoming, technically, servants of the lord. Shakespeare's company were known as the Lord Chamberlain's Men during the 1590s, and after the accession of James I they would become the King's Men.

There was a constant and insatiable demand for plays, and actors became celebrated figures—the first stars. The plays' action combined humor and violence along with musical interludes and dazzling special effects—not unlike modern popular films. Playwrights were typically university graduates, and their lives could be short and turbulent. Christopher Marlowe took Elizabethan audiences by storm. His *Tamburlaine the Great* (1587–88), full of violence, ambition, and horror, was the blockbuster of its day. William Shakespeare began his theatrical career late in Elizabeth's reign, in the early 1590s with works including his history plays, *Romeo and Juliet* and *Midsummer Night's Dream;* Ben Jonson entered the scene later in the same decade.

In addition to the permanent theaters in London, there were less formal settings for theatrical performances. The London companies occasionally toured the smaller cities and towns, performing in innyards and civic halls, and there were plenty of minor performers, part-time folk players, puppeteers, magicians, acrobats, and other entertainers.

LITERATURE

The other principal form of commercial entertainment was literature. Elizabethan presses churned out all manner of texts: technical works, political and religious tracts (some of them considered highly seditious by the authorities, who punished the authors severely if they were caught), ballads, almanacs, histories, and even news reports. These texts varied in format from lavish volumes richly illustrated with fine engravings— sometimes even colored by hand—down to cheap pamphlets and *broadsides* (single printed sheets) illustrated with simple woodcuts, produced for the mass market and selling for just a penny. The volume of printed material expanded substantially: from the arrival of printing in England in the 1470s to Elizabeth's accession, a bit over 5,000 books were published of which copies still survive; from 1558 to 1579, the figure is 2,760; and from 1580 to 1603, it is 4,730. Readership was not limited to those who purchased copies, or even to those who could read them, since people sometimes read aloud in groups.

The most important text to the Elizabethan reader was the Bible. The law required a copy to be kept in every church, along with the *Book of Common Prayer*, which described the liturgy of the church of England. The Bible was the one book you would count on finding in any literate household. The most popular version was the translation known as the Geneva Bible, which appeared at about the time Elizabeth came to the throne; the version authorized by the English church was the Bishops' Bible of 1568, which was less reformist in tone. Perhaps the second most common volume on the bookshelf in an English home was John Foxe's *Acts and Monuments of these Latter and Perilous Days, Touching Matters of the Church*—familiarly known as the *Book of Martyrs*. First published in 1563 and reissued many times thereafter, Foxe's work told of the faithfulness of English Christians throughout history, with special emphasis on Protestants who had died under the persecutions of Bloody Mary. The law also required a copy of Foxe to be kept in the parish church.

MUSIC

If theater and literature were predominantly consumer entertainments, most other Elizabethan pastimes involved people as producers as well as consumers. Perhaps the most prominent example is music. The Elizabethans, like people today, liked to hear music. Unlike people today, they had no access to recording technology: all music had to be performed live. To some degree, people made use of professional musicians to satisfy their desire for music. A wealthy householder might hire musicians to play during dinner, and major towns had official musicians known as *waits* who sometimes gave free public concerts—beginning in 1571, such concerts were given at the Royal Exchange in London after 7 P.M. on Sundays and holidays.

For the most part, people made their own music. Laborers and craftsmen sang while working; gentlefolk and respectable townspeople sang part-songs or played consort music after a meal. Barbershops kept musical instruments so that patrons could entertain themselves while they waited. The ability to hold one's own in a part-song or a round (known to the Elizabethans as a *catch*) was a basic social skill. In fact, musical literacy was expected in polite society, and well-bred people could often play or sing a piece on sight. Even those of Puritanical leanings found pleasure in singing psalms; the reform-minded Lady Margaret Hoby liked to sing, accompanying herself on a lute-like instrument called the orpharion.

Favored instruments among the upper classes included the lute, the virginals (a keyboard instrument in which the strings are plucked rather than struck), the viol (resembling a modern viola or cello), and the recorder. Among common folk the bagpipe was popular, especially in the country; other common instruments were the fiddle and the pipe-and-tabor (a combination of a three-hole recorder played with the left hand and a drum played with the right). Public music was most often performed on loud instruments such as the shawm (a powerful double-reeded instrument) and sackbut (a simple trombone). In the countryside, the ringing of church bells was a popular pastime.

DANCING

Dancing was also a common entertainment. It was considered a vital skill for an aristocrat (the Queen was said to look favorably on a man who could dance well), but was equally important to ordinary people: it was not merely a pleasant diversion but one of the best opportunities for interaction between unmarried people. The Puritan moralist Phillip Stubbes complained in his *Anatomy of Abuses*,

What clipping and culling, what kissing and bussing, what smooching and slavering one of another, what filthy groping and unclean handling is not practiced everywhere in these dancings?[3]

THE PURITAN CRITIC PHILIP STUBBES
DESCRIBES MORRIS DANCING AT A PARISH ALE

All the wild-heads of the Parish . . . choose them a Grand-Captain . . . whom they ennoble with the title of "my Lord of Mis-rule," and him they crown with great solemnity, and adopt for their king. This king anointed chooseth forth twenty, forty, threescore or a hundred lusty guts, like to himself, to wait upon his lordly Majesty, and to guard his noble person. Then every one of these his men he investeth with his liveries of green, yellow, or some other light wanton colour. . . They bedeck themselves with scarves, ribbons & laces hanged all over with gold rings, precious stones, & other jewels; this done, they tie about either leg 20 or 40 bells, with rich handkerchiefs in their hands, and sometimes laid across over their shoulders & necks, borrowed for the most part of their pretty Mopsies & loving Besses, for bussing [kissing] them in the dark. Thus all things set in order, then have they their hobby-horses, dragons & other antiques [spectacles], together with their bawdy Pipers and thundering Drummers to strike up the devil's dance withall. Then march these heathen company towards the Church and Church-yard, their pipers piping, their drummers thundring, their stumps dancing, their bells jingling, their handkerchefs swinging about their heads like madmen, their hobby horses and other monsters skirmishing amongst the route. . . . Then . . . about the Church they go again and again, & so forth into the church-yard, where they have commonly their Summer-halls, their bowers, arbors, & banqueting houses set up, wherin they feast, banquet & dance all that day & (peradventure) all the night too.

Phillip Stubbes, *The Anatomie of Abuses* (London: Richard Jones, 1583), 92v-93r.

The preferred type of dancing varied between social classes. Those of social pretensions favored the courtly dances imported from the Continent, especially Italy and France. These dances were mostly performed by couples, sometimes by a set of two couples; they often involved intricate and subtle footwork. Ordinary people were more likely to do the traditional country dances of England. These were danced by groups of couples in round, square, or rectangular sets, and were much simpler in form and footwork, relatives of the modern square dance. The division was not absolute: ordinary people sometimes danced almains, which were originally a courtly dance from France, while Elizabeth herself encouraged country dances among the aristocracy. In addition to social dances, there were performance and ritual dances. Foremost among these was morris dancing, characterized by the wearing of bells, and often performed as a part of summer festivals.

HUNTING AND ANIMAL SPORTS

Elizabethan pastimes were not all as gentle as music and dance. One of the preferred sports of gentlemen was hunting—particularly for deer,

The actor Will Kemp morris-dancing to the pipe and tabor. [*Shakespeare's England*]

sometimes for foxes or hares. Modern greyhound racing had its origins in hare hunting, in which a pair of dogs would be set loose after a hare, and wagers were laid on which one would catch the quarry. Birds were also hunted, in two different ways. One was the ancient and difficult sport of falconry in which trained falcons were sent after the prey. The alternative involved crossbows or, increasingly, firearms. Rather more sedate was fishing, enjoyed by many who found hunting too barbarous or expensive. All these sports might be enjoyed by women as well as men. Ordinary people did not generally hunt or fish for sport. Indeed, they were not allowed to do so. The rights of hunting and fishing were normally reserved for landowners, although poaching was still common as a means of obtaining extra food.

Hunting was a mild pastime in comparison with some Elizabethan animal sports, especially bullbaiting, bearbaiting, and cockfighting. Cockfighting involved pitting roosters against each other in a *cockpit*, a small round arena surrounded by benches—sometimes a permanent structure was built for the purpose. In bullbaiting, a bull was chained in the middle of a large arena and set upon by one or more mastiffs. The dogs were trained to clamp their jaws closed on the bull's nose or ears and hang on until the bull fell down exhausted; the bull meanwhile tried to shake the dogs free and gore them to death. Bearbaiting was very similar, with the bull replaced by a bear. In all of these sports, the onlookers would place wagers on the outcome of the combat. Bullbaiting usually ended in the death of the animal: when an old bull was to be butchered, it was common practice to bait the animal to make its meat more tender. Bearbaiting was usually more fatal to the dogs, as the bears were expensive and the sport was weighted in their favor—in fact, several bears became entertainment stars in their own right, known to Londoners by names like George Stone, Harry Hunks, and Sackerson. These entertainments, brutal though they seem to modern sensibilities, were widely enjoyed—even Elizabeth liked to attend bearbaitings. The main voice of criticism was from Puritan commentators like Philip Stubbes: "What Christian heart can take pleasure to see one poor beast to rend, tear, and kill another, and all for his foolish pleasure? . . . For notwithstanding that they be evil to us, and thirst after our blood, yet are they good creatures in their own nature and kind, and made to set forth the glory, power, and magnificence of our God . . . and therefore for his sake we ought not to abuse them."[4]

Some animal-related activities were not so violent. Horse racing was increasing in popularity—England's first formal racecourses were built during the 1500s. Animals were also kept as pets. Dogs and cats were usually working members of the household, serving for home protection and rodent control, but upper-class households sometimes kept lapdogs, birds, or even monkeys as pets.

MARTIAL SPORTS

The violence of Elizabethan animal sports had parallels in human combat games. The aristocracy sometimes practiced the medieval sport of the tournament, a colorful but expensive pastime that typically served as the centerpiece of a major public festival. Featured activities might include jousting, pitting one horseman against another at lancepoint, or foot combat with swords or spears. Participants used blunt weapons and specialized tournament armor that maximized protection, and the combatants were usually separated by a wooden barrier that further reduced the level of risk.

Fencing was popular both as a spectator entertainment and a participatory sport. Fencing weapons had blunted edges and rounded tips but the sport was dangerous nonetheless. The rapier used in fencing was a great deal heavier than a modern fencing weapon; the only protective gear was a padded doublet, and occasionally a large round button secured over the tip of the blade to reduce the risk of putting out an eye. Even so, the risk of personal injury, even death, was always present, and public fencing matches were often played to first blood—the winner was the first one who could draw blood from his opponent.

Fencers with sword and dagger. [Castle]

Sometimes the rapier was supplemented by a small round shield, called a *buckler,* or by a larger one, either round or square, called a *target*. Alternatively, the fencer might use a rapier in one hand and a dagger in the other, or even two rapiers.

The rapier was considered an Italian weapon; those who preferred English traditions might fight with a backsword instead. Where the rapier was purely a civilian weapon, the backsword was designed to be suitable for military use. It was typically shorter than the rapier, with a thicker blade, optimized for cutting blows instead of thrusts with the point. Sometimes the combatants used wooden swords called wasters or cudgels. Other weapons used by fencers included quarterstaves, pikes, two-handed swords, and halberds. Somewhat less fashionable was wrestling, which had traditionally been a skill of the medieval knightly class, but was now increasingly seen as an entertainment of country folk.

Such martial arts had some practical application. There was a certain amount of lawlessness in Elizabethan England: even in London, street fights and brawls were known to break out in broad daylight. For many people, the ability to defend oneself was an important life skill.

Other martial sports were geared toward military rather than civilian purposes. By law, every English commoner was required to practice archery regularly. The law was originally introduced in the 1300s, when archery was still very important on the battlefield. By Elizabeth's time archery had declined in military significance, but Elizabeth encouraged it nonetheless (she sometimes engaged in the sport herself, as did many English aristocrats). There were archers in the militia, and some military theorists still preferred the bow to the gun. Laws promoting archery were not strictly observed, but the sport remained popular among all classes and was widely seen as an especially patriotic pastime.

More useful for the national defense was the practice of military drill with pike and shot. Elizabeth's government made a concerted effort to improve England's defenses by training a national militia known as the Trained Bands. Sixteenth-century warfare involved more training of the ordinary soldier than had once been the case. The matchlock musket required less physical strength and skill than the bow, but it was a fairly complex weapon to fire, requiring 20 to 30 seconds for each shot and some two dozen distinct motions—all of this while holding a slowly burning length of saltpeter-impregnated rope (called the *match*) and charging the weapon with gunpowder. An error could be fatal.

The pike, a 16- to 24-foot spear designed to ward off cavalry, was less dangerous to its user but even more demanding. There were about a dozen positions in which the pike might be held, and the pikemen had to learn to move from each position to all the others in precise coordination with the rest of the pikemen—in a tight block of pikeman, every weapon had to be aligned with all the others to avoid entanglement. The government's efforts to promote military training met with extraordinary success, for military drill actually became a fashionable pastime, as well as a popular spectator entertainment.

PHYSICAL GAMES

A tendency toward violence can be seen even in some of the nonmartial pastimes of the Elizabethans. The most characteristic English outdoor game of the period was football, especially favored by the lower classes. Elizabethan football was rough, loud, and perilous to bystanders as well as players. The game was roughly the same as modern European football (soccer in America), but with fewer rules. Two teams would try to kick a ball through their opponents' goal. The ball was made of a farm animal's bladder, inflated, tied shut, and sewn into a leather covering. A major part of the game was the subtle art of tripping up one's opponents on the run. Richard Mulcaster, a London schoolteacher who believed that the game "had great helps, both to health and strength," acknowledged that "as it is now commonly used, with thronging of a rude multitude, with bursting of shins, and breaking of legs, it be neither civil, neither worthy the name of any train to health," but he argued that the game could be made safer by the use of a referee, assigned positions for the players, and rules about the permissible levels of physical contact.[5] Even more violent were the

PHILIP STUBBES ON FOOTBALL

Football playing . . . may rather becalled a friendly kind of fight than a play or recreation, a bloody and murdering practice, than a fellowly sport or pastime. For doth not everyone lie in wait for his adversary, seeking to overthrow him, and to pitch him on his nose, though it be upon hard stones, in ditch or dale, in valley or hill, or what place so ever it be, he careth not, so he may have him down? And he that can serve the most of this fashion, he is counted the only fellow, and who but he? . . . They have slights to meet one betwixt two, to dash him against the heart with their elbows, to hit him under the short ribs, with the gripped fist, and with their knees, to catch him upon the hip, and to pitch him on his neck, with an hundred such murdering devises. And hereof groweth envy, malice, rancor . . . and sometimes fighting, brawling . . . homicide and great effusion of blood.

Phillip Stubbes, *The Anatomy of Abuses* (London: Richard Jones, 1583), 120r-v.

versions known as *camp-ball* in England, *hurling* in Cornwall, or *cnapan* in Wales. In these games, a ball or other object was conveyed over open country to opposing goals by any means possible—even horsemen might be involved. These games frequently led to serious injuries.

Similar to football in concept if not equipment was the game of bandy-ball, the ancestor of modern field hockey. The object of the game was to drive a small, hard ball through the opponents' goal with hooked clubs (almost identical to field hockey sticks).

Bat-and-ball games were known, but are poorly attested in Elizabethan sources. Stoolball in later years would be a game similar to cricket, with the ball thrown at a stool and a batsman trying to fend it off, but the earliest description of the game does not mention a bat (see the end of this chapter for an interpretation). Stoolball was one of few sports played by women as well as men. It is often confused with Stowball, a game played in Wiltshire and adjoining counties—a distant relative of croquet, in which one team tried to bat the ball around the course, while the other team would try to hit it back. A family of bat games were played with a *cat*, a cylinder of wood tapered at both ends so that the batsman could strike it on the ground, making it fly up in the air for him to swing at. In the game of trap or trapball a levered device was used to achieve the same effect.

Tennis, a game introduced from France during the Middle Ages, called for expensive equipment and an equally expensive court, so it was played only by the rich. The tennis ball was made of woolen scraps tightly wrapped in packing thread and encased in white fabric; the rackets were made of wood and gut. The game was played on a purpose-built, enclosed court with a complex shape—the Elizabethan game survives today under the name *real tennis*. Tennis was one of the most athletic games played by

Reția dum pilulam faciunt hinc inde volantem.   *Nam pila reſtaurat maleſano in corpore vires,*
Exercet leſeais corpus, et ingenium.   *Torpet at aſsiduis obruta mens ſtudijs*

Tennis. [Allemagne]

the upper classes, and it was only played by men. The plebeian version was handball: as the name suggests, the ball was hit with the hands rather than with a racket. A similar game was shuttlecock, comparable to modern badminton. The shuttlecock was a cylinder of cork rounded at one end with feathers stuck in it; it was batted back and forth with wooden paddles known as *battledores*.

A less demanding outdoor game was bowls, similar to the modern English game of that name, or to Italian *bocce*. Each player threw two balls at a target, trying to get them as close as possible once all the balls had been thrown. Bowls was so popular that there were commercial bowling alleys, and the game could be quite sophisticated, involving various shapes of balls, an elaborate terminology for describing the lay of the ground and the course of the ball, and a formalized system of betting. Moralists often criticized the game, yet when betting was not involved it was played by even the most respectable men and women.

A slightly more dangerous variant was quoits, in which a stake or spike was driven into the ground and players tossed stones or heavy metal disks at it. The game seems to have been played with vigor rather than finesse, and serious injury was known to result. The modern game of horseshoes is a variant of quoits.

Another game in the same family was Penny Prick. In Penny Prick, a peg was set in the ground with a penny on top; players would throw their knives at it, trying either to knock the penny off or to lodge their knife in the ground closest to the peg. A very simple game in this class, played by children, was Cherry Stone, in which the contestants tried to throw cherry pits into a small hole in the ground.

Similar to modern American bowling was the game known by such names as nine-pegs, ten-pins, skittle pins, skittles, or kittles. Nine conical pins were set up on the ground, and players would try to knock them down with a wooden ball. In a related game called kayles or loggats, the pins were knocked down with a stick instead of a ball. Country folk sometimes used the leg bones of oxen for pins.

Some games involved a great deal of running and little or no equipment. The game known in modern schoolyards as Prisoner's Base was played under the name Base or Prison Bars. A particular favorite in this period was Barley Break, a chasing game in which two mixed-sex couples tried to avoid being caught by a third couple, with the couples changing partners each time. The game, with its grabbing and constant changing of partners, was proverbially an opportunity for rustic flirtation.

Other athletic sports included footraces, swimming, and tug-of-war (probably known by multiple names—the attested version was called Sun-and-Moon). Men threw spears, heavy stones, or iron bars, and they competed at jumping for distance or height, sometimes with a pole. Vaulting, a sport once practiced by knights as a way to develop strength and

Playing with inflated bladders. [Allemagne]

skill as horsemen, still had some currency, and the vaulting-horse was still made to resemble an actual animal. People also liked simply to ride or take walks for exercise; members of the upper classes were especially fond of strolling in their gardens after a meal.

A variety of parlor-games were played by children, merrymakers at times like Christmas, and flirtatious young men and women. In Hot Cockles one player hid his head in another's lap while the others slapped him on the rear—if he could guess who had slapped him last, the two traded places. Blindman's Buff, also known as Hoodman Blind, was a similar game in which a blinded player tried to catch the others while they dealt him *buffs* (blows). If he could identify the person he caught, they would trade places.

TABLE GAMES

Many games were purely for indoor recreation. Among table games, chess was the most prestigious. Its rules were essentially the same as they are today. Chess was unusual among table games in that it did not normally involve betting. For those who wanted a simpler game, the chess board could be combined with *table men* (backgammon pieces) for the game of draughts (now known in North America as checkers), again with essentially the same rules as today.[6]

Fox and Geese and Nine Men's Morris were two simple board games in which each player moved pieces about on a geometric board, trying to capture or pin his opponent's pieces. Boards for these games could be made by cutting lines into a wooden surface or by writing on it with chalk or charcoal. A simpler relative was Three-Men's Morris, played on a three-by-three unit board with three men on a side—the progenitor of Tic-Tac-Toe, but allowing the pieces to be moved once they were placed.

There were several games in the family known as Tables, played with the equipment used in modern backgammon. Backgammon itself was not invented until the early 17th century, but the game of Irish was almost identical to it, although without the rules applying to doubles on the dice, which made it slower. Games at Tables varied enormously. The childish game of Doublets involved only one side of the board: each player stacked his pieces on the points of their side, then rolled dice first to unstack them, then to bear them off the board. Perhaps the most complex game was Ticktack, in which the general idea was to move all one's pieces from one end of the board to the other, with several alternative ways of winning the game at single or double stakes en route.

Dice were the classic pastime of the lower orders of society—they were cheap, highly portable, and very effective at whiling away idle time (for which reason they were especially favored by soldiers). Dice games were played by the aristocracy as well; Elizabeth herself was known to indulge in them. The dice were typically made of bone, and the spots were called the *ace, deuce, tray, cater, sink,* and *sise*—thus a roll of 6 and 1 was called *sise-ace.* The classic dice game was Hazard, a relative of modern Craps.

Cards were widely popular throughout society, and inexpensive block-printed decks were readily available. Elizabethan playing cards were unwaxed, and the custom had not yet evolved of printing a pattern on the back to prevent marking. For this reason, it was customary to retire the deck every Christmas—the old cards often being recycled as matches.

Playing cards were divided according to the French system, essentially the same one used in English-speaking countries today. The French suits were the same as in a modern deck, and each suit contained the same range of cards. The first three were called the Ace, Deuce, and Trey, and the face cards were called King, Queen, and Knave (there was no Joker). The cards had only images on them, no letters or numbers. The images on the face cards were similar to modern ones, save that they were full-body portraits (unlike the mirror-image on modern cards).

Many Elizabethan card games have disappeared from use, but some still have modern derivatives. One and Thirty was similar to the modern Twenty-One, except that it was played to a higher number. Noddy was an earlier variant of Cribbage (which first appeared in the early 17th century). Ruff and Trump were ancestors of modern Whist, and Primero was an early version of Poker.

POPULAR GAMES AND SPORTS, 1600

Man, I dare challenge thee to throw the sledge [hammer],
To jump or leap over a ditch or hedge,
To wrestle, play at stoolball, or to run,
To pitch the bar, or to shoot off a gun,
To play at loggats, nineholes or tenpins,
At Ticktack, Irish, Noddy, Maw and Ruff,
At hot-cockles, leap-frog, or blindman-buff,
To drink half-pots or deal at the whole can;
To play at base, or pen-and-inkhorn Sir John,
To dance the Morris, play at barley-break,
At all exploits a man can think or speak;
At shove-groat, venter-point or cross and pile,
At "Breshrew him that's last at yonder stile,"
At leaping o'er a Midsummer bonfire
Or at the "Drawing Dun out of the mire."
At any of these, or all these presently,
Wag but your finger, I am for you, I.

Samuel Rowlands, *The Letting of Humour's Blood in the Head-Vein* (London: W. White, 1600), sig. D8v-E1r.

Shovelboard or shove-groat was an indoor game in which metal discs (which could be coins—*groat* was a name for a fourpenny piece) were pushed across a table to land as close as possible to the other end without falling off. A series of lines were drawn across the board, and points were scored according to where the piece stopped. Wealthy households sometimes had special tables built for this game. The simplest coin game was Cross and Pile, identical to Heads or Tails—the *cross* was the cross on the back of English coins, and the *pile* the face of the Queen on the front.

Another very simple game involved the tee-totum, a kind of top, used exactly like a Hanukkah dreidel. It had four sides, each bearing a letter: *T* for *take*, *N* for *nothing*, *P* for *put*, and *H* for *half*. Depending on which side came up, the player would take all the stakes out of the pot, get nothing, put another stake into the pot, or take out half the stakes.

A few new table games appeared during Elizabeth's reign. Billiards appears to have been introduced from the Continent during this period. The Game of Goose is first attested in England in 1597. This was the earliest ancestor of many of today's commercial board games. Goose came as a commercially printed sheet bearing a track of squares spiraling toward the center. Players rolled dice to move their pieces along the track. Some of the squares bore special symbols: the player who landed on such a square might get an extra roll or be sent back a certain number of squares. The first player to reach the end won.

Some entertainments involved nothing more than words. Jokes were as popular then as now—there were even printed joke books. Riddles were another common form of word game. In general, Elizabethans greatly enjoyed conversation and were especially fond of sharing news: in a world without mass or electronic media, people were always eager for tidings of what was going on in the world around them.

PLAY AND SOCIETY

In a world where most people spent the bulk of their waking hours earning a living, recreation played an especially important cultural role. People's work-time activities were heavily governed by practical factors, but their pastimes, unconstrained by the same material considerations, tell us much more about who they were and what they valued.

A person's choice of pastimes said much about their cultural affiliations, rank, and gender. Tennis, hunting, and riding were pursued by the wealthy and fashionable. Football and wrestling were favored by country people and plebeian townsfolk. Archery was seen by some as old-fashioned, yet it had a strongly patriotic flavor, recalling the source of medieval England's military might.

Women did not engage in martial, dangerous, or extremely vigorous sports like fencing, football, or tennis. However, they might take part in lighter physical games such as Stoolball, Blindman's Buff or Barley Break.

Games with minimal physical activity such as bowls and card games were especially common pastimes for women, and they often participated as spectators at sports that they did not play themselves, even violent sports like fencing or bearbaiting.

Most Elizabethan games were less rules oriented and standardized than is true today. Rules were often minimal and might vary from one locality to the next. This was especially true of children's games and folk games, less true of table games and games of the upper classes, which were more elaborate and formalized.

Violence was much more a part of Elizabethan pastimes than is true today: not only were martial sports highly popular, but games like football were much rougher than their modern counterparts, and a degree of violence was present even in parlor games like Hot Cockles. In general, Elizabethans—or Elizabethan men at least—were much more willing to run the risk of personal injury in play than is commonly true today, and society as a whole was more willing to countenance real violence as a form of entertainment.

Closely related to the penchant for personal risk was the prevalence of gambling, which pervaded Elizabethan culture. A wager might be laid on almost any game, and in many cases, betting was an integral part of the game itself. People developed a taste for gambling in childhood, playing for lacing-points, pins, cherry stones, or various sorts of counters. Even the government got in on the act, organizing several national lotteries as a means of raising funds.

The disorder, violence and gambling involved in many plebeian pastimes contributed to a swelling tide of disapproval in official circles. Disapproval was exacerbated by practical factors: for most people, free time was largely confined to Sundays and holy days, and the chief space available for public festivities was the parish church. Puritan-minded commentators railed against ungodly conduct on the Sabbath or on church grounds, while secular authorities were concerned about the impact of boisterous plebeian pastimes in a society that seemed increasingly turbulent and unpredictable. Feelings among the governing classes were mixed—Elizabeth herself saw traditional entertainments as a means of fostering national unity and identity—but bit by bit, church and secular authorities were starting to curtail activities that seemed irreligious or riotous.

The results were mixed. Bishops and town authorities in many regions succeeded in withdrawing official support from traditional festivities, leading to a precipitous decline in activities like summer wakes and ales. On the other hand, direct actions against popular pastimes, such as a series of laws passed in the 1580s to prohibit football, dicing, cards, and blood sports on Sundays, were intermittent and minimally effective.

The overall outcome was a shift in plebeian culture away from the public sector toward the private. Robin Hood folk-plays had been an integral part of parish festivals and were tied to their fate, and so they had become rare by 1600, but morris dancing survived, since it was privately supported by gathering money from spectators. Public May games declined, while private Christmas celebrations endured. Traditional entertainments still held their ground in the more remote parts of the country, but in London folk culture was rapidly being displaced by commercial entertainments like theater and penny-broadsides, pointing the way toward the popular culture of the modern world.

RULES FOR ELIZABETHAN GAMES

Almost no rules for games survive from the late 16th century, but there are quite a few from the late 17th century. As games tend to be conservative, these rules are probably quite close to their Elizabethan forms; most of the rules given below are interpretations of such sources.[7]

Physical Games

Barley Break

Barley Break is played by three mixed-sex couples, AB and EF at the ends of the field, and CD in the middle, called *Hell*. All three couples hold one another by the hands. To initiate play, AB shout "Barley!" and EF respond "Break!" All three couples drop hands. AB and EF break, B and F running to meet each other, and A and E likewise. C and D try to catch any one of them.

If C and D can catch anyone before that person meets his or her new partner, those two must go in the middle next time. If both new pairs meet each other before any of them is caught, C and D remain in Hell. Both C and D must catch their target before the new partner reaches them, or it does not count. The new pairs go to the ends of the field for the next round.

Another variation is to have just one person from each end run toward the opposite side, with the middle couple trying to catch that person before he or she reaches the players on the far side. This variation can be played with more than six people, with the one who just ran going to the end of the line at the far side.

A   C D   E

B   F

The starting positions for Barley Break.

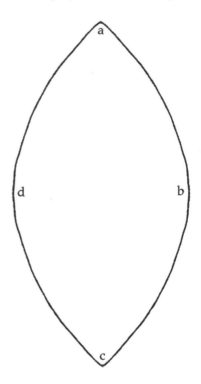

Pattern for the ball covering. [Forgeng]

Stoolball

Equipment

—1 leather ball (see instructions below)

—1 stools or similar target

Stoolball is another running game in which both men and women participated. It may have been played in several versions; the version here is based on the earliest known description of the game.

The first step is to make a ball. Cut four pieces of leather (designated I, II, III, and IV) in the shape shown.

Right sides together, stitch **abc** on I to **adc** on II; do likewise with III and IV. You will now have two roughly hemispherical pieces. Right sides together, stitch III to I/II, with the two hemispheres at 90 degrees to each other (so that the point **a** on III matches with **d** on I, **d** on III matches with **a** on I and II, **c** on III matches with **b** on II). You will now have a single sphere, with one seam still open. Turn the sphere right side out. Grab a bundle of fabric scraps (preferably wool, since it is springy). When squeezed, they should be about the size to stuff the sphere. Too many is better than too few.

Tie a piece of twine tightly around the scraps, and pass it around a few times in various directions, pulling tightly (you may want to wear gloves).

B

B   B   B

B   B   Stool   B

B

A

A

A

A

A

A   A   Arrangement of teams for
Stoolball.

Check the fit. If the bundle is too big, pull a few pieces out, wrap tightly a few more times and try again. If it is significantly too small, you will have to untie the twine, add some more pieces, and try again. Once the fit is reasonably close, wrap the twine tightly many times about the fabric so that most of the surface is covered. Squeeze the stuffing into the cover, and stitch it shut. A well-made ball will actually bounce on a hard surface (this is essentially what tennis balls were like in the days before rubber).

To set up the game, a stool is laid on its side with the seat facing the playing field (any target of comparable size will do one alternative is a pair of stones marking the left and right boundaries). Ideally, the ground should slope slightly downward from the stool: the team standing at the stool is therefore up, and the other is down.

Toss a coin to determine which side is up first. That team stands at the stool, the other is down in the field.

The first player stands at the stool and *posts* the ball to the opposing team—tossing it up and hitting it like a volleyball.

If no one on the down team can catch the ball, they pick it up and throw it at the stool. If they hit the stool, the player who first posted the ball is out, and the next one comes up. If they miss, the player scores 2 points for the team and posts again.

If the down team catch the initial posted ball, they post it back to the up team, who try to catch it. If no one can catch it, the player who first posted is out. If they catch it, they post it back again.

From here on, the teams post back and forth. If the down team is the first to miss the ball, they must throw at the stool, either hitting and making the initial player out, or missing, and that player scores 1 point and posts again. If the up team are the first to miss the ball, the player is out.

The up team continues until all players have posted, and the two teams change places. The first team to score 31 points is the winner.

Bowls/Quoits

Equipment

—2 hardwood balls for each player, about 3½″ in diameter (each pair of balls should be color coded to distinguish them from other pairs)

—1 *Mistress* (a stake that can be set upright in the ground) or 1 *Jack* (a ball smaller than the others, preferably of a bright contrasting color)

A point is designated as the casting spot and is indicated with some sort of mark, such as a piece of wood or metal called a *trig*. If using a Mistress, it is set up on the ground some distance away—the distance will depend on the players. Two Mistresses can be set up, each serving as the other's casting spot; this will save walking back and forth. If using a Jack, the first player casts it out onto the ground. Each player in turn casts one ball, trying to get it as close to the Jack or Mistress as possible; then each in turn casts the second ball. The player whose ball is closest at the end scores 1 point, 2 points for the two closest balls. A ball touching the target counts double. Balls can be knocked about by other balls, and the Jack can be repositioned in this way. The first player to reach a certain number of points (generally 5 or 7) wins the game.

Quoits is played in the same manner, save that the bowls are replaced by quoits, large flat stones or pieces of metal. The Mistress in quoits is an iron stake or *hob* driven into the ground; the Jack is a smaller quoit.

Board and Dice Games

Fox and Geese

Equipment

—1 game board. This could be as small as 4″ square or as big as you like. It can be made by carving a board, by drawing, painting, and so on.

—15 *Geese*. These are small counters: they can be pegs (in which case the board needs to have holes at all the intersections), stones, or other small items.

—1 *Fox*. This is a counter visibly larger than the Geese.

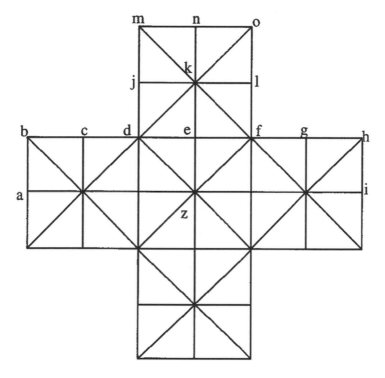

The board for Fox and Geese. [Forgeng]

One player has the Geese, which start on points **a, b, c, d, e, f, g, h, i, j, k, l, m, n, o.** The other player has the Fox, starting on point **z.** Each player moves in turn, along the lines to adjacent intersections. The Geese can move only sideways, downward, or diagonally downward. The Fox can move in any direction. The Fox can also jump over a Goose and capture it, as in checkers; multiple jumps are allowed in a single move. The Geese win if they pen up the Fox so that it cannot move; the Fox wins by capturing all the Geese.

Irish

Equipment

—1 backgammon set

Irish was one of the commonest *games at tables* (i.e., games played on a backgammon board). The rules are exactly the same as for modern backgammon, save that the special rules for doubles do not apply. The 15 men are placed as indicated by the numbers on the diagram, the upright numbers belonging to player 1, the upside-down ones to player 2. Player 1

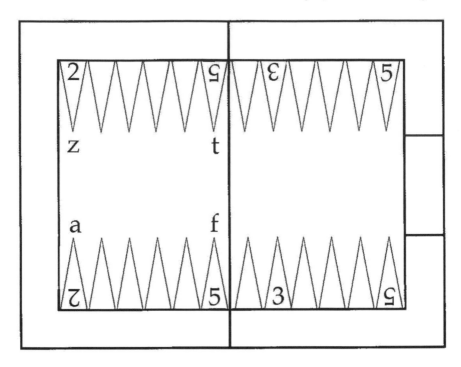

The setup for Irish. [Forgeng]

moves his men clockwise around the board from **z** toward **a** (his *home point*), player 2 counterclockwise from **a** toward **z** (his home point). The six points from **a** to **f** are player 1's home points, the six from **z** to **t** are player 2's home points.

The players each roll one die, and the higher roll moves first (if the rolls are equal, roll again). The first player rolls two dice for his move and may move one man for the number on each die (the same man may move for both). Once touched, a man must be played. After the first player has moved, it is the second player's turn.

A man cannot be moved onto a point already occupied by two or more opponents. If a man is left alone on a point and an opponent's man lands on it at the end of one die's move, that man is removed from the board and must be played on again from the far end.

Any player who has a man off the board must play it on before he can move any other men. This means that if the roll would require placing the entering man onto a point already occupied by two or more opponents, he must forfeit his turn. If a player has two or more men on all of his six home points and his opponent has a man to enter, one of those points must be *broken*: both players roll two dice, and the higher chooses a point from which all but one of the men are removed. The removed men must reenter the board again.

The player who removes all his men from the board first wins. No man may be played off the board until all of the player's men are in the six home points. It does not require an exact roll to play a man off the board.

Hazard

This was by far the most popular and enduring game at dice. The rules here derive from 17th-century sources.

Order of play is determined by the roll of one die—the highest roll goes first.

The first player rolls two dice until he gets a *Main*, which can be any number from 5 through 9.

He then rolls again.

—On a 2 or 3, he loses (a roll of 2 was called *ames-ace*).

—If the Main is 5 or 9 and the player again rolls the Main, he wins. This is called a *nick*. If he rolls an 11 or 12, he loses.

—If the Main is 6 or 8 and the player rolls the Main or a 12, it is a nick. If he rolls 11, he loses.

—If the Main is 7 and the player rolls the Main or an 11, it is a nick. If he rolls a 12, he loses.

—Any other roll is called the *Mark*. The player continues to roll until he gets the Mark and wins, or gets the Main and loses. If the player wins, he starts again rolling for a Main; if he loses, play moves clockwise to the next player.

Card Games

To determine order of play in any card game, each player lifts a random number of cards from the deck and looks at the bottom card. The highest card deals; ties lift again. As in modern usage, cards are shuffled and cut before play. The player to the left of the dealer is called the *eldest*. The eldest hand plays first and will be the next dealer.

Put

This game had a particularly low reputation as an alehouse pastime. All cards are used, of which the 3 ranks highest, the 2 next, and then the Ace, King, Queen, and so on. Suits are irrelevant to this game. This game is usually played with two players but can be played with more.

Each player is dealt one more card than there are players. The eldest leads a card, and the other players play cards to it until all players have laid down a card. Whoever plays the highest card takes the trick. Ties go to nobody. Each round consists of as many tricks as the players have cards,

A party at cards in the early 1600s. [By permission of the Folger Shakespeare Library]

and whoever wins two of the tricks scores 1 point. If nobody wins two tricks, nobody scores a point. Once the round is played, the next player deals. Play is normally to either 5 or 7 points, as agreed on by the players before the game.

At any point a player may knock on the table and say "Put!" If the other says, "I see it," whoever wins that round wins the game, regardless of the score, and takes the stakes. If the other does not see, the first player automatically wins the round and scores a point.

Maw

This is perhaps the simplest of trick-taking games involving suits. Each player pays one chip or coin to the pot and receives five cards. The aim is to either sweep the pool by winning three or more tricks, or, at least, to prevent anyone else from doing the same, thereby carrying the pot into the next round. The ordinary ranking of cards is Ace high and Deuce low.

The eldest hand plays a card to the table. Each player in turn must *follow suit*, if possible, by playing any card of the same suit led by the eldest. If the player does not have a card of that suit, he may play any card he chooses. The highest card in the suit led wins the trick. That player places all the cards from that trick next to him to keep score and leads the first card of the next trick. Once the current hand is played out, the deal passes to the eldest hand.

A player winning the first three tricks may claim the pot without further play, but if he leads to the fourth he is said to *jink* it, thus undertaking to win all five tricks. If he succeeds, all players must pay a second stake; if he fails, he loses the pot and it carries over into the next round.

This basic idea can be elaborated with all sorts of complications to make it more amusing to play. One version involves ranking two of the suits (usually the black suits or the red suits) in reverse order (Deuce high and Ace low).

Trumps can also be added. When the cards have been shuffled and dealt, turn over the top card of the deck. The suit of that card is the trump suit, and cards of that suit will beat cards of the suit led in any trick, with higher trumps beating lower trumps. Another variation is to have the top three cards of the deck be the Five of Trumps (called Five Fingers), Jack of Trumps, and Ace of Hearts (regardless of current trump suit), in that order.

Primero

To judge by contemporary references, this appears to have been one of the most popular card games in Elizabethan England. It is obviously related to modern poker.

Discard the 8s, 9s, and 10s of each suit. All players ante in. The dealer deals two cards to each, proceeding counterclockwise. Starting on the dealer's right, each player may choose to bet or to trade in one or both cards. As soon as one player bets, no one else may trade in cards. Once a player trades cards, the play passes to the next player. If all players trade cards (including the dealer), the hand is redealt.

Once a player bets, the others may play with the cards they have or drop out of the hand. However, if no other player chooses to continue, the last player after the one who laid the bet must match it and continue.

Except for the ante and the above provision, any bet may be refused. If each subsequent player refuses the bet, it must be withdrawn and play continues with the betting at the previous level.

After the initial round of betting, each player remaining receives two more cards. At this point, there is another round of betting, during which players declare the rank of their hands as they place their bets. Players may declare their hands at a level equal to or higher than what they actually have, but not lower. The one exception is if a previous player has declared a Flush or Primero and your hand is a Chorus (see hand rankings below), in which case you may declare your hand to be equal to the hand already declared.

After this round of betting, players may trade in one or two cards. Finally all remaining players reveal their hands, and the highest hand takes the pot.

The ranks of hands are as follows:

Numerus, the lowest hand, consists of two or three cards of the same suit. The point value is equal to the sum of the cards in that one suit.

Primero, or *Prime,* ranks next, consisting of one card of each suit. The value of a Primero is the sum of the cards in the hand.

Supreme, or *Fifty-Five,* is a hand containing the Ace, 6, and 7 of one suit. The value of this hand is always 55.

Flush consists of four cards of the same suit. Its value is the sum of the cards in the hand.

Chorus, the highest hand, is four of a kind.

Card values are as follows:

7:	21
6:	18
Ace:	16
5:	15
4:	14
3:	13
2:	12
Face Cards:	10

If two hands tie, the one closest to the right of the dealer wins.

SONGS

Quite a large number of songs of the Elizabethan period survive, including popular and folk-type songs. The following pages offer a selection of a few fairly simple ones, mostly from Thomas Ravenscroft's collections *Pammelia, Deuteromelia,* and *Melismata* [1609–11].

Lord Willoughby

[Chappell]

The fifteenth day of Ju - ly, with glist'-ning spear and shield, A famous fight in Flan - ders was fought-en in the field: The most cou-ra-geous of-fi-cers was Eng-lish cap-tains three; But the bravest man in bat - tle was brave Lord Wil - lough - by.

"Stand to it, noble pikemen,
And look you round about,
And shoot you right, you bowmen,
And we will keep them out.
You muskets and calivermen,
Do you prove true to me,
I'll be the foremost man in fight,"
Said brave Lord Willoughby.

Then quoth the Spanish general,
"Come let us march away,
I fear we shall be spoiled all
If we here longer stay,
For yonder comes Lord Willoughby
With courage fierce and fell,
He will not give one inch of way
For all the devils in hell."

And then the fearful enemy
Were quickly put to flight,
Our men pursued courageously
And caught their forces quite,
But at the last they gave a shout
Which echoed through the sky,
"God and St. George for England!"
The conquerors did cry.

To the soldiers that were maimed
And wounded in the fray
The Queen allowed a pension
Of eighteen pence a day,
And from all costs and charges
She quit and set them free,
And this she did all for the sake
Of brave Lord Willoughby.

Then courage, noble Englishmen,
And never be dismayed,
For if we be but one to ten
We will not be afraid
To fight the foreign enemy
And set our country free,
And thus I end the bloody bout
Of brave Lord Willoughby.

This patriotic song commemorated a victory by Peregrine Bertie, Lord Willoughby, in the Netherlands in the 1580s. The words are preserved in a 17th-century broadside, but the music is found in 16th-century collections.

Tomorrow the Fox Will Come to Town

[Ravenscroft]

He'll steal the Cock out from his flock!
  Keep, keep, keep, keep!
He'll steal the Cock out from his flock!
  O keep you all well there! etc.

He'll steal the Hen out of the pen!
  Keep, keep, keep, keep!
He'll steal the Hen out of the pen!
  O keep you all well there! etc.

He'll steal the Duck out of the brook!
  Keep, keep, keep, keep!
He'll steal the Duck out of the brook!
  O keep you all well there! etc.

He'll steal the Lamb e'en from his dam!
  Keep, keep, keep, keep!
He'll steal the Lamb e'en from his dam!
  O keep you all well there! etc.

The fox was a constant problem for the Elizabethan husbandman—traditionally, when such an animal was found prowling in the village, all the villagers would be called out to pursue it.

Of All the Birds that Ever I See

[Ravenscroft]

"Of all the birds that ever I see" was a common traditional opening for a song—this silly song was a send-up of the type. Cinnamon, ginger, nutmeg, and cloves were used to make spiced ale and wine. This song was originally set for several voices; if you have several singers, all should sing the plain text, and divide into half to sing the italic and bold texts.

Hold Thy Peace

[Ravenscroft]

This is a *catch*, or round, for three voices—it appears in Shakespeare's *Twelfth Night*. "Thou knave" was a common insult, and "Hold thy peace" was essentially the Elizabethan for "Shut up!" This round was obviously intended to be silly and loud.

Hold thy peace, and I pri - thee hold thy peace,

thou knave,   hold thy peace   thou   knave,

thou   knave.

Hey Ho Nobody at Home

[Ravenscroft]

This is a catch for five voices, a version of which is sometimes heard today.

Hey   ho,   no - bo - dy at home,   meat nor drink nor   mo - ney have I none. Fill the pot Ea - die

DANCE

Elizabethans tended to categorize dances according to the country of origin. Italian dances were particularly fashionable; French dances also had a long history in England; and dances of the native English style were known as country dances. Our principal source for English country dancing is *The English Dancing Master,* a collection of dances published by John Playford, which went through 10 editions between 1651 and 1700 and several more in the 18th century.

Elizabethan sources mention quite a number of country dances by name, nearly 20 of which were later to appear in Playford. Three of these appear here. We cannot be certain that these dances were the same in the 16th century as in Playford's day, but Playford's versions probably correspond in general to the Elizabethan form even if they may have differed in detail.

Of the courtly dances imported from France, perhaps the most popular was the almain, which is often found in country as well as courtly contexts. Quite a few almains are described in Elizabethan manuscripts from the Inns of Court, including those printed here: the versions here try to follow Bodleian MS. Douce 280, a manuscript dating to around 1600.

The *measure* was an English development of French dances, and probably similar to the almain in style.

It is relatively easy to recreate the steps of dances; it is harder to recreate their feel. Many Elizabethan dances were rather simple and sedate, and we may presume that they did not rely on exciting choreography for their appeal. There was probably a lot of communication of one sort or another; and there was doubtless considerable emphasis on skill and grace, rather than mere memorization of complex patterns.

Symbols

[A],[B], etc. designate sections of the music.

[Ax2] means that section is performed twice.

[A1] and [A2] are two repetitions of the same music.

LF Left Foot

RF Right Foot

H Honor

s Single

d Double

Up means the "top" of the hall, normally where the musicians are. All dances begin on the left foot. The man normally stands on the lady's left. Couple dances begin with partners taking near hands; if necessary, couples may be arranged in a processional circle, with *up* being clockwise.

Steps

The numbers on the left of each step description are beats of the music (*and* is a half-beat).

Honor (Reverence)

As the music begins, take hands: hands are held low for a country dance, forearms are held horizontal for a measure or almain.

1–2 Slide the right foot back, bending the right leg, and remove the hat with the left hand (women do the same, but do not move the right foot as far or remove the hat).

3–4 Return the right foot to place and replace the hat.

An Honor should always be done at the beginning and end of any dance. For this purpose, the musicians should play the last few measures of the tune to start, and hold the last note at the end.

The reverence.
[Arbeau]

Double (Country Dance)

1   Step onto the left foot

2   Step onto the right foot

3   Step onto the left foot

and Rise on the toes of the left foot

4   Close the right foot to the left foot as you lower your heels.

The next double starts on the right foot. A double can be done in any direction.

Double (Measure or Almain)

1   Step onto the left foot

2   Step onto the right foot

3   Step onto the left foot

4   Kick the right foot forward, either with or without a hop.

The next double starts on the right foot. Doubles may be done in any direction.

Single/Set (Country Dance)

1   Step onto the left foot
and Rise on the toes of the left foot
2   Close the right foot to the left foot as you lower your heels.

The next single starts on the right foot. A single can be done in any direction: in country dances, a single to the side is called a *set*.

Single (Measure or Almain)

1   Step onto the left foot
2   Kick the right foot forward, either with or without a hop.

The next single starts on the right foot. Singles may be done in any direction.

Slip Step ("French slide")

1   Step left foot to the left
and Move the right foot next to the left as you hop onto it.

The next slip steps will be onto the left foot again—they do not alternate.

"French" Dances

Earl of Essex Measure

[Cunningham 26; Pugliese & Cassaza 17]

[A] Double forward, single back. Repeat a total of four times.
[B] Slow set left and right, double forward, single back.

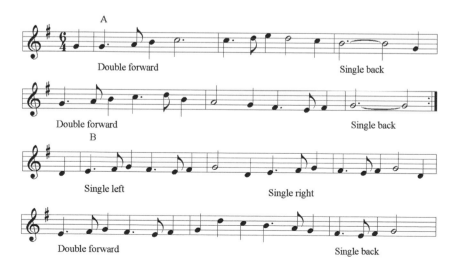

Black Almain

[Cunningham 27, 33; Pugliese & Casazza 31]

[A] All dance four doubles forward.

[B1] Turn to face partner and drop hands: double back, then double forward.

[B2] All make a quarter-turn left: double forward. All make a half-turn right: double forward.

[C] All turn to face partner. Men do two singles and a double, turning in place. Women do likewise on the repeat.

[D] All take both hands: double clockwise to partner's place. All do four slip-steps up the hall. All double clockwise back to own place, and do four slip-steps down the hall. All drop hands: double backward, then double to meet again.

The second time through the dance, the women set first, then the men.

Country Dances

Steps and Terms

Unless indicated otherwise, steps are a lively walking step. According to one late-17th-century Continental observer, English country dances were noteworthy for the dancers' freedom in choosing such types of steps as pleased them.

Set: A single step to the side.

Turn single: The dancer turns alone in place with a double step. The feet trace out a small circle on the floor, and the dancer ends up where he started.

Turn each other: Partners take one or both hands and turn around each other, giving weight (i.e., leaning or pulling back slightly) as they go around.

Lead a double and back: Partners take near hands and do a double step forward in the specified direction and a double backward.

Partners, Corners, Opposites: Partners stand with the man on the left, the woman on the right. The *corner* is the dancer of the opposite sex on the other side of you from your partner. The *opposite* is the person of the opposite sex across from you in the set.

Numbering of Couples: The 1s are the couple closest to the top of the hall, the 2s the couple next to them, and so on.

Circle: All join hands in a circle and slip-step around for a certain number of steps (clockwise first).

Cast: The dancer turns away from the set and goes around the outside.

Arming: The two dancers link arms, left arms for *arm left* and right arms for *arm right,* and walk around once in a circle, ending back in their original places.

Siding: The two dancers move toward each other with a small double step, to meet left shoulder to left shoulder (for *side left*), or right shoulder to right shoulder (for *side right*).

Trenchmore (The Hunting of the Fox)

[Playford (1653) 103; Millar 85]

This dance is mentioned as early as 1551 and seems to have been extremely popular for a very long period. Any number may dance: partners stand in a longways set, men on the left side, women on the right.

The melody is that of "Tomorrow the Fox Will Come to Town" (p. 212).

Top of Hall

M   W
M   W
M   W
etc.

1st Verse

Partners lead up a double and back twice [Playford: three times]. 1s, followed by the rest, cast off, going separately down the outside, then meet at the bottom to lead back up to their original place [Playford: three times].

2nd Verse

Arched hey: All take hands; 2s make an arch, which 1s pass under; 1s make an arch, which 3s pass under; 1s pass under 4s while 2s pass under 3s, etc., until all are back in their original places [Playford: "Do this forward and back twice or thrice"].

3rd Verse

1s cross to set to the 2s (the first man setting to the second woman, and the first woman to the second man), then to each other, then to the 3s, then to each other, and so on down the line. Once all the way through the set, they turn back and arm the last couple by the right (the man arming the last woman, the woman the last man), then each other by the left, and so on back up the set to place.

4th Verse

1s turn each other by the right hand, then the 2s by the left, the 3s by the right, and so on to the bottom of the set. The dance begins again with a new couple at the top.

The version here is somewhat shortened from Playford's. The dance has also been adjusted to make the 3rd and 4th verses work; from the way Playford describes it, it is obviously not too rigidly structured anyway. Millar offers a slightly shorter version in which the 3rd verse consists of arming to the bottom, and the 4th verse is omitted.

Sellenger's Round (The Beginning of the World)

[Playford (1675) 1; Keller & Shimer 96; Millar 8]

This dance is first mentioned in 1593 but was probably popular for some time before that; the melody is recorded in 16th-century collections. Any number of couples stand in a circle facing inward, with each man on his partner's left.

1st Verse

[A] All circle eight steps clockwise and eight steps back.

Chorus

[B] All do two single steps advancing toward the middle of the circle, then fall back a double to places, face partners, then set and turn single. Repeat.

2nd Verse

[A] Partners lead in a double and back. Repeat.

[B] Chorus.

3rd Verse

[A] Partners side right and left.

[B] Chorus.

4th Verse

[A] Partners arm right and left.

[B] Chorus.

Playford's version of the first chorus omits the double in and back, but the music seems to demand it.

Heartsease

[Playford (1651); Keller & Shimer 45; Millar 20]

This dance is attested as early as 1560. Two couples stand facing each other in a square, each man with his partner on his right, and his corner in front of him.

1st Verse

[A] Partners lead forward a double and back. Repeat.

Chorus

[B1] All face partners, fall back a double, then forward a double. Then face corners and turn your corner once around by the right hand.

[B2] Still facing corners, fall back a double, then forward a double. Then face partners and turn your partner once around by the left hand.

2nd Verse

[A1] Partners side right.

[A2] Face your corner. Corners side left.

[B] Chorus.

3rd Verse

[A1] Partners arm right.

[A2] Face your corner. Corners arm left.

[B] Chorus.

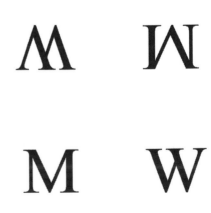

Positions of the dancers for Heartsease.

NOTES

1. Moryson, Fynes. *Shakespeare's Europe*, ed. Charles Hughes (London: Sherratt and Hughes, 1903), 475–77.

2. P. Razzell, ed., *The Journals of Two Travellers in Elizabethan and Early Stuart England* (London: Caliban Books, 1995), 27–28.

3. Phillip Stubbes, *The Anatomie of Abuses* (London: Richard Jones, 1583), fol. 99r.

4. Stubbes, *Anatomie*, fols. 115v–116r.

5. Richard Mulcaster, *Positions Wherein Those Primitive Circumstances Be Examined Which Are Necessary for the Training Up of Children* (London: Thomas Chare, 1581), 104–5.

6. Randle Holme, *The Academy of Armory* [1688] (Menston: Scolar Press, 1972), 3.264.

7. The outdoor games and board games are taken from Francis Willughby, *Francis Willughby's Book of Games: A Seventeenth-Century Treatise on Sports, Games, and Pastimes*, eds. David Cram, Jeffrey L. Forgeng, and Dorothy Johnston (Aldershot: Ashgate Press, 2003). The dice games are from Holme, *Academy*, and Charles Cotton, "The Compleat Gamester [1674]," in *Games and Gamesters of the Restoration* (London: Routledge, 1930). The card games are from Cotton, *Gamester*; Holme, *Academy*; Willughby, *Book of Games*; and David Parlett, *The Oxford Guide to Card Games* (Oxford: Oxford University Press, 1990).

9

The Elizabethan World

Elizabeth came to the throne in the middle of a century when the globe was being swiftly and radically transformed. European mariners had found their way to the Indian Ocean and the Americas at the end of the 1400s: in a very short time, societies separated by miles and millennia suddenly found themselves in direct contact with each other. Elizabethans became familiar with plants, places, and peoples undreamt of by their grandparents. Even the shape of the universe was changing, as the astronomical theories of scientists like Copernicus found their way from the margin to the mainstream. Such alterations in the external world were mirrored by changes within the Elizabethan mind as individuals began to revise fundamental assumptions about their place in the world around them.

Then as now, people's horizons were shaped by their participation in networks of travel and communication. Local Elizabethan society could be very insular. Farmers did not often need to travel, beyond visiting a nearby fair or market to sell produce or purchase supplies. When villagers contrasted their countrymen with foreigners, they were usually speaking of people from the village as contrasted with nonlocals.

Yet overall there was a surprising degree of mobility. In southeastern England, perhaps 70 to 80 percent of the population moved at least once in their lives. Some livelihoods required ongoing travel: servants in search of a new master, chapmen and factors plying their trades, and wage laborers following the market. Migration tended to be toward the south and east of the country, from the countryside to the towns, and from small towns toward larger ones. Prosperous landholders were unlikely to migrate: it was the poor, the landless, and the young who most often had to move. The population of London was especially fluid: it was estimated in the 1580s that the population of any given parish was mostly changed over any given period of 12 years or so.

For those who moved only once in their lives, the move was probably local, as when young people left their parents' house for a new household either through marriage or employment. Such moves often took the person to a new community, but not necessarily far from their place of birth. The distance was more likely to be significant if there was a major career move involved. Craftsmen, tradesmen, and professionals relocated to pursue advancement in their careers, and there was a constant migration of unskilled workers into the towns, especially London.

Although relocation was rare among the upper classes, travel was common: merchants traveled to oversee their enterprises; major landowners owned multiple estates in different parts of the country; and upper-class families from the provinces spent part of the year in London, pursuing the social contacts and cultural opportunities that the city afforded

This mobility created networks of people that extended well beyond the travel ranges of any individual. A countryman who had never traveled beyond the nearest market town might have friends or relatives who had ended up in London. Urban con artists made a living by playing on these connections: seeing a prosperous but naive countryman on the city streets, they would introduce themselves and invent a personal connection to work their way into their victim's trust, calling him *cousin*—so that *to cozen* came to mean "to cheat."

These networks of travel and communication contributed to a sense of national identity that was unusually strong compared to other parts of Europe at the time. In spite of regional differences, most English people felt a deep sense of belonging to England. This nationalism was both expressed and perpetuated in popular culture (as in the song "Lord Willoughby" in the previous chapter); it was also fostered by the Queen's impeccable talent for public relations. As the reign progressed, it was heightened by a sense of national danger: war with Spain and the threat of invasion, rebellion in Ireland, and papal efforts to subvert English Protestantism. London played a crucial role in crystallizing this sense of national identity: few European capitals dominated national life or were as connected to their provinces as England's. A constant stream of travelers to and from the city ensured a close connection between London and the rest of the nation.

LAND TRAVEL

Travel was an important part of Elizabethan life and the Elizabethan economy, yet Elizabethan systems of transportation were so haphazard that it is misleading to call them systems at all. The roads were problematic. Unpaved, and for the most part without foundations (with the exception of the roads left over from Roman days), they were difficult to use in adverse weather. Parliament passed Highways Acts in the mid-1500s requiring each parish to maintain its roads, but as with many ambitious reforms of the period, the goals outreached the capacity for enforcement. In practice, conditions depended on local custom and initiative. Moreover, weak law enforcement left travelers vulnerable to the depredations of highwaymen. There were long stretches of lonely road even on major thoroughfares, with ample greenery by the wayside to conceal an ambush. The main roads out of London were favored haunts of highway robbers, who preyed on the substantial wealth that passed in and out of the city on any given day.

Although the roads were bad, travel accommodations were surprisingly good. The better English inns had private rooms with fireplaces and food service; the lodger was given a key and could expect clean sheets on the bed. Of course, people traveling on a tight budget might not be so well accommodated, and most people could expect to share their bed with other wayfarers. If you weren't close to a large town at nightfall, you might have to make arrangements at a village alehouse or a private home. The least fortunate had to take shelter under hedgerows as best they might. Even a seemingly good inn might have its drawbacks. Inn staff sometimes collaborated with highway robbers, sending report of particularly promising victims who stayed at their inn.

The speed of travel was a fraction of modern rates. A person journeying on foot could cover 15 miles a day by road in fair weather. On horseback one could travel twice or even three times as far, although a horse could not be pushed that fast indefinitely. Purchasing a horse could be expensive, but the cost could be reduced by renting or by buying the animal used. Horse dealers, called *horsecoursers*, had much the same reputation among Elizabethans as used-car salesmen today. Various tricks of the trade could make a horse seem younger or healthier than it was, and there was extensive trafficking in stolen mounts. Owners branded their horses or nicked them on the ear as a means of identification, but there were ways to obliterate or alter the markings. One could also fasten a large padlock (called a *fetterlock*) on the horse's leg to prevent theft.

Riders by post, with regular changes of horses awaiting them at official post-houses, could cover 10 miles an hour and as much as 100 or even 160 miles in a day. Post-houses were kept by postmasters, typically innkeepers specially licensed by the Queen; the post-houses were located at about 10-mile intervals along major roads. They had originally been established as a network to ensure the speedy expedition of royal business, but private individuals were also allowed to hire post-horses, although they also had to hire a postboy or guide to bring the horses back.

Those who wished might travel by cart, wagon, or coach. Carts were two-wheeled vehicles, mostly used for carrying small quantities of goods. Wagons had four wheels and might carry over 6,000 pounds. They mostly

ENGLISH INNS DESCRIBED, 1577

Our inns are . . . very well furnished with napery, bedding, and tapestry. . . . Each comer is sure to lie in clean sheets, wherein no man hath been lodged since they came from the laundress or out of the water wherein they were last washed. . . . The traveler . . . may carry the key with him, as of his own house, so long as he lodgeth there. If he lose aught whilst he abideth in the inn, the host is bound by a general custom to restore the damage, so that there is no greater security anywhere for travelers than in the greatest inns of England. . . .

Many an honest man is spoiled of his goods as he traveleth to and fro, in which feat also the counsel of the tapsters, or drawers of drink, and chamberlains is not seldom behind or wanting. Certes I believe not that chapman or traveler in England is robbed by the way without the knowledge of some of them; for when he cometh into the inn and alighteth from his horse, the hostler forthwith is very busy to take down his budget or capcase [traveling bag] in the yard from his saddlebow, which he peiseth [weighs] slyly in his hand to feel the weight thereof. . . . The tapster in like sort for his part doth mark his behavior and what plenty of money he draweth when he payeth. . . .

Each owner . . . contendeth with other for goodness of entertainment of their guests, as about fineness and change of linen, furniture of bedding, beauty of rooms, service at the table, costliness of plate, strength of drink, variety of wines, or well using of horses.

William Harrison, *The Description of England*, ed. Georges Edelen (Ithaca, NY: Folger Shakespeare Library, 1968), 397–99.

served for carrying goods, but travelers could also book passage—the coach might have an awning to provide some protection against sun and dust. Coaches were more expensive but more comfortable since they were fully enclosed vehicles designed specifically for passengers. Regular coach and wagon service was developing between major towns over the course of Elizabeth's reign: by 1575 there was a weekly wagon between Oxford and London, leaving on Saturday and returning the following Wednesday. All of these vehicles were slower than riding, and none had springs, so the journey was a boneshaker. Overland transport of small volumes of goods could also be by packhorse: packhorses could carry only about 225 pounds each, but they were better on rough terrain or in bad weather.

The post system provided the royal government with an effective means of transporting messages, but private citizens had to make shift as best they could. One might hire a courier; local letters might be entrusted to a servant (large aristocratic households had footmen who specialized in running these sorts of errands); over long distances, the letter might

THE ACTOR EDWARD ALLEYN WRITES TO HIS WIFE, 1593

My good sweet mouse, I commend me heartily to you, and to my father, my mother, and my sister Bess, hoping in God, though the sickness be round about you, yet by His mercy it may escape your house, which by the grace of God it shall. Therefore use this course: keep your house fair and clean (which I know you will) and every evening throw water before your door . . . and have in your windows good store of rue and herb of grace . . . Now good mouse I have no news to send you but this, that we have all our health, for which the Lord be praised. I received your letter at Bristol by Richard Couley, for the which I thank you. I have sent you by this bearer (Thomas Pope's kinsman) my white waistcoat, because it is a trouble to me to carry it. . . . If you send any more letters, send to me by the carriers of Shrewsbury or to West Chester or to York, to be kept till my Lord Strange's Players come. . . .

Your loving husband, E. Alleyn

[*Postscript*] Mouse, you send me no news of any things you should send of your domestical matters, such things as happens at home, as how your distilled water proves, or this or that or any thing what you will.

[*Address*] This be delivered to Master Henslowe, one of the grooms of Her Majesty's Chamber, dwelling on the Bankside right over against the Clink.

R. A. Foakes and R. T. Rickert, eds. *Henslowe's Diary* (Cambridge: Cambridge University Press, 1961), 274–75.

simply be given to someone who was known to be traveling toward the letter's destination. The letter would be folded over and sealed with wax, and the recipient's name written on the outside, with some indication of where he or she might be found.

WATER TRAVEL

Water routes played a much more visible role in transportation than they do today, in part due to cost: for bulk goods, transport by water could cost ¼ to ¹/₁₂ of the price by land. Speed was not a factor, since travel by boat was no quicker than land travel and could take much longer depending on weather and the directness of the route. The journey between Dover and Calais, a distance of about 25 miles, took two to four hours with favorable winds and could take as long as seven. The voyage to the New World normally lasted a month or two.

Water transport was especially important to England, an island nation that had no contact with the outside world except by sea. The heavily indented coastline (second in Europe only to Norway) and numerous

A post rider in the early 1600s. [By permission of the Folger Shakespeare Library]

navigable rivers also made water transport accessible to a large part of the country.

Since bridges were comparatively rare, boats were essential in some places as a means of crossing rivers. London had only a single bridge: transportation along and across the Thames was provided by a multitude of small rowing-boats called *wherries*, giving Elizabethan London something of the flavor we associate with Venice. A wherry ride across the river cost 1d.; the trip between London and Greenwich cost 8d. with the tide, 12d. against it. The Swiss visitor Thomas Platter was favorably impressed with these boats: "The wherries are charmingly upholstered and embroidered cushions are laid across the seats, very comfortable to sit on or lean against, and generally speaking the benches only seat two people next to one another; many of them are covered in, particularly in rainy weather or fierce sunshine."[1]

Warships and commercial ships were not very different from each other. The seas were a dangerous place: merchant ships were generally fitted with at least a few guns and were often pressed into military service in times of war. There were a few significant distinctions. Ships built specifically for war tended to be narrower in proportion to their width, and the largest warships were much larger than any merchant ship. There were no passenger ships as such—travelers overseas would book passage on a merchant ship of some sort. Merchant ships tended to be of about 200 tons (a figure that estimated the number of barrels—*tuns*—that could be carried in its hold), rarely reaching 300 or 350, and almost never anything above; the keel would be around 60 feet long. Warships might be of 500 tons or more, with keels of about 100 feet and beams of 35 feet, carrying 30–40 guns and crews of 200–300. Yet many ships were much smaller. The *Golden Hind*, on which Francis Drake circled the globe, was 100 feet long, 18 feet broad, and of 140 tons, and it carried 16 principal guns and 90 crew.

Hulls were rounded toward the fore, tapering toward the aft, and built up high and narrow at deck level—this served in part to reduce tolls, which were often levied on ships based on deck area. Sails were few: a three-masted ship would carry two square sails each on the fore- and mainmasts, another square sail on the bowsprit, and a triangular lateen sail on the mizzenmast. Under favorable conditions, such ships might make some four to six knots (around five to seven miles per hour).

TOURISM

During the Middle Ages, travel had been generally for professional or military reasons, or for the purpose of pilgrimage. By the late 1500s, personal secular travel—tourism—had become well established. Within England one popular tourist attraction was Drake's *Golden Hind*, which was ultimately destroyed by visitors taking chips of wood from it. Another favored destination was the Tower of London, where visitors might pay the staff to show them the royal armories, menagerie, and crown jewels. St. Paul's Cathedral and Westminster Abbey were also tourist sites. Perhaps the most eccentric tourist attraction in England was the Great Bed of Ware in Hertfordshire—this palatial bed, which survives today in the Victoria and Albert Museum in London, was over 11 feet wide.

However, the favorite destination for English travelers was the Continent. A young man of the upper classes might follow his formal schooling with a journey to France and Italy, in the company of a tutor hired by his parents: such a trip, it was thought, gave the final polish to his education and breeding. Even older men and women were known to visit the Continent out of sheer interest. Traditionalists viewed such excursions with mistrust, and Italy in particular was seen as a bad influence. William Harrison expressed a view typical of many of his countrymen: "This . . . is generally to be reprehended in all estates of gentility, and which in short time will turn to the great ruin of our country, and that is, the usual sending of noblemen's and mean gentlemen's sons into Italy, from whence they bring home nothing but mere atheism, infidelity, vicious conversation, and ambitious and proud behaviour, whereby it cometh to pass that they return far worse men than they went out."[2]

Those who wished to travel, both internally and overseas, had to secure passports. People traveling outside their home parish needed to be able to prove that they were not mere vagrants—an easy thing to do for someone who was obviously well-to-do, or if you were going only as far as a nearby market town, but if you weren't rich and were traveling far afield, it was best to get a document signed by two justices of the peace. Those who were found to be vagrants could be whipped and sent home.

Anyone who wanted to journey overseas needed a passport from the Privy Council. This requirement helped the government keep tabs on the dealings of Englishmen overseas, and permission was not always easy to obtain: it was reported that when someone applied for a passport, Lord Burghley "would first examine him of England. And if he found him ignorant, would bid him stay at home, and know his own country first."[3]

Then as now, tourism could be an expensive hobby: Fynes Moryson, one of the greatest travel writers of the day, recommended allowing expenses of £50–60 a year, several times the annual income of the middling sorts of commoners.

GEOGRAPHY

Travel was not the only way people could broaden their horizons. A growing body of geographical literature was becoming available in English. English scholars compiled substantial volumes detailing the geography, history, and culture of their native country: William Harrison's broad-reaching and detailed *Description of England* first appeared in 1577; William Camden published his *Britannia* in 1586; and a series of local studies of individual shires came out during Elizabeth's reign. Other works offered the stay-at-home Englishman a glimpse of the wider world. The most famous was Richard Hakluyt's monumental bestseller *Principal Navigations, Voyages, and Discoveries of the English Nation*. First published in 1589, and reissued in an enlarged edition in 1598–1600, Hakluyt's work in many ways laid the foundation for England's reputation as a nation of global explorers.

The emerging science of cartography quickly permeated the daily lives of the educated. The Flemish cartographer Gerard Mercator first published his ground-breaking atlas in 1569, and before long maps were becoming a familiar sight in English homes, both as a source of information and as a fashionable form of interior decoration. According to John Dee, people collected maps, charts, and globes, "some to beautify their halls, parlors, chambers, galleries, studies or libraries with; other some for things past, as battles fought . . . and such occurrences in histories mentioned; . . . some other presently to view the large dominion of the Turk, the wide empire of the Muscovite, and the little morsel of ground where Christendom . . . is

LEONARD DIGGES'S PREFACE TO
HIS TRANSLATION OF COPERNICUS, 1576

In this our age one rare wit . . . hath by long study, painful practice, and rare invention, delivered a new theoric or model of the world, showing that the earth resteth not in the center of the whole world, but only in the center of this our mortal world or globe of elements which environed and enclosed the moon's orb. . . . Reason and deep discourse having opened these things to Copernicus, and the same being with demonstrations mathematical most apparently by him to the world delivered, I though it convenient together with the old theoric also to publish this, to the end such noble English minds as delight to reach above the baser sort of men might not be altogether defrauded of so noble a part of philosophy. . . . If . . . the earth be situate immoveable in the center of the world, why find we not theorics upon that ground to produce the effects as true and certain as these of Copernicus? . . . Why shall we so much dote in the appearance of our sense, which many ways may be abused, and not suffer ourselves to be directed by the rule of reason, which the great God hath given us as a lamp to lighten the darkness of our understanding and the perfect guide to lead us to the golden branch of verity amid the forest of errors?

Leonard Digges, *A Prognostication of Right Good Effect* (London: Thomas Marsh, 1576), sig. M1r-v.

certainly known; . . . some other for their own journeys directing into far lands, or to understand other men's travels."[4] A series of county maps of England were published by Christopher Saxton in the 1570s: by the end of the century, Saxton's maps had become "usual with all noblemen and gentlemen, and daily perused by them."[5]

Before the Elizabethan age, Englishmen had mostly known their world from a ground-level perspective. Travelers found their way from place to place by landmarks such as bridges, hills, and towns and often had to rely on local advice and guides to help them on their way. Now it was becoming increasingly possible to visualize the world from the bird's-eye perspective of the mapmaker, suggesting the possibility that humans could rise above their natural environment.

SYSTEMS OF BELIEF

The shape of the universe was itself changing, as the geocentric cosmos of the Middle Ages was gradually displaced by the heliocentric model proposed by Copernicus (first published in 1543). Originally seen as heretical, and still highly controversial in parts of Europe, the Copernican model was rapidly gaining acceptance in England during Elizabeth's reign.

The changing physical model of the universe was part of a broader process of transformation that was beginning to redefine the relationship between people and the cosmos they inhabited. This process unfolded principally in the domain of religion, which provided the framework and vocabulary through which people understood their place in the world.

Religion ranked with profession and family as a core defining feature of an Elizabethan person's life. It was seen as the key ingredient in the recipe for a successful society, and it was the primary criterion by which one judged a life successfully lived. God was invoked on waking in the morning and retiring at night, at the beginning and end of meals, in greetings and in partings. People interpreted the course of human history and the cycles of their own lives through religious stories, particularly the stories of personal and national salvation that pervade the New and Old Testaments. Birth, baptism, marriage, and death were waypoints on an individual's road to heaven, following in the footsteps of Christ. The political history of Tudor England was seen as the story of a people chosen by God for tribulation and greatness, paralleling the experiences of the Jews in the Old Testament.

To the degree that religious skepticism, atheism, and irreligion were present, they operated within an essentially religious framework. When Lady Monson in 1597 consulted an astrologer "because she doubteth whether there is a God," her doubts actually confirmed the importance of religion in her life.[6] One contemporary complained that it was "a matter very common to dispute whether there be a God or not," but in reality, few people voiced such questions, which could lead to the severest punishment. Christopher Marlowe is sometimes cited as an example of Elizabethan atheism, and he certainly ran considerable risk in claiming (as reported by a hostile informant) "that the first beginning of religion was only to keep men in awe," and "that Christ deserved better to die than Barabbas and that the Jews made a good choice though Barabbas was both a thief and a murderer."[7] Marlowe's words went unpunished, probably because of his shadowy connections to the government spy network, but in reality, they were in large part a posture of transgression by a self-made "bad boy"—a posture that had shock power precisely because he lived in a pervasively religious environment.

Marlowe's provocative statements were ultimately sacrilegious rather than atheistic, and sacrilege is well documented in Elizabethan culture, whether in the form of swearing, blasphemy, or profanation of religious sacraments. On one occasion, a goose and gander were married; on another, a horse's head was baptized; on yet another, an entire dead horse was brought to receive communion. Such impious actions were the ritual equivalent of Marlowe's sacrilegious speech: their topsy-turvydom deliberately violated accepted cultural propriety but was not necessarily intended as a serious challenge to the established cultural order.

Most people adhered to at least outward conformity with the religious status quo, in part because of the sanctions for failing to do so, but also because it was widely agreed that religious conformity was essential to the well-being of society. Hardly anyone advocated freedom of worship. Catholic recusants and Protestant separatists alike believed that only a single religion should be permitted, disagreeing only in what that religion should be.

The nature of the dominant religious model changed significantly during Elizabeth's lifetime. When she came to the throne, most adults had grown up in an environment shaped by medieval Catholicism. For such people, religion was a ritualized activity rooted in material things: doing pious works, honoring established religious institutions, observing the cycle of religious holy days that embodied the defining stories of the received faith. Respect for tradition encompassed not only specifically religious practices, but the host of secular observances that came with them, such as the festive rituals that attached to religious holidays.

The emerging Protestant generation of Elizabeth's day were moving toward a mode of religion that was more cerebral and less reverent toward tradition. In its place, Protestants emphasized study of the Bible as the universal guide and reflection on its meaning in the life of the reader. Lady Margaret Hoby's diary records daily religious reading and reflection, searching her own soul before bedtime to judge her own conduct, and often meeting with others to read and discuss religious texts. Indeed the diary begins to emerge as a literary form in this period, particularly among reformist Protestants for whom it served as a means of cultivating religious self-awareness.

As literacy spread, more people were able to participate in this process of spiritual inquiry and reflection. Even those who could not read had ample opportunities to take part in contemporary religious culture. Weekly church services included sermons and biblical readings, large towns offered public sermons outside of the regular services, and small-group reading was a common activity among reformists like Lady Hoby. Public discussions on religious themes, known as *prophesyings,* were widely attended in the early part of Elizabeth's reign; these provided a fertile ground for the development of increasingly reformist Protestantism, to the degree that the Queen had them suppressed in 1577.

All of these factors shifted the midpoint of English religious belief in a Protestant direction, but most people fell somewhere between Catholic and Protestant extremes. Practicing Catholics were few, but a majority of the population observed customs that would be regarded as superstitious by the reformists: one critic complained in 1584 that "three parts at least of the people [are] wedded to their old superstition still."[8] In 1590 in the conservative county of Lancashire, many observing members of the English church were still bringing prayer beads to services and habitually crossing

Consulting an astrologer. [*Shakespeare's England*]

themselves. At the other end of the spectrum, ardent reformists called for the abolition of bishops, yet most Protestants were willing to accept their continued existence. Some of the leading reformers were bishops themselves: Edmund Grindal, archbishop of Canterbury, was suspended from his office for resisting the Queen's order to suppress prophesyings.

Not every aspect of belief fell on a spectrum between Catholic and Protestant. At the margins of the Christian worlds of heaven, hell, and earth was another realm that did not fit comfortably into the geography of salvation: a world of angels, fairies, and witches, of astrology and divination—some of them perhaps mentioned in scripture, but none having a clear place in Christian theology.

Such phenomena had roots in the more inclusive, less rationalistic spiritual environment of the Catholic Middle Ages. Yet belief in these forces was widespread across all sectors of society, regardless of religious leanings. Witchcraft was accepted as real by both church and state and carried the death penalty. Witchcraft accusations were most numerous in the highly Protestantized regions of southeastern England. They peaked in the 1580s and 1590s, although they were never as numerous as they tend to be in the modern popular imagination. Indictments for witchcraft in Essex, one of the counties most active in prosecuting witchcraft cases, amounted to 174 over the 40-year period 1563–1603; fewer than half of these led to executions. Reginald Scot, a justice of the peace in Kent at a time when witchcraft accusations were at their height, summed up the situation in terms that resonate with modern interpretations of the witchcraft craze:

The fables of witchcraft have taken so fast hold and deep root in the heart of man, that few or none can nowadays with patience endure the hand and correction of God. For if any adversity, grief, loss of children, corn, cattle or, liberty happen unto them, by and by they exclaim upon witches—as if there were no God in Israel that ordereth all things according to his will, punishing both just and unjust with griefs, plagues, and afflictions in manner and form as he thinketh good; but that certain old women here on earth, called witches, must needs be the contrivers of all men's calamities—and as though they themselves [the accusers] were innocents, and had deserved no such punishments.[9]

Belief in a non-Scriptural world of the supernatural permeated even the highest and most learned levels of society. John Dee, one of the most erudite men in England and a leading promoter of scientific, geographic, and mathematical discovery, was also a noted astrologer and spent much of his life and fortune trying to summon angels and discover the alchemist's elusive Philosopher's Stone. Elizabeth herself chose the date of her coronation based on a horoscope cast by Dee.

In fact, it is somewhat misleading in an Elizabethan context to distinguish between science and magic. Science was the body of human lore passed down over the centuries in the writings of learned men; it was the domain of numbers and logic, and much that today would be classed as magic was preeminently numeric and logical. Astrology and alchemy were as much a part of science as geometry and mathematics.

At the heart of both scientific and magical thinking was a system of correspondences that unified different aspects of the cosmos in a network of analogies. Physical matter was categorized by the ancient theory of the Four Elements, in which all matter consisted of one of the four elements, each defined by two properties: Fire (hot and dry), Air (hot and moist), Water (cold and moist), and Earth (cold and dry). This two-by-two division aligned with a grid of correspondences that connected the elements with directions on the compass, seasons of the year, signs of the zodiac, and parts of the human body. This system for classifying the physical world underlay much of Elizabethan science and medicine as well as supernatural disciplines like astrology and alchemy.

The study of magic actually played a role in the development of scientific thought. John Dee's diary meticulously records personal events in his life—dreams, good and bad fortune, even instances of sex with his wife. Dee's aim was to collate this data with his astrological calculations in order to place his astrological work on a more secure footing. It was

Table 9.1.
The "Correspondences"

Humor in the Body	Element of Matter	Qualities	Wind	Celestial Quarter / Season	Time of Day / Gender	Zodiacal Sign	Body Part	Planet
Blood	Air	Hot-Moist	South	West/Spring	Day / Male	Gemini	Shoulders, arms	Mercury
						Libra	Loins, kidneys	Venus
						Aquarius	Shins, ankles	Saturn
Choler (Yellow bile)	Fire	Hot-Dry	East	East/Summer		Aries	Head, face	Mars
						Leo	Heart, back	Sun
						Sagittarius	Thighs, hips	Jupiter
Melancholy (Black bile)	Earth	Cold-Dry	North	South/Autumn	Night / Female	Taurus	Neck, throat	Venus
						Virgo	Bowels, belly	Mercury
						Capricorn	Knees, back of the thighs	Saturn
Phlegm	Water	Cold-Moist	West	North/Winter		Cancer	Breast, ribs, stomach	Moon
						Scorpio	Genitals, bladder	Mars
						Pisces	Feet, toes	Jupiter

This table illustrates the system of correspondences between various aspects of the physical universe as understood by Elizabethan science. The humors are the four substances that compose the human body; the elements are the substances that compose the physical world. All of these substances are integrated into an orderly scheme of associations, as shown above.

precisely this mode of thought that would pave the way for Sir Francis Bacon, an up-and-coming figure of the late Elizabethan years, to articulate his influential model of scientific empiricism in *Novum Organum* (1620).

Educated Elizabethans distinguished scholarly magic from the superstitious folk-beliefs of the uneducated. Many people still believed in supernatural creatures, particularly fairies; they used magical charms and recipes and consulted people believed to have supernatural skills or powers, especially in matters such as illness, childbirth, loss of property, love-longing, or predicting the future. A common charm for recovering stolen goods involved balancing a sieve on a pair of shears as a kind of divinatory compass: in 1598 a defendant in the Archdeaconry Court of Nottingham admitted that "a wether [sheep] being lost in their parish, there was a device used to know what was become of the said wether by taking a sieve and a pair of shears and saying, 'In the name of the Father and of the Son and of the Holy Ghost,' after which words the sieve would turn about—which device he and his sister . . . once without any ill intent tried."[10]

The position of any individual amidst these cross-currents of belief was complex, even contradictory: any given person might embrace multiple strands of potentially incompatible belief. If there is a common theme that unites these kaleidoscopic perspectives, it is perhaps a preoccupation with change. Elizabethans feared change: some commended it; many condemned it; all paid at least lip-service to the importance of stability and tradition. Yet everyone could sense that change was in the air. Change could be seen in the shrinking populations of villages and growing populations in the towns; it could be seen in rising standards of living for some, in growing levels of poverty for many; it could even be seen in the transformation of clothing from year to year, as the wealthy and powerful cultivated new fashions to distinguish themselves from those around them.

Regardless of their perspective, people across the spectrum of society were leading lives that propelled the country toward change. Catholics longed to see a restoration of the papacy; Puritans yearned for a more Protestant English church; both were undermining the traditional authority of the state to dictate religious practice to its subjects. Landowners worked to increase returns from their holdings; laborers sought new homes in hopes of finding better work opportunities; merchants explored unfamiliar seas in search of new markets for trade; educated young men gravitated toward London looking for personal advancement. But few could have dreamed of the tumultuous transformation for which they were setting the stage. Within less than a century of the Queen's death, Parliament would execute a king for treason, the state would cease to require religious uniformity, books would no longer be censored, and Newton would posit a universe fundamentally comprehensible through mathematics. In some ways, the Elizabethan period was the Indian Summer of the Middle Ages; in many ways it prepared the way for a definitive break with the medieval past.

NOTES

1. P. Razzell, ed., *The Journals of Two Travellers in Elizabethan and Early Stuart England* (London: Caliban Books, 1995), 12.

2. William Harrison, *Description of England* [1587] (Ithaca, NY: Folger Shakespeare Library, 1968), 8.

3. D. M. Palliser, *The Age of Elizabeth* (London: Longman, 1992), 10.

4. Nicholas Crane, *Mercator: The Man Who Mapped the Planet* (New York: Holt, 2002), 217.

5. Palliser, *Age of Elizabeth*, 10.

6. Keith Thomas, *Religion and the Decline of Magic* (New York: Scribner, 1971), 199, 201; Palliser, *Age of Elizabeth*, 395.

7. Christopher Marlowe, *Complete Plays and Poems*, ed. E. D. Pendry (London: Everyman, 1976), 513.

8. Keith Wrightson, *English Society, 1580–1680* (New Brunswick, NJ: Rutgers University Press, 1982), 200.

9. Reginald Scot, *The Discoverie of Witchcraft* (London: n.p., 1584), 1.

10. Thomas, *Religion*, 213–14.

Glossary

alderman—A member of a city council.

ale—An early form of beer made without hops; also, another name for a parish wake.

anon—Soon, shortly.

apprentice—A young person learning a craft or trade.

archdeacon—A church officer assigned to assist the bishop in administering his bishopric, having especial authority for church courts.

assizes—A periodic court held by circuit judges for trying major criminal cases.

breeches—Underwear, shorts.

broadside—A single printed sheet, often a ballad, sold for a penny.

buckler—A small round shield carried by civilians.

buckram—Linen impregnated with a stiffening gum.

burgage tenure—The system of landholding in towns, allowing free purchase and sale of the land, unlike manorial tenure in the countryside.

burgess—See **citizen.**

carrier—A wagoneer plying a regularly scheduled trade route.

cassock—A loose coat.

champion settlement—A system of agricultural organization in which each holding consists of strips of land scattered about a village, as contrasted with **woodland settlement.** Also called **open-field settlement.**

chandler—A candlemaker.

churchwarden—A parish officer chosen periodically from among the inhabitants of the parish and responsible for upkeep of the parish church.

citizen—An inhabitant of a town having the full rights and privileges of the town.

clothes-press—A shelved cupboard for clothing.

coif—A linen cap worn by women.

commoner—Anyone not of the gentlemanly class; a person obliged to work for a living.

communion—The religious ceremony in which the communicants receive wine and/or bread as representing the blood and body of Christ.

confirmation—The religious ceremony by which a young person is fully admitted as a member of the church.

constable—A local officer chosen periodically from among local residents and responsible for law and order.

cottager—The smallest sort of landholding commoner, holding insufficient land to support a family without doing additional labor.

cutler—A knifemaker.

cutwork—A form of decoration combining cutting of the fabric and embroidery.

deacon—A church officer responsible for assisting a priest.

demesne—The manorial land that belongs to the manor lord, not held by manorial tenants.

distaff—A long staff used in spinning flax fibers into linen thread.

doublet—A fitted jacket with buttons worn by both men and women.

esquire—A substantial gentleman, especially one who has a knight among his ancestors.

ewer—A jug used for pouring water.

factor—An agent, often itinerant, working on behalf of a merchant or entrepreneur.

falling band—A detachable collar.

fallow field—A field out of use for a season to allow it to recover for future crops.

farthingale—An underskirt made to flare by means of hoops.

flock bed—A bed stuffed with wool.

freeholder—The most privileged class of common landholder, holding his land in perpetuity, generally for insignificant rent.

gaol—A jail, used for holding the accused prior to trial.

garter—A strip of leather or fabric used to hold up one's stockings.

gentleman—A man of the class traditionally holding sufficient lands not to be required to work for a living; any man of a gentlemanly family.

gentleman-usher—A personal servant of gentle birth, serving in an aristocratic household.

girdle—A belt.

glazier—A craftsman specializing in glasswork.

goodman—A commoner who is the independent head of a household.

gossip—Originally, a relative through godparentage; also used more generally of close friends.

grocer—A retailer selling nonperishable consumables, such as dried fruit, spices, and soap.

guild—An organization regulating the practice of a craft or trade in a particular town. *Guild* is the modern term; the Elizabethans usually called it a *company*.

haberdasher—A retailer specializing in clothing accessories.

hall—The main room in a home.

holding—A parcel or quantity of land rented to a holder in accordance with the custom associated with that holding. Also called a **landholding.**

hose—A general term for garments worn on the legs. The plural is *hosen*.

house of office—See **privy.**

husbandman—A small but self-sufficient landholding commoner.

joint stool—A stool made with mortice-and-tenon joints, superior to a *boarded* stool made without joints.

journeyman—A craftsman or tradesman who has completed apprenticeship but does not possess a business of his own, working instead for others.

justice of the peace—A gentleman empowered by the crown to administer minor legal matters in a locality.

kersey—An inexpensive woolen cloth.

kirtle—A long fitted garment for women; an ankle-length, close-fitting dress.

lady-in-waiting—A female servant of gentle birth, serving in an aristocratic household.

landholding—See **holding.**

lay peers—The secular aristocracy of the House of Lords in Parliament, as opposed to the bishops who also sat in the House of Lords.

Lent—The period from Ash Wednesday until Easter, during which Elizabethans were supposed to abstain from eating meat and poultry.

lime—Calcium oxide, which can be obtained from limestone and is useful for enhancing soil and as a component in mortar, plaster, and similar building materials.

marl—A heavy clay useful for enriching agricultural soil.

master—A craftsman or tradesman who has his own shop.

master of arts—A university graduate.

open-field settlement—See **champion settlement.**

page—The lowest rank of servant, usually a young boy.

pallet—A mattress stuffed with straw.

petticoat—A skirt.

pickadill—One of a row of decorative tabs on the edge of a garment.

point—A lace used for fastening clothing.

privy—An outhouse or secluded indoor toilet. Euphemistically called **a house of office**.

Privy Council—The committee of royal officers with primary responsibility for advising the queen and carrying out her policies.

proctor—A lawyer in the system of ecclesiastical courts.

roll—A padded roll of fabric worn about a woman's hips.

sacring bell—A small bell used in church services.

saint's day—A holy day traditionally commemorating a particular saint.

sarcenet—A kind of silken cloth.

squire—See **esquire.**

Statute of Artificers—A law regulating work and wages, passed by Parliament in 1563.

trencher—A wooden plate.

vintner—A merchant or retailer dealing in wine.

wake—A parish festival (sometimes called an ale); also, a social event held at the home of a deceased person prior to burial.

watch—An urban nighttime patrol, staffed by part-time volunteers.

Whitsun—The Sunday seven weeks after Easter (Pentecost), traditionally an occasion for summer festivals.

winnowing—The process of separating cracked grain husks from the seed.

woodland settlement—A system of agricultural organization in which each holding is a discrete parcel of land, as contrasted with **champion settlement.**

yeoman—The upper rank of landholding free commoners.

Appendix:
The
Elizabethan Event

The text on which this book is based was originally written as a living-history manual for the Elizabethan period. It has since been expanded and reworked to provide an introduction to Elizabethan daily life for the general-interest reader, but it can still be used for organizing a period event such as an Elizabethan fair, festival, or feast. It can also prepare the individual reader to participate in such an event.

For the individual preparing to take part in an event, the first steps will be to choose what sort of character you will be representing and to assemble an appropriate kit of personal equipment. A character toward the lower end of the social scale would be easier to portray well: an upper-class character would not only have expensive clothing but would probably be attended by a servant and would certainly be well versed in all manner of social graces. A minimum outfit for a man would be a **shirt, hose, garters, Venetians, doublet, hat** or **cap,** and **shoes.** For a woman, it would be a **smock, petticoat, bodice, coif,** and **shoes.** Depending on the circumstances of the event, you may also need to provide basic eating equipment such as a **bowl** and/or **trencher, knife, spoon,** and **drinking vessel.** Some ideas for identifying suppliers of such items can be found in A Guide to Digitally Accessible Resources.

ORGANIZING AN EVENT

To host a successful event, you will need to attend to the following essentials.

Define and Disseminate the Goals

First, decide precisely what you are trying to achieve, as this will govern the balance struck between practicality and authenticity. Every group must make its own decisions about the degree of authenticity it wishes to achieve. If the principal goal is entertainment of yourselves or your guests, then historical accuracy may not be a priority although we hope this book will convince you that reasonable accuracy can be both fun and easy. If you are a living-history group putting on a demonstration for the public, you have more of a responsibility to be true to the past. In any case, the most important thing is to be as honest as possible with yourselves and your guests or audience as to what you are actually doing.

Even the best living-history group needs to remember that perfect accuracy is impossible. Bearing this in mind, it is important to define the degree of accuracy your group actually expects. If you expect people to meet a certain standard of authenticity, that standard needs to be clearly articulated. It is worthwhile to compile a list of authoritative sources, people or texts one can turn to as a guide for how to prepare for the event. A source need not be perfect to be considered authoritative: it need only represent a degree of authenticity that you consider adequate for the purposes of your reenactment. This book is in part written to provide an authoritative source of this sort.

Provide for Creature Comforts

No event can succeed without a supply of food and drink, as well as adequate seating, utensils, and the like. The food in particular can require a lot of effort, so if your organizing group is small, you may want to keep it as simple as possible, choosing such dishes as will provide the greatest satisfaction for the least preparation. You will make things easier on yourselves if you prepare dishes ahead of time and serve them cold or reheated.

Define the Space

As Tudor buildings are few and far between, some effort is required to make the setting feel right. In the absence of an Elizabethan hall, an outdoor event is one possibility, especially if you can provide appropriate tentage. If the event is held indoors in a modern-looking setting, it will help to furnish the site with period household accoutrements of some sort: wall hangings will do much to disguise concrete, and much modernity can be overlooked by candlelight. It is also very important to define the physical and temporal space of the re-creation. Decide what area is to be used and mark it off somehow so that people know where to go when they are in the mood for the past and where to slip off for a modern break if they need one. Demarcate the beginning and end of the re-creation by some prearranged signal; for example, someone might welcome the guests at the official beginning and thank them at the end. A clear boundary is essential if you want to keep the modern world from spilling into the re-creation.

Arrange Entertainment

If the event is not fun, it will not succeed. This book includes a selection of easily recreated entertainments. They will not only provide enjoyment for the participants but will help them to act as Elizabethans: it is easier to play an Elizabethan game than to discuss Elizabethan politics. For the entertainments to succeed, you will need to ensure that the proper equipment is available, and it will help if the participants have some practice beforehand.

Another kind of entertainment is *scripting*. If some sort of plot or plots are happening at the event comparable perhaps to the "host-a-murder-mystery idea, which has been a popular party theme in recent years this will add to the interest of the occasion. For this purpose, it will help if your group has some idea beforehand of the characters who will be represented at the event.

Prepare the Participants

It is not always easy to re-create the past, and it will help if the group takes an active part in preparing people for the event. Try to ensure that beginners have guidance in assembling their outfits sewing get-togethers are a good way of doing this. It may even be worthwhile to set up a buddy system whereby each beginner has an experienced person responsible for making sure they have everything they need.

The event will work best if there is a core of people who know what they are doing. For this reason, it is worth having a series of workshops prior to the event at which people can practice games, dances, songs, and social interaction. In addition, the day of the event is a good time to hold workshops for the benefit of out-of-town visitors.

You should also be prepared to take an active hand in arranging the social relationships between the participants' characters. Left to their own devices, people often all choose characters of the same rank (usually aristocratic), with few relationships among them. This tends to make the event both unrealistic and dull. Encourage people to come with prearranged social relationships. One possibility is service: it is relatively easy and inexpensive to portray a servant, and it can be a great deal of fun as well (there are plenty of good examples in the comedies of Shakespeare and Jonson). Other possible relationships include relatives, neighbors, and boon-companions. Again, you may find it worthwhile to organize a session to make this happen before and/or on the day.

A Guide to Digitally Accessible Resources

When the first edition of this book was published, the Internet was only just starting to become widely accessible. A bit over a decade later, it has transformed the landscape for people who are interested in studying cultures of the past: museum collections from around the globe can be searched online; manuscripts and early printed books are available in digital facsimile; makers of reproduction artifacts can easily be found through the Web; people with similar interests are in constant contact through a variety of digital media.

It is impossible to map fully the ever-changing terrain of digital resources. The following survey is intended to suggest the range of resources that are out there and how to use them.

Among the many research resources now available, printed books remain essential. The classified bibliographies at the end of this book are intended to identify especially useful print resources.

REFERENCE RESOURCES

A general Web search engine such as Google or a partially filtered engine like Google Scholar can yield plenty of hits for any given topic. The information from Web sites needs to be viewed with skepticism, but playing around with a few search terms can be a good way to do some preliminary investigation and find your bearings on a topic. It is also important to remember that not everything that is available on the Web is accessible through these search engines: many specialized databases can only be searched by going to the database itself.

An essential tool for any kind of meaningful research is a union database of books and articles, such as WorldCat, which runs unified searches on the databases of libraries across North America and (to a lesser degree) around the world. Such resources are usually accessible through university and public libraries. An increasing number of digital books are accessible on the Web, either in full (generally only if they are out of copyright) or in limited previews. Tools like Google Book Search can help you locate some of these.

Since WorldCat is less global than its name implies, it is also worth knowing about the union catalog *The European Library* (**www.theeuropean library.org**), which offers similar searching for European libraries.

It is also worth remembering that a growing number of books have been digitized and put up on the Web. Excellent old reference works like *Shakespeare's England* (Oxford: Clarendon Press, 1916) can now be downloaded from your home PC by running a quick search on a site like **www.archive. org.**

An outstanding resource is *British History Online* (**www.british-history. ac.uk**), a massive site with extensive online versions of primary and secondary source material relating to British history, searchable by period, region, topic, and other filters.

Among the most valuable specialized resources not accessible through a general search engine is the online version of the *Oxford English Dictionary* (**dictionary.oed.com**). If you can identify a few relevant keywords for your topic, the *OED* can quickly put you in touch with pertinent primary source material: each entry includes not only definitions but also primary source quotes in which the word appears, with information on where the quotes came from.

INTERNET PORTALS

A variety of specialized Internet sites offer research leads for Elizabethan England. Some good general examples are *Luminarium* (**www.lumi narium.org/renlit**); *Renaissance: The Elizabethan World* (**www.elizabethan. org**); and *Tudor History* (**www.tudorhistory.org**). These sites provide lists of useful links including primary sources, modern scholarship, databases, discussion groups, and organizations. Personal Web sites can be quirky to navigate but with some patience can yield excellent results; a prime example is **www.pbm.com/~lindahl,** a treasure-trove of links to resources across the Web.

There are also specialized portals. *The Elizabethan Costume Page* (**www. elizabethancostume.net**) has an excellent selection of links to a variety of sites relating to Renaissance costume.

PRIMARY SOURCE TEXTS ONLINE

Large quantities of primary source material are now available online. Transcribed copies of a selection of texts can be found at the *Internet Modern History Sourcebook* (**www.fordham.edu/halsall/mod/modsbook.html**), the Shakespeare Authorship Sourcebook (**www.sourcetext.com/sourcebook/e-texts.htm**), the University of Oregon's *Renascence Editions* (**www.uoregon.edu/~rbear/ren.htm**), and the University of Birmingham's *Library of Humanistic Texts* (**www.philological.bham.ac.uk/library.html**). Accessible through major research libraries are the PDF versions of large numbers of Elizabethan books in the *Early English Books Online* (**eebo.chadwyck.com**). See also *British History Online* under Reference Resources.

VISUAL RESOURCES

Using a general images search engine (such as Google Images) can be a quick way to locate visual sources about the Elizabethan era, but not every image available on the Web will be picked up by such a search. Visiting online databases of museums and other collections such as those mentioned below can turn up valuable materials that the general search engines will miss. Some sites with powerful image search capacity include the following:

www.npg.org.uk/live/collect.asp. The online collections of the National Portrait Gallery, London, which includes a very large number of important Elizabethan portraits.

www.bridgeman.co.uk. A commercial firm that brokers rights for the publication of images their Web site has a well developed apparatus for searching by place, period, and subject matter.

MUSEUMS AND OTHER COLLECTIONS

An increasing number of museums, libraries, and other institutions with Elizabethan-period artifacts among their holdings are putting parts of their collections online; the list below is only a sampling.

Museum of London (**www.museumoflondon.org.uk**). Probably the world's premiere museum collection in the domain covered by this book, with extensive holdings of artifacts from the daily life of Londoners across the centuries. Parts of the collection are searchable online.

Higgins Armory Museum (**www.higgins.org**). North America's only specialized museum of armor, and also the center for a program of study of early European martial arts treatises. The entire collection is accessible online.

Weald and Downland Museum (**www.wealddown.co.uk**). Includes an outstanding collection of surviving medieval buildings, accessible through a virtual tour.

Folger Shakespeare Library (**www.folger.edu**). A major collection specializing in books, manuscripts, and other materials from Shakespeare's period.

SITES

Various sites reconstruct aspects of English Renaissance life in reconstructed or original settings. A few examples:

The Globe Theatre (**www.shakespeares-globe.org**). A reconstruction of Shakespeare's theater in the heart of modern London, near its original site.

Kentwell Hall (**www.kentwell.co.uk/Re-Creations/Tudor**). A manor estate of the 1500s that hosts multiple elaborate recreations of Tudor-period life during the course of a year.

Plimoth Plantation (**www.plimoth.org**). Plimoth recreates the world of the Pilgrim settlers in Massachusetts in 1627 a bit after the Elizabethan period, and in a very different location, but Plimoth nonetheless offers one of the best modern evocations of the Elizabethan world.

SHAKESPEARE

As one of the best known and most studied figures in the history of the English-speaking world, William Shakespeare (1564–1616) has been a staple of Elizabethan studies for centuries, and Shakespeare-related Web sites can be a good point of access for further information on the Elizabethan world. A few examples are listed below:

internetshakespeare.uvic.ca/Library/SLT/intro/introsubj.html. A site with information on history, society, and other aspects of Shakespeare's world.

shakespeare.palomar.edu/life.htm. A Shakespeare portal with a variety of links to sites on Shakespeare and his historical context.

search.eb.com/shakespeare. The Encyclopedia Britannica Guide to Shakespeare, with links to encyclopedia entries on various topics relating to Elizabethan England.

dewey.library.upenn.edu/SCETI/furness/index.cfm. The Furness Shakespeare Collection hosts digital versions of numerous texts from Renaissance England.

SUPPLIERS

One benefit of the Internet is the ease with which a person can now find highly specialized wares. Reproductions of Elizabethan artifacts are a case in point. There are a very large number of firms trading in such things; below are a few examples.

Syke's Sutlery (**sykesutler.home.att.net**). Carries a variety of clothes and accessories, somewhat leaning toward the 17th century.

Sarah Juniper (**www.sarahjuniper.co.uk**). Outstanding-quality reproduction shoes and other leatherware.

Arms and Armour (**www.armor.com**). Offers museum-quality reproductions of 16th-century weaponry.

Caliver Books (**www.caliverbooks.com**). A rich source of books on the period, some of them privately published and harder to acquire through other channels.

Buying goods through the Web can be tricky; a good strategy is to consult beforehand with someone who has experience with the sellers. Living-history groups can be a great resource in this respect, and they are typically very generous with their time and knowledge.

AUDIOVISUAL SOURCES

Various educational films relating to the subject matter of this book have been produced over the years. An example is *The Elizabethans [Seven Ages of Fashion Part 1]* (Films Media Group, 1992). This and other audiovisual media sources are available through Films for the Humanities (**ffh.films. com**).

Quite a few recordings of Elizabethan music have been produced over the years. A few good examples:

1588. Music from the Time of the Spanish Armada. The York Waits (Saydisc).

In the Streets and Theatres of London. Elizabethan Ballads and Theatre Music. The Musicians of Swanne Alley (Virgin Classics).

"New Fashions." Cries and Ballads of London. Circa 1500 and Redbyrd (CRD Records).

Watkins Ale. Music of the English Renaissance. The Baltimore Consort (Dorian Recordings).

Some Elizabethan music is available on the Web: the page **www.pbm. com/~lindahl/music.html** has links to a wide variety of early music resources, among them extensive MIDI files of Renaissance music, including songs and dances in this book (the page can be hard to navigate, but try a Web search on the keywords *Ravenscroft* and *MIDI*).

There are also a number of feature films that offer interpretations of the Elizabethan world. The television mini-series *Elizabeth R* (BBC, 1972) remains one of the best efforts to date in this direction, both for its fidelity to history and for capturing the drama of the real historical events. The more recent *Elizabeth* (Polygram Filmed Entertainment, 1998) and *Elizabeth: The Golden Age* (Motion Picture ZETA Produktionsgesellschaft, 2007) are much less true to the history, though they have their inspired moments. *Shakespeare in Love* (Universal Pictures, 1999) is something of a fantasy on a Shakespearean theme but is informed by a real understanding of Shakespeare and his world. Not really historical, but an inspired piece of historical lunacy, is the television comedy series *Blackadder II* (Fox Video, 1989).

RESEARCH ORGANIZATIONS

There are a variety of specialist organizations involved in researching areas relating to the subjects in this book. Below are just a few examples:

Records of Early English Drama (**www.reed.utoronto.ca**). A longstanding project at the University of Toronto for the study of English theater prior to 1642; the closely allied Poculi Ludique Societas stages performances of medieval and Renaissance plays.

Higgins Armory Sword Guild (**www.higginssword.org**). Studies, teaches, and demonstrates historical combat techniques at the Higgins Armory Museum.

LIVING-HISTORY GROUPS

There are a variety of groups in various parts of the globe involved in recreating aspects of Elizabethan life, and others specializing in a slightly earlier or later period (often either the age of Henry VIII or the English Civil War).

Trayn'd Bandes of London (**www.gardinerscompany.org**). Recreates the civilian and military world of members of the London militia in the Elizabethan age.

The Tudor Group (**www.tudorgroup.co.uk**). An organization that specializes in the recreation of late-16th-century England.

Classified Bibliographies

SUGGESTED READING

There are quite a number of very good sources for information on Elizabethan daily life. Those that relate to particular topics covered in this book have been included in the footnotes, but a few general sources are worth particular mention.

Two very useful anthologies of articles on various aspects of life in this period are *Shakespeare's England. An Account of the Life and Manners of His Age* (Oxford: Clarendon Press, 1916), and *William Shakespeare: His World, His Works, His Influence. Vol. 1: His World*, ed. John F. Andrews (New York: Scribner, 1985). For an overview of Elizabethan society, a particularly good introduction is D. M. Palliser's *The Age of Elizabeth* (London and New York: Longman, 1992). A good introductory narrative of Elizabethan history is J. E. Neale, *Queen Elizabeth I* (London: Cape, 1954); a readable account of the Armada is Garret Mattingly's *The Armada* (Boston: Houghton Mifflin, 1959).

Two vivid modern interpretations of daily life, although they deal with colonial life in the 1620s, are Kate Waters's *Sarah Morton's Day. A Day in the Life of a Pilgrim Girl* (New York: Scholastic, 1989) and *Samuel Eaton's Day. A Day in the Life of a Pilgrim Boy* (New York: Scholastic, 1993). Geared toward younger readers, they are nonetheless interesting and enjoyable at any level and richly illustrated with photographs taken at the Plimoth Plantation living-history site.

Many useful primary sources have been published in modern editions. Probably the best single description of Elizabethan society and life by a contemporary is William Harrison's *Description of England*, dating to 1587 (Ithaca, NY: Folger Shakespeare Library, 1968). An intimate glimpse into daily life is provided by contemporary dialogues from language-instruction manuals, edited in M. St. Clare Byrne, *The Elizabethan Home* (London: Cobden-Sanderson, 1930). For pursuit of specific topics in a wide variety of fields, including social structure, games, music, technology, agriculture, and many more, Randle Holme's *Academy of Armory* is an indispensable source, even though it dates to the late-17th century. Most of the book was published in Holme's lifetime and has been reprinted in facsimile (Menston: Scolar Press, 1972); a few remaining manuscript chapters were published centuries after Holme's death (London: Roxburghe Club, 1905).

The plays of Ben Jonson, especially *Bartholomew Fair*, provide a literary image of the Elizabethan world. Although Jonson's heyday was slightly after Elizabeth's reign, his works offer a lively picture of people in this period as they imagined themselves.

GENERAL AND REFERENCE SOURCES

Andrews, John F., ed. *William Shakespeare: His World, His Works, His Influence. Vol. 1: His World.* New York: Scribner, 1985.

Dodd, A. H. *Life in Elizabethan England.* New York: Putnam, 1961.

Emmison, F. G. *Elizabethan Life: Home, Work and Land.* Chelmsford: Essex County Council, 1976.

Emmison, F. G. *Elizabethan Life: Morals and the Church Courts.* Chelmsford: Essex County Council, 1973.

Fritze, Ronald H. *Historical Dictionary of Tudor England, 1485–1603.* New York: Greenwood Press, 1991.

Garret, George. "Daily Life in City, Town, and Country." In *William Shakespeare: His World, His Works, His Influence. Vol. 1: His World,* ed. John F. Andrews, 215–32. New York: Scribner, 1985.

Glanville, Philippa. *Tudor London.* London: Museum of London, 1979.

Harrison, William. *Description of England.* Ithaca, NY: Folger Shakespeare Library, 1968.

Hartley, Dorothy. *Lost Country Life.* New York: Pantheon, 1979.

Hartley, Dorothy, and Margaret M. Elliot. *Life and Work of the People of England. A Pictorial Record from Contemporary Sources. The Sixteenth Century.* London: G. P. Putnam's Sons, 1926.

Hughes, Paul L., and James F. Larkin. *Tudor Royal Proclamations.* New Haven, CT: Yale University Press, 1964.

Hurstfield, Joel, and Alan G. R. Smith. *Elizabethan People: State and Society.* New York: St. Martin's Press, 1972.

Laslett, Peter. *The World We Have Lost.* London: Methuen, 1971.

McMurtry, Jo. *Understanding Shakespeare's England. A Companion for the American Reader.* Hamden, CT: Archon, 1989.

Morril, J., ed. *The Oxford Illustrated History of Tudor and Stuart Britain.* Oxford: Oxford University Press, 1996.

O'Day, Rosemary. *The Longman Companion to the Tudor Age.* London and New York: Longman, 1995.

Palliser, D. M. *The Age of Elizabeth*. London and New York: Longman, 1992.

Palmer, Alan, and Veronica Palmer. *Who's Who in Shakespeare's England*. New York: St. Martin's Press, 1981.

Picard, Liza. *Elizabeth's London: Everyday Life in Elizabethan London*. New York: St. Martin's Press, 2004.

Shakespeare's England. An Account of the Life and Manners of His Age. 2 vols. Oxford: Clarendon Press, 1916.

Sharpe, J. A. *Early Modern England: A Social History 1550–1760*. 2nd ed. London and New York: Arnold, 1997.

Smith, Lacey Baldwin. "'Style Is the Man': Manners, Dress, Decorum." In *William Shakespeare: His World, His Works, His Influence. Vol. 1: His World*, ed. John F. Andrews, 201–14. New York: Scribner, 1985.

Spufford, Margaret. *Contrasting Communities: English Villagers in the Sixteenth and Seventeenth Centuries*. Cambridge: Cambridge University Press, 1974.

Stubbes, Phillip. *Phillip Stubbes's Anatomy of the Abuses in England in Shakespeare's Youth A.D. 1583*, ed. F. J. Furnivall. New Shakespeare Society 6:6. London: Trübner, 1879.

Thirsk, Joan. *The Agrarian History of England and Wales 1500–1750. Vol. 4: 1500–1640*. Cambridge: Cambridge University Press, 1967.

Tittler, Robert, and Norman L. Jones. *A Companion to Tudor Britain*. Malden, MA: Blackwell, 2004.

Tusser, Thomas. *Five Hundred Points of Good Husbandry*. Edited by Geoffrey Grigson. Oxford: Oxford University Press, 1984.

Wagner, John A. *Historical Dictionary of the Elizabethan World*. Phoenix, AZ: Oryx Press, 1999.

Wilson, Sir Thomas. *The State of England, A.D. 1600 [De Republica Anglorum]*. Edited by F. J. Fisher. Camden Miscellany 3:52. London: Offices of the Camden Society, 1936.

Wood, Eric S. *Historical Britain*. London: Harvill Press, 1995.

Wrightson, Keith. *Earthly Necessities: Economic Lives in Early Modern Britain*. New Haven, CT: Yale University Press, 2000.

Wrightson, Keith. *English Society, 1580–1680*. New Brunswick, NJ: Rutgers University Press, 1982.

Wrigley, E. A., and R. S. Davies, J. E. Oeppen, and R. S. Schofield. *English Population History from Family Reconstitution, 1580–1837*. Cambridge: Cambridge University Press, 1997.

Wrigley, E. A. and R. S. Schofield. *The Population History of England 1541–1871*. Cambridge, MA: Harvard University Press, 1981.

JOURNALS, DIARIES, AND TRAVELOGUES

Barrons, C., C. Coleman, and C. Gobbi, eds. "The London Journal of Alessandro Magno 1562." *The London Journal* 9 (1983): 2.

Fenton, Edward, ed. *The Diaries of John Dee*. Charlbury, Oxfordshire: Day Books, 1998.

Hentzner, Paul. *A Journey into England in the Year 1593*. Translated by R. Bentley and edited by Horace Walpole. Edinburgh: Aungervyle Society, 1881.

Hentzner, Paul. *Paul Hentzner's Travels in England during the Reign of Queen Elizabeth*. London: Edward Jeffery, 1797.

Hoby, Lady Margaret. *Diary of Lady Margaret Hoby 1599–1605.* Edited by Dorothy M. Meads. London: Routledge, 1930.

Machyn, Henry. *The Diary of Henry Machyn, Citizen and Merchant-Taylor of London, from A.D. 1550 to A.D. 1563.* Edited by John Gough Nichols. London: Camden Society, 1848.

Moryson, Fynes. *An Itinerary.* Amsterdam and New York: Da Capo Press, Theatrum Orbis Terrarum, 1971.

Moryson, Fynes. *Shakespeare's Europe.* Edited by Charles Hughes. London: Sherratt and Hughes, 1903.

Perrin, W. G., ed. *The Autobiography of Phineas Pett.* N.p.: Navy Records Society, 1918.

Platter, Thomas. *Thomas Platter's Travels in England 1599.* Translated by Clare Williams. London: J. Cape, 1937.

Razzell, P., ed. *The Journals of Two Travellers in Elizabethan and Early Stuart England.* London: Caliban Books, 1995.

Rowse, A. L. *Sex and Society in Shakespeare's Age: Simon Forman the Astrologer.* New York: Scribner, 1974.

Rye, William Brenchley. *England as Seen by Foreigners in the Days of Elizabeth and James the First.* New York: Benjamin Blom, 1967.

PRIMARY-SOURCE ANTHOLOGIES

Aughterson, Kate. *The English Renaissance: An Anthology of Sources and Documents.* London and New York: Routledge, 1998.

Harrison, Molly, and O. M. Royston. *How They Lived: An Anthology of Original Accounts Written between 1485 and 1700.* New York: Barnes and Noble, 1963.

Houlbrooke, Ralph A. *English Family Life, 1576–1716: An Anthology from Diaries.* Oxford and New York: Basil Blackwell, 1988.

Manley, Lawrence. *London in the Age of Shakespeare: An Anthology.* London: Croom Helm, 1986.

Orlin, Lena Cowen. *Elizabethan Households: An Anthology.* Washington, DC: Folger Shakespeare Library, 1995.

Pritchard, R. E. *Shakespeare's England: Life in Elizabethan and Jacobean Times.* Stroud: Sutton, 1999.

Swisher, Clarice. *Elizabethan England: Primary Sources.* San Diego: Lucent Books, 2003.

Tawney, R. H., and Eileen Power. *Tudor Economic Documents.* 3 vols. London: Longmans, 1924.

Wilson, John Dover. *Life in Shakespeare's England.* Harmondsworth: Penguin, 1949.

POLITICAL HISTORY

Brigden, Susan. *New Worlds, Lost Worlds.* London: Viking, 2000.

Lockyer, Roger. *Tudor and Stuart Britain.* 3rd ed. Harlow and New York: Pearson/ Longman, 2005.

Neale, J. E. *Elizabeth I.* London: Folio Society, 2005.

Weir, Alison. *Elizabeth the Queen.* London: Random House, 1998.

SOCIETY

Barry, Jonathan. *The Tudor and Stuart Town: A Reader in English Urban History 1530–1688*. London and New York: Longman, 1990.

Beier, A. L., and Roger Finlay. *London 1500–1700: The Making of the Metropolis*. London and New York: Longman, 1986.

Collinson, Patrick. 1985. "The Church: Religion and Its Manifestations." In *William Shakespeare: His World, His Works, His Influence. Vol. 1: His World*, ed. John F. Andrews, 21–40. New York: Scribner, 1985.

Emmison, F. G. *Elizabethan Life: Morals and the Church Courts*. Chelmsford: Essex County Council, 1973.

Harrison, William. *Description of England*. Ithaca, NY: Folger Shakespeare Library, 1968.

Houston, R. A. *The Population History of Britain and Ireland, 1500–1750*. Basingstoke: Macmillan Education, 1992.

Loades, David. *Tudor Government: Structures of Authority in the Sixteenth Century*. Oxford: Blackwell, 1997.

Palliser, D. M. *The Age of Elizabeth*. London and New York: Longman, 1992.

Rappaport, Steve. *Worlds within Worlds: Structures of Life in Sixteenth-Century London*. Cambridge: Cambridge University Press, 1989.

Sharpe, J. A. *Crime in Early Modern England, 1550–1750*. London and New York: Longman, 1984.

Sharpe, J. A. *Early Modern England: A Social History 1550–1760*. 2nd ed. London and New York: Arnold, 1997.

Smith, A.G.R. *The Government of Elizabethan England*. New York: Norton, 1967.

Smith, Sir Thomas. *De Republica Anglorum: The Manner of Government or Policy of the Realm of England*. London: Gregory Seton, 1584.

Wrightson, Keith. *Earthly Necessities: Economic Lives in Early Modern Britain*. New Haven, CT: Yale University Press, 2000.

Wrightson, Keith. *English Society 1580–1680*. New Brunswick, NJ: Rutgers University Press, 1982.

HOUSEHOLDS AND THE LIFE CYCLE

Abbott, Mary. *Life Cycles in England 1560–1720: Cradle to Grave*. London and New York: Routledge, 1996.

Adair, R. *Courtship, Illegitimacy, and Marriage in England, 1500–1850*. Manchester: Manchester University Press, 1996.

Amussen, Susan. *An Ordered Society: Gender and Class in Early Modern England*. Oxford and New York: Blackwell, 1988.

Byrne, M. St Clare, ed. *The Elizabethan Home*. London: Methuen, 1949.

Byrne, M. St. Clare. *Elizabethan Life in Town and Country*. London: Methuen, 1950.

Clarkson, L. A. *Death, Disease, and Famine in Pre-Industrial England*. New York: St. Martins' Press, 1975.

Cooke, A. J. *Making a Match: Courtship in Shakespeare and His Society*. Princeton, NJ: Princeton University Press, 1991.

Cressy, David. *Birth, Marriage, and Death. Ritual, Religion, and the Life-Cycle in Tudor and Stuart England*. Oxford: Oxford University Press, 1997.

Cressy, David. *Education in Tudor and Stuart England*. London: Edward Arnold, 1975.

Cressy, David. *Literacy and the Social Order: Reading and Writing in Tudor and Stuart England*. Cambridge: Cambridge University Press, 1980.

Eccles, A. *Obstetrics and Gynaecology in Tudor and Stuart England*. Kent, OH: Kent State University Press, 1982.

Forsyth, Hazel, and Geoff Egan. *Toys, Trifles, and Trinkets: Base-Metal Miniatures from London 1200 to 1800*. London: Museum of London/Unicorn, 2004.

Grafton, Anthony. "Education and Apprenticeship." In *William Shakespeare: His World, His Works, His Influence. Vol. 1: His World*, ed. John F. Andrews, 55–66. New York: Scribner, 1985.

Houlbrooke, Ralph A. *Death, Religion and the Family in England, 1480–1750*. Oxford: Oxford University Press, 1998.

Houlbrooke, Ralph A. *The English Family 1450–1700*. London: Longman, 1984.

Houlbrooke, Ralph A., ed. *English Family Life, 1576–1716: An Anthology from Diaries*. Oxford and New York: Basil Blackwell, 1988.

Ingram, Martin. *Church Courts, Sex, and Marriage in England, 1570–1640*. Cambridge: Cambridge University Press, 1987.

Kussmaul, Ann. *Servants in Husbandry in Early Modern England*. Cambridge: Cambridge University Press, 1981.

O'Day, Rosemary. *Education and Society, 1500–1800: The Social Foundations of Education in Early Modern Britain*. London and New York: Longman, 1982.

Palliser, D. M. *The Age of Elizabeth*. London and New York: Longman, 1992.

Pearson, Lu. *The Elizabethans at Home*. Stanford, CA: Stanford University Press, 1957.

Rappaport, Steve. *Worlds within Worlds: Structures of Life in Sixteenth-Century London*. Cambridge: Cambridge University Press, 1989.

Sandys, Sir John. "Education." In *Shakespeare's England. An Account of the Life and Manners of His Age*. Oxford: Clarendon Press, 1916. 1.224–50

Stone, Lawrence. *The Family, Sex, and Marriage in England 1500–1800*. New York etc.: Harper and Row, 1977.

Thompson, Sir Edward. "Handwriting." In *Shakespeare's England. An Account of the Life and Manners of His Age*, 1.284–310. Oxford: Clarendon Press, 1916.

Wrightson, Keith. *English Society 1580–1680*. New Brunswick, NJ: Rutgers University Press, 1982.

WOMEN

Amussen, Susan. *An Ordered Society: Gender and Class in Early Modern England*. Oxford and New York: Blackwell, 1988.

Bradford, Gamaliel. *Elizabethan Women*. Cambridge, MA: Houghton Mifflin, 1936.

Camden, Carroll C. *The Elizabethan Woman*. Mamaroneck, NY: P. P. Appel, 1975.

Eccles, Audrey. *Obstetrics and Gynaecology in Tudor and Stuart England*. Kent, OH: Kent State University Press, 1982.

Mendelson, S., and P. Crawford. *Women in Early Modern England 1550–1720*. Oxford: Clarendon Press, 1998.

Moody, Joanna, ed. *The Private Life of an Elizabethan Lady: The Diary of Lady Margaret Hoby 1599–1605*. Stroud: Sutton, 1998.

Sim, Alison. *The Tudor Housewife*. Stroud: Sutton, 1996.

CYCLES OF TIME

Byrne, M. St. Clare, ed. *The Elizabethan Home.* London: Methuen, 1949.

Byrne, M. St. Clare. *Elizabethan Life in Town and Country.* London: Methuen, 1950.

Cressy, David. *Bonfires and Bells: National Memory and the Protestant Calendar in Elizabethan and Stuart England.* London: Weidenfeld and Nicholson, 1989.

Harrison, William. *Description of England.* Ithaca, NY: Folger Shakespeare Library, 1968.

Hutton, Ronald. *The Rise and Fall of Merry England: The Ritual Year 1400–1700.* Oxford: Oxford University Press, 1994.

Hutton, Ronald. *The Stations of the Sun: A History of the Ritual Year in Britain.* Oxford and New York: Oxford University Press, 1996.

MacQuoid, Percy. "The Home." In *Shakespeare's England. An Account of the Life and Manners of His Age,* 2.134. Oxford: Clarendon Press, 1916.

Wilson, John Dover. *Life in Shakespeare's England.* Harmondsworth: Penguin, 1949.

MATERIAL CULTURE

Ayres, James. *Domestic Interiors: The British Tradition 1500–1850.* New Haven, CT: Yale University Press, 2003.

Barley, Maurice W. *Houses and History.* London: Faber and Faber, 1986.

Bishop, W. J. "Personnel and Practice of Medicine in Tudor and Stuart England. Part 1: The Provinces." *Medical History* 6 (1957): 363–82.

Bishop, W. J. "Personnel and Practice of Medicine in Tudor and Stuart England. Part 2: London." *Medical History* 8 (1957): 217–34.

Challis, C. E. *The Tudor Coinage.* New York: Barnes and Noble, 1978.

Charleston, R. J. *English Glass and the Glass Used in England circa 400–1940.* London: Unwin, 1984.

Chinnery, Victor. *Oak Furniture. The British Tradition.* Woodbridge: Antique Collectors' Club, 1979.

Copeman, W.S.C. *Doctors and Disease in Tudor Times.* London: Dawson's, 1960.

Evans-Thomas, Owen. *Domestic Utensils of Wood, 16th to 19th Century.* London: Owen Evan-Thomas, 1932.

Fitzherbert, Anthony. *The Book of Husbandry* [1598]. London: Trübner, 1882.

Hall, Hubert, and Frieda Nicholas, eds. *Select Tracts and Table Books of English Weights and Measures.* London: Camden Society, 1929.

Harrison, William. *Description of England.* Ithaca, NY: Folger Shakespeare Library, 1968.

Holme, Randle. *The Academy of Armory.* London: Roxburghe Club, 1905. [This consists of the final chapters of the *Academy,* which were not published in Holme's lifetime.]

Holme, Randle. *The Academy of Armory.* Menston: Scolar Press, 1972.

Holme, Randle. *Living and Working in Seventeenth-Century England: An Encyclopedia of Drawings and Descriptions from Randle Holme's Original Manuscripts for The Academy of Armory* (1688) [CD-ROM]. Edited by N. W. Alcock and Nancy Cox. London: British Library, 2001.

Holmes, Martin. *Elizabethan London.* London: Cassell, 1969.

Hornsby, Peter R. G., Rosemary Weinstein, and Ronald F. Homer. *Pewter: A Celebration of the Craft 1200–1700.* London: Museum of London, 1989.

Jekyll, Gertrude. *Old English Household Life. Some Account of Cottage Objects and Country Folk.* London: Batsford, 1925.

Lindsay, J. Seymour. *Iron and Brass Implements of the English House.* London, Boston: Medici Society, 1927.

MacGregor, Arthur. *Bone, Antler, Ivory, and Horn: The Technology of Skeletal Materials Since the Roman Period.* London and Sydney: Croom Helm, 1985.

MacQuoid, Percy. "The Home." In *Shakespeare's England. An Account of the Life and Manners of His Age,* 2.119–52. Oxford: Clarendon Press, 1916.

Markham, Gervase. *The English Housewife.* Edited by Michael R. Best. Kingston and Montréal: McGill-Queen's University Press, 1986.

McCarthy, Michael R., and Catherine M. Brooks. *Medieval Pottery in Britain A.D. 900–1600.* Leicester: Leicester University Press, 1988.

Mercer, Eric. *English Vernacular Houses.* London: Her Majesty's Stationery Office, 1975.

Michaelis, Ronald F. *A Short History of the Worshipful Company of Pewterers, and a Catalogue of Pewterware in Its Possession.* London: published by the authority of the Court of Assistants, 1968.

Palliser, D. M. *The Age of Elizabeth.* London and New York: Longman, 1992.

Pelling, Margaret. "Medicine and Sanitation." In *William Shakespeare: His World, His Works, His Influence. Vol. 1: His World,* ed. John F. Andrews, 75–84. New York: Scribner, 1985.

The Pewter Society. *Pewter: A Handbook of Selected Tudor and Stuart Pieces.* London: the Pewter Society in association with the Museum of London, 1983.

Prothero, R. E. "Agriculture and Gardening." In *Shakespeare's England. An Account of the Life and Manners of His Age,* 1.346–80. Oxford: Clarendon Press, 1916.

Rappaport, Steve. *Worlds within Worlds: Structures of Life in Sixteenth-Century London.* Cambridge: Cambridge University Press, 1989.

Rogers, James E. Thorold. *A History of Agriculture and Prices in England.* Oxford: Clarendon Press, 1882.

Singer, Charles Joseph, ed. *A History of Technology.* 5 vols. Oxford: Clarendon Press, 1954–1978.

Spufford, Margaret. *The Great Reclothing of Rural England.* London: Hambledon Press, 1984.

Thirsk, Joan. *The Agrarian History of England and Wales 1500–1750. Vol. 4: 1500–1640.* Cambridge: Cambridge University Press, 1967.

Thirsk, Joan. *Chapters from the Agrarian History of England and Wales 1500–1750.* Cambridge: Cambridge University Press, 1990.

Thornton, Peter. *Seventeenth-Century Interior Decoration in England, France and Holland.* New Haven, CT: Yale University Press, 1978.

Treswell, Ralph. *The London Surveys of Ralph Treswell.* Edited by John Schofield. London: London Topographical Society, 1987.

Tusser, Thomas. *Five Hundred Points of Good Husbandry.* Edited by Geoffrey Grigson. Oxford: Oxford University Press, 1984.

Unwin, George. "Commerce and Coinage." In *Shakespeare's England. An Account of the Life and Manners of His Age,* 1.311–45. Oxford: Clarendon Press, 1916.

Waterer, John W. *Leather Craftsmanship.* London: Bell, 1968.

Wear, Andrew. *Knowledge and Practice in English Medicine, 1550–1680.* Cambridge: Cambridge University Press, 2000.

Wheatley, Henry B. "London and the Life of the Town." In *Shakespeare's England. An Account of the Life and Manners of His Age,* 2.153–81. Oxford: Clarendon Press, 1916.

Wolsey, S. W., and R.W.P. Lanff. *Furniture in England: The Age of the Joiner.* New York: Praeger, 1968.

Wood, Eric S. *Historical Britain.* London: Harvill Press, 1995.

Wrightson, Keith. *Earthly Necessities: Economic Lives in Early Modern Britain.* New Haven, CT: Yale University Press, 2000.

Yarwood, Doreen. *The English Home.* London: Batsford, 1979.

CLOTHING AND ACCESSORIES

Arnold, Janet. "Elizabethan and Jacobean Smocks and Shirts." *Waffen- und Kostümkunde* 19 (1977): 89–110.

Arnold, Janet. *Patterns of Fashion: The Cut and Construction of Clothes for Men and Women c.1560–1620.* New York: Drama Books, 1985.

Arnold, Janet. "Three Examples of Late Sixteenth and Early Seventeenth Century Neckwear." *Waffen- und Kostümkunde* 15 (1973): 109–24.

Cunnington, Phyllis, and Anne Buck. *Children's Costume in England.* London: Black, 1965.

Davenport, Millia. *The Book of Costume.* New York: Crown, 1948.

Flury-Lemberg, Mechtild. *Textile Conservation and Research.* Bern: Schriften der Abegg-Stiftung, 1988.

Geddes, Elisabeth, and Moyra McNeill. *Blackwork Embroidery.* New York: Dover, 1976.

Goubitz, Olaf, Carol van Driel-Murray, and Willy Groenman-Van Waateringe. *Stepping through Time: Archaeological Footwear from Prehistoric Times until 1800.* Zwolle: Stichting Promotie Archeologie, 2007.

Hunnisett, Jean, *Period Costume for Stage and Screen.* Los Angeles: Players Press, 1991.

Köhler, Carl. *A History of Costume.* Translated by Alexander K. Dallas. New York: Dover, 1963.

Linthicum, M. Channing. *Costume in the Drama of Shakespeare and His Contemporaries.* Oxford: Clarendon Press, 1936.

MacQuoid, Percy. "Costume." In *Shakespeare's England. An Account of the Life and Manners of His Age,* 2.91–118. Oxford: Clarendon Press, 1916.

Mikhaila, Ninya, and Jane Malcolm-Davies. *The Tudor Tailor: Techniques and Patterns for Making Historically Accurate Period Clothing.* Hollywood: Costume and Fashion Press, 2006.

Nevinson, John L. *Catalogue of English Domestic Embroidery of the Sixteenth and Seventeenth Centuries.* London: His Majesty's Stationery Office, 1938.

Norris, Herbert. *Costume and Fashion. Vol. 3, The Tudors. Book 2: 1547–1603.* New York: Dutton, 1924.

Rutt, Richard. *A History of Hand Knitting.* Loveland, CO: Interweave Press, 1987.

Spufford, Margaret. *The Great Reclothing of Rural England.* London: Hambledon Press, 1984.

Stubbes, Phillip. *Phillip Stubbes's Anatomy of the Abuses in England in Shakespeare's Youth A.D. 1583.* Edited by F. J. Furnivall. London: Trübner, 1879.

Tilke, Max. *Costume Patterns and Designs*. New York: Praeger, 1957.

Trump, R. W. *Drafting & Constructing a Simple Doublet & Trunkhose of the Spanish Renaissance*. Eugene, OR: Alfarhaugr Publishing Society, 1991.

Waugh, Norah. *Corsets and Crinolines*. London: Batsford, 1954.

Waugh, Norah. *The Cut of Men's Clothes 1600–1900*. London: Faber and Faber, 1964.

Waugh, Norah. *The Cut of Women's Clothes 1600–1930*. New York: Theater Arts, 1968.

Weaver's Guild of Boston. *17th Century Knitting Patterns as Adapted for Plimoth Plantation*. Boston: n.p., 1990.

Willet, C., and Phyllis Cunnington. *Handbook of English Costume in the Sixteenth Century*. London: Faber and Faber, 1954, rev. ed. 1970.

FOOD AND DRINK

Byrne, M. St. Clare, ed. *The Elizabethan Home*. London: Methuen, 1949.

Dawson, Thomas. *The Good Huswifes Jewell* [1596]. Edited by Susan J. Evans. Albany, NY: Falconwood Press, 1988.

Dawson, Thomas. *The Second Part of the Good Huswifes Jewell*. [1597]. Edited by Susan J. Evans. Albany, NY: Falconwood Press, 1988.

Garret, George. "Daily Life in City, Town, and Country." In *William Shakespeare: His World, His Works, His Influence. Vol. 1: His World*, ed. John F. Andrews, 215–32. New York: Scribner, 1985.

Harrison, William. *Description of England*. Ithaca, NY: Folger Shakespeare Library, 1968.

Hess, Karen. *Martha Washington's Booke of Cookery*. New York: Columbia University Press, 1981.

Loram, Madge. *Dining with William Shakespeare*. New York: Atheneum, 1976.

MacQuoid, Percy. "The Home." In *Shakespeare's England. An Account of the Life and Manners of His Age*, 2.119–52. Oxford: Clarendon Press, 1916.

Markham, Gervase. *The English Housewife* [1615]. Edited by Michael R. Best. Kingston and Montréal: McGill-Queen's University Press, 1986.

McCarthy, Michael R., and Catherine M. Brooks. *Medieval Pottery in Britain A.D. 900–1600*. Leicester: Leicester University Press, 1988.

Monckton, H. A. *A History of English Ale and Beer*. London: Bodley Head, 1966.

Murrell, John. *A Daily Exercise for Ladies and Gentlewomen* [1617]. Edited by Susan J. Evans. Albany, NY: Falconwood Press, 1990.

Murrell, John. *A Delightful Daily Exercise for Ladies and Gentlewomen* [1621]. Edited by Susan J. Evans. Albany, NY: Falconwood Press, 1990.

Murrell, John. *A New Booke of Cookerie*. London: J. Browne, 1615.

Peachey, Stuart, ed. *The Good Huswifes Handmaide for the Kitchin* [1594].Bristol: Stuart Press, 1992.

Sim, Alison. *Food and Feast in Tudor England*. Stroud: Sutton, 1997.

Sim, Alison. *The Tudor Housewife*. Stroud: Sutton, 1998.

Spurling, Hilary, ed. *Elinor Fettiplace's Receipt Book*. New York: Viking, 1987.

Thirsk, Joan. *Food in Early Modern England: Phases, Fads, Fashions, 1500–1760*. London: Hambledon Continuuum, 2006.

Tusser, Thomas. *Five Hundred Points of Good Husbandry.* Edited by Geoffrey Grigson. Oxford: Oxford University Press, 1984.

Wilson, C. Anne. *Food and Drink in Britain.* London: Constable, 1973.

ENTERTAINMENTS: GENERAL

Cotton, Charles. "The Compleat Gamester [1674]." In *Games and Gamesters of the Restoration.* London: Routledge, 1930.

Fortescue, J. W., Gerald Lascelles, A. Forbes Sieveking, H. Walrond, and Sir Sidney Lee, "Sports and Pastimes." In *Shakespeare's England. An Account of the Life and Manners of His Age,* 2.334–483. Oxford: Clarendon Press, 1916.

Heninger, S. K. "The Literate Culture of Shakespeare's Audience." In *William Shakespeare: His World, His Works, His Influence. Vol. 1: His World,* ed. John F. Andrews, 159–74. New York: Scribner, 1985.

Holme, Randle. *The Acudemy of Armory* [1688]. Menston: Scolar Press, 1972.

Hutton, Ronald. *The Rise and Fall of Merry England: The Ritual Year 1400–1700.* Oxford: Oxford University Press, 1994.

Pringle, Roger. "Sports and Recreations." In *William Shakespeare: His World, His Works, His Influence. Vol. 1: His World,* ed. John F. Andrews, 269–80. New York: Scribner, 1985.

Sim, Alison. *Pleasures and Pastimes in Tudor England.* Stroud, Gloucestershire: Sutton, 1999.

Vale, Marcia. *The Gentleman's Recreations: Accomplishments and Pastimes of the English Gentleman, 1580–1630.* Cambridge: D. S. Brewer; Totowa, NJ: Rowman and Littlefield, 1977.

Willughby, Francis. *Francis Willughby's Book of Games: A Seventeenth-Century Treatise on Sports, Games, and Pastimes.* Edited by David Cram, Jeffrey L. Forgeng, and Dorothy Johnston. Aldershot: Ashgate Press, 2003.

ENTERTAINMENTS: MUSIC AND DANCE

Arbeau, Thoinot. *Orchesography* [1589]. Translated by Mary Stewart Evans. New York: Dover, 1967.

Bantock, Granville, and H. Orsmund Anderton, eds. *The Melvill Book of Roundels.* London: Roxburghe Club, 1916.

Caroso, Fabritio. *Nobiltà di Dame* [1600]. Translated by Julia Sutton. Oxford: Oxford University Press, 1986.

Chappell, William. *Popular Music of the Olden Time.* London: Chappell, 1859.

Cunningham, James P. *Dancing in the Inns of Court.* London: Jordan and Sons, 1965.

Greenberg, Noah, W. H. Auden, and Chester Kallman. *An Elizabethan Song Book.* London and Boston: Faber and Faber, 1957.

Inglehearn, Madeleine. *Ten Dances from Sixteenth Century Italy.* Witham, Essex: Compagnie of Dansers, 1983.

Keller, Kate van Winkle, and Genevieve Shimer. *The Playford Ball.* Chicago: A Cappella Books, 1990.

Playford, John. *The English Dancing Master* [1651]. Edited by Margaret Dean-Smith. London: Schott, 1957.

Pugliese, P., and J. Cassaza. *Practice for Dauncinge.* Cambridge, MA: privately published, 1980.
Ravenscroft, Thomas. *Pammelia, Deuteromelia, and Melismata* [1609, 1611]. Philadelphia: American Folklore Society, 1961.
Thomas, Bernard, and Jane Gingell. *The Renaissance Dance Book.* London: London Pro Musica, 1987.

THE ELIZABETHAN WORLD

Bayne, Rev. Ronald. "Religion." In *Shakespeare's England. An Account of the Life and Manners of His Age,* 1.48–78. Oxford: Clarendon Press, 1916.
Braun, Georg, and Franz Hogenberg. *Civitates Orbis Terrarum, 1572–1618.* Edited by R. A. Skelton. Cleveland: World Publishing, 1966.
Collinson, Patrick. "The Church: Religion and Its Manifestations." In *William Shakespeare: His World, His Works, His Influence. Vol. 1: His World,* ed. John F. Andrews, 21–40. New York: Scribner, 1985.
Harrison, William. *Description of England.* Ithaca, NY: Folger Shakespeare Library, 1968.
Hughes, Charles. "Land Travel." In *Shakespeare's England. An Account of the Life and Manners of His Age,* 1.198–223. Oxford: Clarendon Press, 1916.
Kassell, Lauren. *Medicine and Magic in Elizabethan London: Simon Forman, Astrologer, Alchemist, and Physician.* Oxford: Clarendon, 2005.
Knobel, E. B., Robert Steele, Percy Simpson, C. T. Onions, and Sir William T. Thiselton-Dyer, "The Sciences." In *Shakespeare's England. An Account of the Life and Manners of His Age,* 1.444–515. Oxford: Clarendon Press, 1916.
Laughton, "The Navy." In *Shakespeare's England. An Account of the Life and Manners of His Age,* 1.141–69. 2 vols. Oxford: Clarendon Press, 1916.
MacDonald, Michael. "Science, Magic, and Folklore." In *William Shakespeare: His World, His Works, His Influence. Vol. 1: His World,* ed. John F. Andrews, 175–94. New York: Scribner, 1985.
Ortelius, Abraham. *Theatrum Orbis Terrarum* [1606]. London: Theatrum Orbis Terrarum, 1968.
Palliser, D. M. *The Age of Elizabeth.* London and New York: Longman, 1992.
Platter, Thomas. *Thomas Platter's Travels in England 1599.* Translated by Clare Williams. London: J. Cape, 1937.
Quinn, David. "Travel by Sea and Land." In *William Shakespeare: His World, His Works, His Influence. Vol. 1: His World,* ed. John F. Andrews, 195–200. New York: Scribner, 1985.
Thomas, Keith. *Religion and the Decline of Magic.* New York: Scribner, 1971.

NOVELS

A fair number of novels have been set in Elizabethan England below are some of the more recent ones. An extensive list can be found in John A. Wagner, *Historical Dictionary of the Elizabethan World* (Phoenix, AZ: Oryx Press, 1999).

Buckley, Fiona. *The Doublet Affair.* New York: Scribner, 1998.

Burgess, Anthony. *A Dead Man in Deptford*. London: Hutchinson, 1993.
Burgess, Anthony. *Nothing Like the Sun*. New York: Norton, 1996.
Chisolm, P.F.A. *A Surfeith of Guns*. New York: Walker, 1997.
Cowell, Stephanie. *Nicholas Cooke: Actor, Soldier, Physician, Poet*. New York: Norton, 1993.
Cowell, Stephanie. *The Players*. New York: Norton, 1997.
Emerson, Kathy Lynn. *Face Down upon an Herbal*. New York: St. Martin's Press, 1998.
Finney, Patricia. *Firedrake's Eye*. London: St Martin's Press, 1991.
Finney, Patricia. *Unicorn's Blood*. London: St Martin's Press, 1998.
Garrett, George. *The Succession. A Novel of Elizabeth and James*. Garden City, NY: Doubleday, 1983.
Garrett, George. *Death of the Fox*. Garden City, NY: Doubleday, 1971.
Harper, Karen. *The Poyson Garden*. New York: Delacorte, 1999.
Scott, Melissa, and Lisa A. Barnett. *The Armor of Light*. New York: Baen, 1988.
Tourney, Leonard. *The Bartholomew Fair Murders*. New York: St. Martin's Press, 1986.
Tourney, Leonard. *Familiar Spirits*. New York: St. Martin's Press, 1984.
Tourney, Leonard. *Knaves Templar*. New York: St. Martin's Press, 1991.
Tourney, Leonard. *Low Treason*. New York: Dutton, 1982.
Tourney, Leonard. *Old Saxon Blood*. New York: St. Martin's Press, 1988.
Tourney, Leonard. *The Players' Boy Is Dead*. New York: Harper-Row, 1980.
Tourney, Leonard. *Witness of Bones*. New York: St. Martin's Press, 1992.

VISUAL AND ILLUSTRATION SOURCES

Allemagne, Henri Réné d'. *Sports et jeux d'adresse*. Paris: Hachette, 1903.
Amman, Jost. *Gynaeceum sive Theatrum Mulierum*. Frankfurt, 1586.
Arbeau, Thoinot. *Orchésographie*. Lengres: J. des Preyz, 1596.
Ashdown, Emily Jessie. *British Costume*. London: T. C. and E. C. Jack, 1910.
Beau-Chesne, Jean de. *A Booke Containing Divers Sortes of Hands*. London: Richard Field, 1602.
Besant, Sir Walter. *London in the Time of the Tudors*. London: Adam and Charles Black, 1904.
Castle, Egerton. *Schools and Masters of Fence*. London: Bell, 1892.
Clark, Andrew, ed. *The Shirburn Ballads 1585–1616*. Oxford: Clarendon Press, 1907.
Clinch, George. *English Costume*. Chicago and London: Methuen and Co., 1910.
Furnivall, F. J. *Harrison's Description of England in Shakspere's Youth*. London: Trübner, 1877.
Furnivall, F. J. *Phillip Stubbes' Anatomy of Abuses*. London: Trübner, 1879.
Gay, Victor. *Glossaire Archéologique*. Paris: Librairie de la Société Bibliographique, 1887.
Gilbert, William. *On the Magnet*. London: Chiswick Press, 1900.
Hindley, Charles, ed. *The Roxburghe Ballads*. London: Reeves and Turner, 1837–74.
Holinshed, Raphael. *The Chronicles of England, Scotlande and Irelande*. London: I. Hunne, 1577.
Hymns Ancient and Modern. London: William Clowes and Sons, 1909.

Monroe, Paul. *A Brief Course in the History of Education*. London: Macmillan, 1907.

Ruding, Rogers. *Annals of the Coinage of Great Britain*. London: J. Hearne, 1840.

Shakespeare's England. An Account of the Life and Manners of his Age. 2 vols. Oxford: Clarendon Press, 1916.

Traill, H. D., and J. S. Mann. *Social England*. London: Cassell; New York: Putnam's, 1909.

Weigel, Hans. *Habitus Praecipuorum Populorum*. Nuremberg: Hans Weigel, 1577.

Illustrations by Jeffrey Forgeng, Victoria Hadfield, and David Hoornstra were produced expressly for this volume.

Index

Page numbers in *italics* indicate illustrations.

bearbaiting and bullbaiting,
190–91
bedchamber. *See* chamber
beds, 74, 75, 107, 116–18, 227.
See also furnishings; sleeping
beer. *See* ale
bees, 110
beggars, *13*, 23
belts, 140
Bible, 77, 104, 187, 235
billiards, 199
birth. *See* childbirth
bishops, 20, 27–28, 29, 31, 236
blast furnace, 96
Blindman's Buff, 197, 198, 199
boats. *See* ships and boats
bodices, 132–34, 144–47
books, 104, 187.
See also broadsides; reading
boots, 138
bowls, 195, 200, 204
bread, 164, 165–66, 172, 176
breakfast, 54, 57, 74, 77, 163–64
breeches, 48, 75, 131, 149–50.
See also Venetian breeches
brewing. *See* ale
broadsides, 104, 187, 211
Brownists, 29. *See also* Separatists
brushes, 74, 75, 130, 142
bumroll. *See* roll
burgage tenure, 132, 133–34
busk, 132, 133–34
butter, 104, 164, 165, 167, 168.
See also dairy produce
buttons, 97, 140, 161

cakes, 81, 87, 90, 167, 180
calendar, 18, 69, 79–90
Calvin, Jean, 2, 26
camp-ball, 194
candles and candlesticks, 75, 90,
104, 114, 115, 117. *See also* light
canvas, 104, 107, 110, 118, 127,
136, 137. *See also* hemp
capes, 139

caps. *See* headgear
cards, 184, 198, 200, 207–10
carpets, 114, 116
cassocks, 104, 139, 160–61
catechism, 51, 53, 77
Catholicism, 1–4, 26, 28–29, 30,
235. *See also* Jesuits; Pope
cats, 191
cellars, 109, 113
chaff, 87, 93, 107, 118
chamber, bedchamber, 109, 110,
114, 116–17
chamber pot, 75, 119
champion (open-field) agriculture,
69, 92, 105. *See also* villages
checkers, 197
cheese, 104, 117, 164, 165, 167, 168.
See also dairy produce
chess, 197
chests. *See* furnishings
childbirth, 41, 43–44, 239
children, 43, 46–63, 173–74, 200
chimneys, 89, 107, 109, 110.
See also fire
Christmas, 58, 90, 181, 197, 201
church, 25–30, 37, 77, 78–79, 80,
105. *See also* Catholicism;
Protestantism; Puritans; religion
churchwardens, 16, 27
citizens, 19
cleaning, 82, 114. *See also* laundry;
washing
clergy, 14, 20, 27, 36.
See also archbishops;
archdeacons; bishops; priests
climate, 6
cloth. *See* fabric
clothing, 104, 116, 125–61
coaches, 227–28
coats, 117, 137, 160–61
cockfighting, 190
codpieces, 135–36
coifs, 75, 139–40, 155–56
collars. *See* neckwear
combs, 74, 97, 132, 141

About the Author

DR. JEFFREY L. FORGENG is Paul S. Morgan Curator at the Higgins Armory Museum in Worcester, Massachusetts, and adjunct associate professor of humanities at Worcester Polytechnic Institute. He has published extensively on topics including daily life in the Middle Ages and Renaissance, the Robin Hood legend, and the history of games, as well as medieval and Renaissance martial arts. Forgeng did his doctorate in Medieval Studies at the University of Toronto specializing in medieval and Renaissance languages and cultural history, and was for many years an editor for the *Middle English Dictionary*.